REAL WORLD COMPOSITING WITH ADOBE PHOTOSHOP CS4

DAN MOUGHAMIAN

SCOTT VALENTINE

PEACHPIT PRESS
BERKELEY, CALIFORNIA

REAL WORLD COMPOSITING WITH ADOBE PHOTOSHOP CS4

Dan Moughamian
Scott Valentine

Peachpit Press
1249 Eighth Street
Berkeley, CA 94710
510/524-2178
510/524-2221 (fax)

Find us on the Web at www.peachpit.com
To report errors, please send a note to errata@peachpit.com
Peachpit Press is a division of Pearson Education.

Real World Compositing with Adobe Photoshop CS4 is published in association with Adobe Press.

For the latest on Adobe Press books, go to www.adobepress.com

Acquisitions Editor: Victor Gavenda
Project Editor: Valerie Witte
Technical Editor: Rocky Berlier
Copyeditor: Kim Wimpsett
Proofreader: Elissa Rabellino
Production Editor: Hilal Sala
Compositor: Danielle Foster
Indexer: Rebecca Plunkett
Cover Design: Charlene Charles Will

ISBN-13: 978-0-321-60453-8
ISBN–10: 0-321-60453-9
9 8 7 6 5 4 3 2 1
Printed and bound in the United States of America

This book is dedicated to my wife, Kathy.
—Dan

For Sydney
—Scott

ABOUT THE AUTHORS

Dan Moughamian is a compositor and fine art photographer of landscapes and urban architecture. He has more than 14 years of experience with Adobe Photoshop and is an Adobe Certified Expert. As a veteran member of their testing programs, Dan has worked directly with Adobe Systems and the Photoshop team to help define and enhance many of the core compositing functions in Photoshop. Dan is also an experienced instructor and has channeled his passion for Photoshop and all things digital into a series of new training videos available from designProVideo.com. For live sessions, Dan works with training provider Mac Specialist to deliver in-depth classes and presentations on Photoshop, Lightroom, and Aperture. Dan resides in suburban Chicago with his wife, Kathy.

Scott Valentine is an award-winning experimental photographer and long-time Photoshop user in both artistic and technical capacities. He has been a user group manager for nearly a decade, supporting a range of Adobe products. Scott also contributes considerable time to the Photoshop and digital photography communities at AllExperts.com, is a partner and author for CommunityMX.com and PhotoshopTechniques.com, and is an administrator for PhotoshopTechniques.com, one of the longest-standing Photoshop Web communities. Over the years, Scott has used his Bachelor's degree in physics from the University of California at San Diego to develop a deep understanding of digital imaging and optical physics, and has served as a subject matter expert in microphotography, optical and electron microscopy, digital archiving, and digital image analysis at a national laboratory. As a member of Photoshop's prerelease teams, Scott has access to all the latest features and thinking from Adobe on "what's next."

CONTENTS AT A GLANCE

TABLE OF CONTENTS

INTRODUCTION

If you're reading this book, chances are good that you're a creative professional or serious Adobe Photoshop hobbyist who wants to learn more about how to bring images from different places together to create something new. That's what this book is all about.

But it's also important to understand what this book is not; namely, it's not a collection of 1-2-3 lists or basic techniques for using Photoshop.

We've approached this book from a holistic perspective, taking into account not only cool Photoshop techniques but also vital processes such as brainstorming, staying organized, handling lighting, and working with new 3D tools. We debated whether this book should follow a format in which you watch a series of images progress from beginning to end; however, that approach (though it has its merits) seemed somewhat limiting to us.

Many photographers have image archives stuffed with all kinds of photography we can't even imagine, and what's more, many use third-party photography sources, such as stock agencies, to complete their vision. So, the idea of picking and choosing four or five detailed examples and walking you through each one—although it would have a certain continuity—has limits in terms of showing you the kinds of images you can use in your compositing work. For that reason, we have organized the book by process type. However, we do provide a few start-to-finish examples at the end of the book … so stay tuned!

That being said, we would love to hear feedback that would help us make the next edition even better, so if an idea strikes you about how we can improve the organization or focus of this book, please send your comments to rwcompositing@colortrails.com.

How This Book Is Organized

As noted, we have broken this book down by process, rather than specific kinds of techniques or projects. So if you're already familiar with one topic (or if it's not part of your standard workflow), you can move ahead to the next chapter. We think most readers will benefit from reading this book start to finish, but that isn't a requirement. Though such choices are always subjective, overall we have tried to give the most important topics equal treatment and those that are a little more mundane (but necessary) a little bit less attention.

The core topics covered in this book are as follows:

Brainstorming and planning. Often an overlooked part of the process, taking the time to explore new ideas and work through them in a rough-draft style is very important. Although it's always possible to just open a few files and throw together a cool composite image, the process of looking through different series of photos, works of art, and other inspiring materials can open up creative doors that you would likely otherwise miss.

Photography (including lighting). One of the most rewarding aspects of creating a beautiful or zany composite image is knowing that the content came from within. Having the technical skills to bring images together in Photoshop and also the ability to recognize and capture those images out in the real world are their own rewards. Digital photography has become such a huge phenomenon that we would be remiss to overlook it in a book about compositing, especially since the vast majority of composites use traditional still images for their content!

Organizing and processing raw files. Once you've loaded all those inspirational photographs onto your hard drive, you need to know how to manage and process them efficiently. Few things are more frustrating than searching through a massive pile of six-month-old images that haven't been named, tagged with keywords, or given any other identifying characteristic beyond their thumbnail! Moreover, a big part of getting the right end result is making sure you start with a strong foundation, and that means working with Adobe Camera Raw.

Enhancing and compositing source materials. This is where the "rubber meets the road." We have attempted to cover the most important Photoshop techniques for setting up your composite file, gathering your materials into that file, and working with them to seamlessly hide the stuff you don't want to see, show off the good stuff you want to focus on, and trick the eye into perceiving depth cues and other characteristics that may not have been part of the original materials.

Note that we do assume you have good Photoshop fundamentals, such as working with selection tools, brush tools, the options bar, and the like.

PLATFORM INDEPENDENCE

Although many of the figures supplied in this book are from the Mac OS X environment, we have made efforts to ensure that where important short-cuts are mentioned, both Mac and Windows variants are supplied. Photoshop is a multiplatform environment, and as such we recognize the importance of noting any of the different behaviors, requirements, or short-cuts as we discuss each technique.

It is worth noting that Chapter 9 in this book, "Creating 3D Content," is dedicated to opening up the world of 3D content to those unfamiliar with it, so parts of it necessarily focus on Adobe Photoshop CS4 Extended. Although most of the techniques discussed in this book do not require it, you will need to own the extended version if you wish to use the Photoshop tools discussed in Chapter 9. Photoshop CS4 Extended is more expensive, but it will be a worthwhile upgrade for compositing enthusiasts who are interested in working with 3D.

WHAT'S IN STORE?

One thing we want to do is show you—right up front—some of the cool new features in Photoshop CS4 and Adobe Camera Raw 5.

3D Power

Photoshop CS4 Extended provides some major advances in the world of 3D creation. Although fundamentally still an image editor—Adobe is not trying to build a modeling application into Photoshop as far as we know—Photoshop is part of a growing trend in which 3D content is becoming more popular and accessible to creative software users. Adobe recognizes this and has therefore built in some new tools that allow you to import 3D models in a variety of third-party formats (like Collada and 3DS) and apply various lighting, texture, and painting effects to those models, as shown in **Figure i.1**.

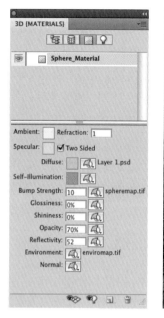

Figure i.1 Photoshop CS4 Extended allows you to create basic 3D shapes and import models from other apps, as well as to adjust their materials, lights, position, and render settings.

Photoshop also provides the means for creating simple 3D shape layers that use empty documents or other images as the basis for their "skin." Naturally, any serious image editor needs to provide the right tools for manipulating specific kinds of media, and Adobe has added several object manipulation and camera tools for framing your 3D content just the way you need it to look.

Target Acquired

Although Adobe Camera Raw (ACR) has long been an indispensable item in just about every photographer's toolbox, the one long-standing complaint has been the lack of localized correction tools. No longer. ACR offers three new tools that can help photographers and compositing artists make Photoshop-like color and tonal corrections as part of the raw-processing workflow. This is a really big deal not only because it saves time later in the process but also because it helps ensure that every image processed in this way has more "headroom" for further edits.

The newest of these three tools is the Targeted Adjustment tool, which arrived with the ACR 5.2 update (Christmas came early in 2008!). The Targeted Adjustment tool (**Figure i.2**) works by allowing you to target tones and colors directly on your document preview and make simple corrections to the hue, saturation, or luminance of that area.

Figure i.2 The Targeted Adjustment tool in Adobe Camera Raw is set to save photographers and compositors a lot of time and effort without sacrificing accuracy. ACR is covered in-depth in Chapter 7, "Processing Raw Source Files."

The Kind of Scale You Can Live With

Photoshop CS4 offers a new type of scale transform that will be of great interest to digital artists. Content Aware Scaling (CAS)—also referred to as *seam carving* in some circles—has arrived, and we can tell you it's a lot of fun to use and pretty powerful as well. CAS takes the familiar scale transform handles and turbocharges them with alpha channel protected regions, allowing you to scale only parts of your document while the rest remains unchanged. This is illustrated in **Figure i.3**, but don't worry: We'll explain what all this means in Chapter 10, "Compositing Source Materials."

Figure i.3 Content Aware Scaling is a great tool for moving objects in an image closer together, without creating seams where content has been removed.

Line 'Em Up!

Another great improvement in Photoshop CS4 (that we also discuss in Chapter 10) is an enhanced Auto-Align Layers command and dialog box. The new dialog box, in addition to leveraging more accurate alignment algorithms for the traditional options, offers several new "perspective types" when setting up images for panoramic photos and other compositing tasks. This tool, shown in **Figure i.4**, and the also-improved Auto-Blend Layers command are two techniques every Photoshop junkie should know about.

Figure i.4 The Auto-Align Layers command has been updated in Photoshop CS4 to cover more options for creating the seamless alignment of your source image content.

Nonmodal Is Good Modal

Finally, another very useful enhancement to the Photoshop toolbox—one you no doubt have heard about by now—is the new Adjustments panel, which houses all your favorite adjustment layers in a non-model panel that you can group and dock with all your favorites for a more streamlined workflow. **Figure i.5** shows the Adjustments panel, along with the new Masks panel.

We'll cover several important adjustment layer concepts in Chapters 8 and 10.

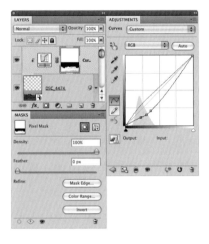

Figure i.5 Photoshop CS4's new Adjustments panel makes using and fine-tuning your image adjustments a much more efficient process.

THANK YOU!

We offer sincere thanks to the people who helped make this book a reality.

First and foremost, a big thank you to Valerie Witte, our editor, for helping us stay on track during the authoring process and for all of your contributions to the book. To Rocky Berlier, our technical editor, as well as Hilal Sala, Danielle Foster, and Charlene Will from Peachpit, thank you for collaborating with us and helping make *Real World Compositing* a better book.

A major shout-out to fellow Photoshop tester and photographer John Weber for producing an outstanding cover while we toiled away with track edits, CMYK conversions, and writer's angst! To Robin Williams and John Tollett, your kindness and insights into the proposal process are greatly appreciated.

To John Nack and the entire Photoshop team, many thanks are in order for putting together another fantastic release in Photoshop CS4. Developing our images and creating digital art would feel a lot more like work were it not for Photoshop! We can't wait to see what you cook up next. And finally, to the many unnamed individuals who helped us along the way with our Photoshop quest, you are not forgotten. We appreciate all that you have done for us.

Dan: Sincerest thanks to my beautiful wife, Kathy, for her love and support and for her patience during the many long hours it took to develop and write this book. To Scott: We made it! Thank you for your hard work and for your sense of humor throughout. Your expertise—specifically in the areas of lighting, human visual perception, and 3D—allowed us to provide readers with a complete look at a complex subject. To Len and Mike: Thank you for more than two decades of friendship, support, and good advice. You guys are the real deal.

Finally, to my father: *Thank you* for providing your children with so many opportunities, for your sound advice, and for the unwavering support that allowed me to build a business and achieve my goals.

Scott: My biggest thanks go to my wife, Carla, and son, Austin, for their patience and love through this work—you've endured many frustrations and long nights, and I love you both for it. Special thanks to Dan, for suggesting that we team up to write a book about compositing, and for all the hard work you put into it.

I also owe a debt of gratitude to my fellow council members and friends at PhotoshopTechniques, without whom I would not have developed this insane addiction to digital imaging. Your encouragement, knowledge, and willingness to help the Photoshop community are second to none; I'm proud to know each of you without exception (the next round is on me, guys!). And my deep appreciation to Greg Vander Houwen for trusting me through the years and helping me find the Tao of Photoshop. Now ... let's be bad guys.

System Considerations

Since you purchased this book, we're assuming you already have a solid understanding of Adobe Photoshop CS4 fundamentals, including the process of optimizing your hardware to run efficiently with Photoshop. For example, we assume you already understand what a scratch disk is and why you'd want to use one. However, because the computer landscape is constantly advancing with new processing, storage, and system technologies, it makes sense to cover some of the more important points. The information provided in this chapter will benefit Windows and Mac OS X users equally.

HARDWARE

Making sure you have a solid hardware setup is crucial to creating an efficient and enjoyable Photoshop compositing workflow. The necessity of some components is obvious. For example, it's always a good idea to buy the most powerful CPU you can reasonably afford as part of your Photoshop system. People also discuss Photoshop's relatively heavy RAM requirements and the need for an extra hard drive for use as a dedicated scratch disk.

Currently, Intel and AMD are focused more on the number of processing "cores" inside a single chip than they are on breaking speed records. As of mid-2008, high-end workstations from Apple, Alienware, and Dell were topping out at about 3.2 GHz. There is some indication we may see multi-core processors in the 3.4 to 3.6 GHz range in 2009, but time will tell.

Generally, any workstation rated between 2 and 3 GHz (or faster) per core should perform nicely in most circumstances. Check your product literature for minimum system requirements.

Less obvious is the importance of having a powerful graphics processor. Now they're called GPUs, but many know them by their former name: video cards. This was the term used in the 1990s—when we had to manufacture our own cards from copper wire and cornmeal wafers. Several Photoshop tools and image display technologies are directly tied to GPU performance. Photoshop is a hungry beast; make sure you have the right hardware on hand!

Memory (RAM)

What holds true for prior versions of Photoshop, with respect to how much RAM you will need, still holds true for Photoshop CS4. Generally, the more memory you have installed, the more performance benefits you will see, up to a point. Your optimum RAM installation and allocation will ultimately be determined by the operating system and hardware you use. Gone are the old formulas of multiplying your image size by 5 and estimating how many images you will have open at one time to determine your Photoshop RAM requirements. Here are the current issues:

64-bits of confusion. Both Microsoft and Apple are making inroads to the world of 64-bit computing and have updated certain products to provide some 64-bit benefits to the scientific and other select user communities. However, limitations in current hardware technology make it difficult to get the full benefits of 64-bit computing without using distributed computing platforms. Despite the marketing hype from Microsoft and Apple, it is not a foregone conclusion that programs such as Photoshop will benefit from 64-bitness in all situations. Some functions and projects, depending on the size of the images you are using, can benefit more than others.

As Photoshop engineer Scott Byer noted on his blog in December 2006, "A 64-bit application … can address a much larger amount of memory. That's pretty much it. 64-bit applications don't magically get faster access to memory, or any of the other key things that would help most applications perform better."

The primary benefit. The best thing about 64-bit computing, as it relates to Photoshop, boils down to memory; 64-bit systems and applications allow you to install and address larger amounts of RAM than their 32-bit counterparts.

In theory, the latest versions of Mac OS X and Windows allow you to install a row of RAM modules that could stretch from Times Square to Toledo, but the truth is, until those modules are the size of a dime, it won't matter.

Currently, most desktop workstations are limited to between six and twelve RAM slots. Using the liberal benchmark of twelve (expensive) DDR-II 8 GB RAM modules, you can in theory set up a Photoshop machine with 96 GB of RAM. However, at the time of this writing, those twelve 8 GB modules would cost approximately $20,000. Twelve 4 GB modules would cost a bargain-basement $5,500 or so—more than the cost of most desktop computers by a fairly wide margin. So, although greater RAM capacities are definitely more feasible than they were just a couple of years ago, budgets are a big consideration until the cost of high-end RAM modules falls considerably.

Another limitation is that most applications (on both platforms) remain 32-bit native, which means they can take advantage of only 2 to 3 GB of RAM each. However, having several gigabytes of RAM installed is still a good idea when running multiple creative programs simultaneously. A general rule of thumb is to make available at least 2 GB of RAM for each creative application you run, and at least 1 GB at all times for the operating system.

Photoshop CS4 has both 32-bit and 64-bit versions available for Windows XP and Windows Vista. Unfortunately, because of some abrupt changes made by Apple to its developer "road map" in 2007, the Mac OS X version of Photoshop remains 32-bit for now. The good news is that Adobe is committed to bringing 64-bit applications to Mac OS X and has already done so with Photoshop Lightroom 2, a fully 64-bit native Mac application.

RAM for desktops. If you have a desktop workstation such as a Mac Pro from Apple or a PC from Alienware and you intend to run multiple applications alongside Photoshop, 8 GB of RAM is a safe bet. This way you can allocate a full 3 GB to Photoshop (or more if you're on a 64-bit Windows operating system) and still have about 5 GB left for other uses. The more RAM you can install, the more leeway you have to push the Memory Usage slider in Photoshop to 100 percent and not risk performance problems with the system or other programs. If you have 4 GB of RAM or less, try using the default memory allocation, usually about 70 percent (**Figure 1.1**).

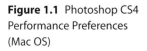

Figure 1.1 Photoshop CS4
Performance Preferences
(Mac OS)

RAM for laptops. If you are working from a laptop, always install the
maximum RAM possible. Often this is 4 GB per slot (and there may be
only one slot), so you won't have as much RAM as if you were using a
desktop workstation. Some laptops will accept two slots, allowing for 8 GB
of total RAM. The cost of 4 GB DDR-II laptop modules was about $500
apiece at the time of this writing.

Graphics Processors (GPUs)

Today's GPUs—such as the AMD Radeon 3870—are miniature systems on
a card (**Figure 1.2**). Using high-bandwidth processors, dedicated memory
called VRAM, and fast connections to your computer's motherboard, GPUs
have given Adobe the ability to enhance the way Photoshop users view and
manipulate their images.

Figure 1.2 Photoshop CS4
takes advantage of the
processing power of
advanced GPUs.

For example, Photoshop offers the possibility of smoothly scaling your images without jagged edges at magnifications like 33.3 percent and 66.7 percent. There is also a new "bird's-eye" function. When zooming to 100 percent magnification or beyond, you can instantly view the whole document by holding down the H key and your mouse button. You can then choose to display a new portion of the image at the original magnification by moving a Navigator-like box and releasing the mouse button when the box is hovering over your target image area.

Unlike with CPUs, choosing the right graphics processor can be a tricky proposition. Because they are designed and brought to market so quickly (making existing cards relatively obsolete), you need to make sure you choose a newer GPU that supports certain standards and specifications.

NOTE Most laptop GPUs are permanent fixtures (that is, you can't remove and replace them).

Usually, if you're going to buy a retail GPU card, the product's specifications page will include everything you need to know. Here are some specs to keep an eye out for when buying your computer or GPU upgrades:

Make and model. Generally, you will have the best luck with the higher-end cards from Nvidia or AMD (whose cards are made by ATI). Look for the GeForce and Radeon brands, respectively. Expect to spend between $200 and $400 per card.

PCI connector type. Make sure the PCI slots in your computer match the PCI type for the card you are considering. PCI slots are located on the motherboard, near the back panel of your computer, and can have different lengths depending on the standard. Several flavors of PCI exist; the most common for new desktops and GPUs is PCI Express (PCI-E).

Display connector type. Make sure your card is compatible with the monitor you have or intend to buy. The most common connector type is called DVI, and it comes in two flavors: DVI-I and DVI-D, which supports commercial HD content via encryption technology called HDCP.

HDMI is a newer connection type, often found on high-end television sets, that is used on some computer LCDs and also allows commercial HD content to be shown (usually Blu-ray content). If your GPU card uses HDMI, make sure there is an HDMI-compatible monitor suited to your budget.

If you plan to drive two monitors from your video card, chances are you will need dual-link DVI. The backs of dual-link GPUs have two female

DVI ports, one to drive each monitor. Be sure the card supports the resolution of your two monitors first!

Video RAM. A good minimum starting point is 512 MB of video RAM.

OpenGL. Look for cards with OpenGL 2.0 technology.

Direct X (Windows only). Look for cards with Shader Model 3 or later.

A good rule of thumb is that you should expect to upgrade your GPU about every two years. About $200 to $400 will usually get you a very capable GPU upgrade, so it's a relatively inexpensive investment for a potentially big performance gain. Besides Photoshop, other digital imaging programs such as Adobe After Effects CS4 are starting to take advantage of GPU technology. Now is a good time to familiarize yourself with the technology so that you can be ahead of the game.

Monitors

LCDs have come a long way over the past three or four years. Currently, one of the more popular professional LCDs is the LaCie 324 (**Figure 1.3**), which can reproduce about 95 percent of Adobe RGB 1998 color space in high detail, and even play back HD video smoothly, for less than $1,200. Adobe RGB coverage is important for the simple reason that it is the workspace of choice for many digital photographers and artists. It is large enough to ensure quality photographic reproductions but also is installed on enough computers to be considered a *de facto* standard.

As time passes, more LCD screens are likely to cover the Adobe RGB gamut at ever-decreasing costs, so don't overlook this when shopping for new LCDs. Cheap monitors—even when calibrated and profiled—will not reproduce the colors from your images as well as a high-end monitor. Just as you would not buy the cheapest PC for Photoshop, you should also consider your LCD an investment toward final image quality.

Figure 1.3 The LaCie 324 LCD

Many users might be tempted to buy an LCD from the company they buy their computer from, such as Dell or Apple. Although these screens are certainly serviceable, they are not color-critical monitors in most cases. To date, original equipment manufacturer (OEM) screens—that is, screens sold under a computer maker's brand name (Apple, Dell, and so on)—typically use cheaper LCD panels and 6- or 8-bit color processing. These produce less even backlighting and reproduce a lower percentage of the Adobe RGB color gamut than screens like the LaCie 324. Most high-end screens use 10-, 12-, or even 16-bit color processing and include technologies to ensure uniform backlighting across the entire screen.

Although you should take any manufacturer's specifications (especially contrast ratio and response time) with a grain of salt, you should look for some important guideposts when LCD shopping:

Color gamut. What percentage of the Adobe RGB 1998 color space can the monitor accurately reproduce? Anything more than 90 percent is likely to yield better results than OEM or inexpensive retail monitors. The benchmark for most high-end LCDs is 95 percent currently, though a few can reproduce 100 percent of Adobe RGB (or beyond), provided you're willing to pay a premium.

Resolution vs. ppi. You may want a larger screen to help you stow your Photoshop panels, instead of cluttering up your desk with two monitors. But be aware that most monitors in the 23-to-26-inch range use the same resolution of 1920 × 1200. The larger the area those pixels are spread across, the lower your pixels per inch (ppi) will be, sometimes resulting in slightly softer images. Look for a screen that performs at 90 ppi or better.

Some of the new high-end 30-inch monitors from NEC and Eizo use a resolution of 2560 × 1600, or 101 ppi. Although these 30-inch monitors will be more expensive than their 23-to-26-inch counterparts, we believe the higher ppi value is worthwhile if you have the budget for it.

Response time. This is one of those specifications that manufacturers love to apply their "marketing fluff factor" to, but it is important. Response time is a measure of how quickly the screen pixels respond to signal changes. Anything more than 12 ms is considered pretty slow by current standards. Single-digit response times are a plus, so that's what you should be shooting for unless you rarely watch video or motion graphics.

Input connection type. Most LCDs use a standard connector called DVI, which comes in two flavors (DVI-D and DVI-I). Either standard is compatible with a wide variety of GPUs. DVI-D is the newer version that includes encryption technology (called HDCP) that allows you to view commercial HD content on your screen. HDMI is a similar standard to DVI-D but uses a very different kind of cable and male-female plug design and is more prevalent in the world of LCD televisions.

The other benefit to choosing a more expensive, higher-end monitor is that it's likely to provide better results when calibrated and profiled, and in general it should give you an extra year or two of life versus a cheaper LCD. Although other manufacturers have some good models, in our experience many professional Photoshop users choose NEC, Eizo, or LaCie as their brand of choice.

One last tip: Make sure as much as possible that the lighting and walls surrounding your monitor do not produce strong color casts. This can interfere with your perception of the colors and tones the monitor is displaying. Invest in a monitor hood if you don't have the option of working in a relatively neutral lighting environment. They typically cost less than $50.

Hard Drives

When it comes to good values, the hard drive market has reached a point of maturation that allows anyone on a budget to get very good performance and large capacities for relatively little money. The bottom line is that there is no reason any longer to skimp on hard drive purchases.

Scratch disks. A dedicated hard drive (for use as a Photoshop scratch disk) can make your workflow more efficient. For the cost of a single GPU, you can get two high-performance, high-capacity hard drives that will last you (most likely) the life of your machine, if you do your homework. For the more technically inclined who want to research their hard drive purchases, sites such as TomsHardware.com and StorageReview.com can be helpful in comparing many hard drives in detail, including specs such as raw transfer speeds and decibel levels.

RAID backups. You can use Redundant Array of Independent Disks (RAID) drives to automatically back up your Photoshop work. Two or more drives formatted to RAID 1 status will create an exact mirror of all the work you save, so if one drive fails, the other will still have the data. Depending on the type of computer you have, you can either install two additional drives internally and format them as a RAID setup, or purchase prepackaged external hard drives, housed in a FireWire or SATA enclosure, that are already set up in a RAID configuration.

RAID speed. Some RAID setups are built for speed rather than redundancy and can be used as a high-performance system disk. One such setup is called RAID 0. This version of RAID offers the fastest throughput by striping two or more hard drives into a single "virtual drive mechanism," but increases the drive's failure rate. It is a riskier setup because if either drive has a bad sector or temporary failure, the entire array will fail, and your data will be lost.

It is not always the case that you need the most "tricked out" hard drive setup to get outstanding Photoshop performance. For many uses, including compositing, a solid-performing SATA drive, such as the Seagate 7200.x series or the Western Digital Caviar series (**Figure 1.4**), may be all you need to make your Photoshop workstation a relatively silent, speedy beast.

NOTE Keep in mind that the fastest hard drives are typically also the hottest, are the noisiest, and draw the most power, so there are trade-offs.

Figure 1.4 High-performance hard drives, like this Seagate® Barracuda® 7200, can help you get the most from Photoshop.

Internal drives. The primary rule has not changed for desktop systems: buy a second internal hard drive (something in the 250 GB range should be fine), install that into one of your empty drive bays such as those found in recent Mac Pro machines (**Figure 1.5**), format it, and leave it *empty*. From there you can assign this drive as your dedicated scratch disk in Photoshop's Performance preferences. Using an internal scratch disk rather than an external hard drive will often result in better performance.

External drives. For most laptops, you will need to use your FireWire or USB 2 ports to connect to a spare external hard drive and use that as your scratch disk. This is important; using a laptop's internal system drive as a scratch disk (which is typically slower than its desktop counterparts) will cause delays in your workflow, especially when working on larger or heavily layered images.

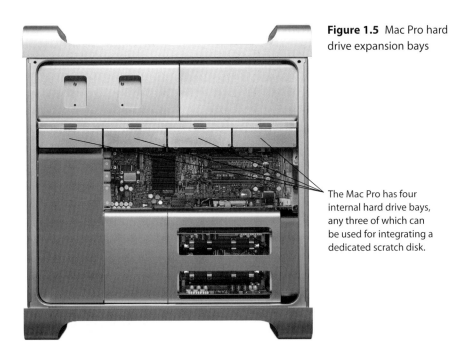

Figure 1.5 Mac Pro hard drive expansion bays

The Mac Pro has four internal hard drive bays, any three of which can be used for integrating a dedicated scratch disk.

Keep in mind that you can maintain your external scratch disk assignment for only as long as the machine and drive are connected and active. As soon as you dismount the drive or shut down the machine, you will have to reassign it the next time you run Photoshop.

Many people are tempted to grab their little mobile hard drive that is half filled with backups or downloads as their laptop scratch disk, but this is unlikely to provide a performance benefit because of both the nonempty status of the drive and the slower data rates for "mini-drives." As an alternative, companies such as Seagate and LaCie offer a range of fast external hard drives (**Figure 1.6**). These drives typically connect to your laptop's FireWire or USB 2 port.

TIP Sometimes a good solution for laptops is to take an old desktop hard drive you're not using, reformat it, and place it inside a compatible FireWire or USB "drive enclosure," which usually costs about $50 to $60 and requires only basic technical skills to install.

Figure 1.6 External desktop hard drives, like this Western Digital My Book Studio Edition, come in different shapes and capacities.

Color Calibration and Profiling

Among the most overlooked hardware devices that are crucial to any successful Photoshop workflow are color calibration devices. Although you can find many inexpensive profiling gadgets on the market, we prefer to work with devices that can calibrate and profile monitors, printers, and cameras:

X marks the spot. The company we recommend (X-Rite) is one that merged with Gretag-Macbeth, a leader in the field for many years. The most popular calibration products, such as the i1XTreme system and the new ColorMunki, are both sold under the X-Rite umbrella. Although a detailed discussion of color calibration and profiling is beyond the scope of this book, take a few minutes to visit XRite.com and see whether the calibration packages offered there suit your workflow and budget.

SOFTWARE

Throughout this book, we reference a few Adobe-made and third-party software products as part of our Photoshop workflow. Although they are not required when compositing images, each of them has proved its worth to us during various Photoshop projects and assignments.

Adobe Bridge CS4

It may seem obvious, but many Photoshop users overlook the value of Adobe Bridge. Although it has endured some growing pains and still has some quirks and missing items that most photographic artists would like to see, Adobe Bridge (**Figure 1.7**) has come a long way over the past three years or so.

Figure 1.7
Adobe Bridge CS4

Adobe Bridge CS4 is more responsive than prior versions in terms of how quickly it processes images for viewing, and is far more flexible in terms of the ways you can navigate, filter, and organize your images. Chapter 6, "Organizing and Evaluating Images," will cover some core functions in Adobe Bridge. So if you haven't paid much attention to Adobe Bridge lately, this book will help you get reacquainted with an old friend. Although Adobe Bridge is not as polished as we'd like it to be ultimately, we use it regularly and think it's a worthwhile investment of your time to learn.

3D Modeling and Rendering

Although Photoshop has some new tricks up its sleeve for creating basic 3D content and enhancing existing 3D content, many compositing artists like to build parts of their artwork in a dedicated 3D application. There are many to choose from, with price points that range from free to $2,000 and beyond for a single license. For the purposes of this book, we will cover a few of the tools we use, including Cinema 4D from Maxon, Strata 3D, and Google Sketchup (which is free and can be found by doing a quick search at Google.com).

Which 3D tools you choose will depend both on your budget and on your appetite for learning and working with 3D environments, but at the very least you should investigate these products and see what they can do for your composite artwork.

For some of the examples in this book, we will use the popular Cinema 4D integrated modeling and rendering application (**Figure 1.8**). Although it is by no means a "learn it in a day" kind of program, it can be more affordable than some of the other pro 3D applications (depending on how you bundle it with other features) and is easier to learn than most of its counterparts; we've also provided some Cinema 4D information later in the book.

Figure 1.8 Cinema 4D R11

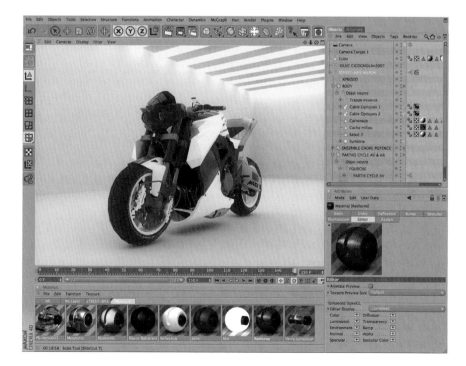

Advanced Masking Tools

One of the most important aspects of creating powerful composite imagery is the ability to create precisely masked areas within your images. Oftentimes the improved masking tools Photoshop provides will be more than powerful enough to accomplish your goals, but occasionally you'll need a little extra help.

A variety of third-party professional masking tools are available, which are not to be confused with matting or "green-screen" tools. The former are designed for use with images shot against a pure green (or sometimes blue) backdrop, which makes it easier to isolate the subject from said backdrop and place it within After Effects and other video-related projects.

Masking software instead requires no special backdrop but rather pulls parts of images directly from their natural surroundings. This can save time and money but might also require a little extra work since the "extraction" process is not as clear-cut as taking shots against a green screen or other matte. You will learn more about one of the masking tools we use when compositing—Mask Pro from onOne software—in Chapter 10, "Compositing Source Materials."

Noise Reduction Software

Another crucial aspect of creating composite imagery in Photoshop is the ability to produce clean-looking photographs. Sometimes, fate conspires against the photographer, forcing a shot in low light with a higher ISO than the photographer would like. The result is usually an image that has a distracting grain-like pattern, or *noise*, to it. Although it is never a bad idea to try the Reduce Noise filter in Photoshop, you will often get the best results from a combination of Adobe Camera Raw (ACR) and third-party noise reduction software, such as Noise Ninja or Noiseware.

Our noise destroyer of choice, because of the amount of control it provides, along with a friendly user interface, is Noiseware (**Figure 1.9**).

Figure 1.9 Imagenomic's Noiseware

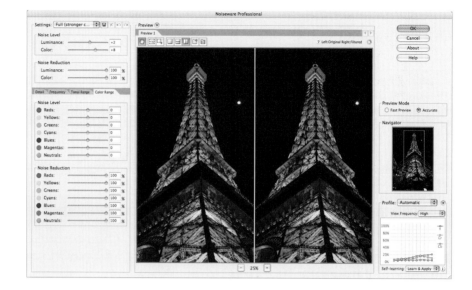

Noiseware looks and feels like it was built as part of Photoshop. Once you understand how it works, it can provide excellent results by removing most of the noise in your images, without oversoftening them. For this reason, we will also be showing how to use Noiseware as part of the compositing workflow in Chapter 8, "Enhancing Source Images."

CHAPTER TWO
Brainstorming

FINDING INSPIRATION

One of the most challenging aspects of building a composite scene is knowing what you want to achieve. You may be working from a professional brief where the ideas have already been laid out for you or even sketched as part of a storyboard. Often, you will start with only a simple concept from which you must build a believable image. The goal is to bring together elements from different images to create something completely new.

Let the ideas flow. Your project could be something as simple as adding color and drama to otherwise empty skies, as shown in **Figure 2.1**, or something more complex such as creating a surreal landscape where the local wildlife wears top hats and drinks lattes while reading *People* magazine! The key is to leverage your creative perceptions of the world to create something that will capture the attention of your viewers, in whatever medium they might ultimately use.

Anything that you find to be inspiring or interesting as a subject is fair game. These topics should be considered in your brainstorming sessions, along with more obvious themes you have in mind. To borrow the cliche: "Don't edit yourself!"

Figure 2.1 Adding drama to empty skies is a common compositing task.

Storing and Evaluating Ideas

Ideas can come from unexpected sources: standing in the shower, taking a walk, or interacting with kids or groups of people. But you can give inspiration a helping hand, as well. One of the most vital steps is something frequently overlooked by most artists: taking notes!

Pen to paper. Whenever something strikes you as having potential, write it down. If you can, take a snapshot of the thing that inspired you or make a sketch. So long as you provide a means of reference, you can come back and thumb through your archives, making connections and remembering things that will help feed your creative mind. If you know you're on the right track but are stuck on the specifics, stepping back from a situation and revisiting it a few days later can often provide enough of a spark to get the energy flowing.

Many digital tools can help you generate ideas. One popular approach is simply to "wander" the Web, searching for and browsing through the creative works of others. Although it can take a lot of time to find the right sites—the ones that really speak to you—seeing the world through the eyes of another artist is often a great way to find inspiration and create new ideas. Obviously, you want your final work to be truly your own, but often the work of others can prompt you to look at the world in different ways, thereby helping you define your own creative styles and viewpoints.

Creative cells. Another method you can use to help manage and generate ideas is to create a spreadsheet with columns of subjects, actions, scenes, and other details. Selecting random cells in each column can help you develop unusual scenarios, such as those shown in **Figure 2.2**. You can include multiple columns of subjects to create complexity, but for this example, we'll stick to one set of each. After your columns are in place, choose a random cell from each column to complete a sentence in the form of "subject action scene." Sometimes you may end up with something surreal, like "puppies bowling on the moon." Certainly some combinations are good only for a few laughs, but others may open your mind to some very cool possibilities. Give it a try!

Brainstorming.xls

Brainstorming List

	Subjects	Actions	Locations	Times	Emotion
1					
2	Architect	Archery	Arena	Morning	Angry
3	Cat	Bowling	Bead of Water	Noon	Confused
4	Doctor	Cricket	Bridge	Night	Content
5	Dog	Diving	Bubble	Winter	Focused
6	Dolphin	Driving	Classroom	Spring	Happy
7	Engineer	Ducking	Corner Office	Summer	Hyper
8	Farmer	Eating	Cubicle	Fall	Quiet
9	Fireman	Floating	Desert	Rain storm	Sad
10	Fisherman	Flying	Gorge	Snow storm	Sneaky
11	Gecko	Foraging	Head of a Pin	Stifling heat	Tired
12	Manikin	Hockey	Hillside		
13	News Anchor	Jumping	In a tree		
14	Painter	Punching	Moon		
15	Physicist	Reading	Mountain Peak		
16	Pilot	Running	Ocean		
17	Polar Bear	Sailing	Riverside		
18	Sculpture	Sleeping	Standing on TV remote		
19	Sprinter	Soccer	Steps		
20	Statue	Watching TV	Temple		
21	Toddler	Writing	Titan		
22	Trucker	Yelling	Traffic		

Sheet1 Sheet2 Sheet3 — Ready — Sum=0 — SCRL CAPS NUM

Figure 2.2
Spreadsheets can be a valuable part of the creative planning process.

The point of this exercise is to free your mind from the obvious and the expected. Although puppies bowling on the moon may not be your final subject, just thinking about the surface of the moon might take you in a direction you would not have considered otherwise.

If you have a large collection of stock images or illustrations, try populating your spreadsheet columns with keywords taken from your image organizer. We also encourage you to add new subjects or concepts that interest you or that are part of planned activities or travel. Naturally, a bit of pragmatism makes sense here as well. "Bikini models skydiving in Peru" didn't impress our wives in the least. Skydiving is dangerous.

Sketching and Visualizing

Once the seed of your idea is planted, you can begin to give life to your ideas by sketching them on paper or onscreen. Just imagining your ideas often isn't enough; you'll need to see them, even if in a very rough form. This is a critical step in visualizing the direction that your composition will take. Since the primary focus of this book is compositing from photographs, it is important to put pencil to paper (or pointer to screen) as early as possible.

You will find that some ideas lend themselves more readily to compositing than others. This can influence how you choose your images and how you plan to photograph a source image—a topic discussed in the next chapter. Using the previous example of puppies bowling on the moon, it might be difficult to build a photorealistic image of a puppy "holding" anything, let alone a 9-pound sphere complete with three finger holes. Sketching ideas can give you a better sense of which image components will be based on photographs and which ones must be based on an illustration or 3D model (to mold a puppy's paw into one that has human-like "fingers," for example).

Focus on the storyline. The goal is to get a basic visual representation of your concept, which you can refine later using Adobe Photoshop CS4 techniques and other software. Some concepts may benefit from *storyboarding* (sketching out a scene concept from multiple angles and points in time). Storyboards like the one in **Figure 2.3** have been part of the artist's toolbox for many years, particularly for moviemakers. However, they are also useful when building a story into a still image, because you can break down the composition into manageable parts.

Figure 2.3 Storyboards can help you plan your composite image more effectively.

Break it down. Separating the background, foreground, and other image components helps clarify and organize your project. Let's take a quick look at some ways you can refine your thoughts in a visual form:

Paper-based sketches. This is probably the quickest and certainly the cheapest option, because sometimes a quick drawing is all you need to see that the idea can evolve into something more or alternatively that it should be scrapped.

Magazine cutouts. Sometimes getting back to your elementary school roots and bringing together some cutout photos from magazines on an art board or desk can also trigger big ideas.

Digital sketches. If you're confident that your idea will work, starting with a digital sketch can speed the compositing process by providing a more permanent storage medium for your concept and aiding source image layout.

Scanned images. Sometimes these different techniques come together as part of the brainstorming process. A common example is when one of your magazine clippings becomes a definite point of inspiration, and you can then scan it into Photoshop and actually use that image or a digital tracing of that image as the starting point of your project.

3D computer models. If you plan to place objects with complex shapes into your composite at some point but you know it has to have a 3D look, a 3D model is the way to go. You can generate 3D content yourself with Photoshop or third-party software (discussed in Chapter 9, "Creating 3D Content"), or you can use online stock agencies (discussed in Chapter 4, "Using Stock Images") as your source for 3D content.

Try each technique to see what works best for you. We have found that digital techniques can make the transition from concept to working project easier. With Photoshop, your photographic elements can reside on distinct layers (see **Figure 2.4**), which allow you to move and manipulate elements independently. You can also organize your layers into logical groups, making it easier to find and work with your digital elements as the project gets under way.

Keep in mind that you are giving yourself a starting point. It may turn out that you run through the visualization process a few times before you settle on a specific concept, and that's perfectly OK. In fact, it may be a good idea to create a few variations of your concept just so you can have some alternatives,

Figure 2.4 Layering documents aids workflow and organization.

should you find you need to make changes during the photography or compositing components of this workflow.

Once more, with depth. 3D applications such as Google SketchUp (which is free of charge, happily enough) can be a great help in evaluating perspective, especially for those of us who are not natural illustrators. Even classically trained artists may find that adjusting features such as perspective and focal length is cumbersome using traditional media. Another advantage to using 3D applications is that you can add 2D images onto the surface of a 3D shape and get a better idea of how to deal with depth, location, and light falloff, all of which are key to building a believable image.

To make your sketches as useful as possible, pay careful attention to the linear and aerial perspectives, as well as the placement of your subjects within the overall composition. Even in a basic way, you should be able to use your sketches as a guide to positioning your 3D camera and laying out your scene. We discuss the new 3D capabilities in Photoshop CS4 Extended, as well as core 3D design concepts and the capabilities of dedicated 3D design environments like Cinema 4D R11, in Chapter 9.

Choosing a Final Concept

As you begin to examine the art of other designers, photographers, and compositors, and as you experiment with different media types and technologies, such as merging 2D and 3D imagery, new ideas will come to light. Here are a few questions to ask yourself in the process:

Mission possible. Can you get the shots you need (assuming you won't be using illustrations)? That may sound trivial, but think about what you will need to do to accomplish the goal. You will have to think about physical locations and timing, as well as equipment and transportation. If you think you have the equipment and availability to take the images you need for your project's scenery and subjects, it's a good idea to prioritize them so that you can tackle the most difficult ones first.

Taking stock of the situation. If you can't take the shots you need, can you use stock images or 3D tools to acquire or create those elements? It may take more time digging through stock catalogs or building a 3D model than to just go shoot, but it may be your only alternative. Although most of this book addresses compositing and photography from the perspective of shooting your own source images, alternative sources are something you will want to consider in case you run into a time crunch or other situation that demands that you acquire image components from other sources.

Tech-know. Do you have the Photoshop skills you need? We hope you will by the time you're done with this book! The next chapter will discuss in more detail how to plan the photographic process so that you can put yourself in a position to get exactly the shots you want for your compositing project.

CHAPTER THREE

Choosing the Scene and Subject

When beginning an artistic project in Adobe Photoshop CS4, you might be tempted to skip the relatively boring details of planning and preparation and dive right into the process of crafting your imagery. Although this can lead you in unexpected directions (sometimes with good results), more often than not "leaping without looking" will result in frustration unless you have unlimited time (and even budget) for endless experimentation.

Photoshop compositing projects are like any other project: You need a clear objective and some semblance of a plan to achieve that objective in a reasonable amount of time with the tools and capabilities you have on hand. Two big parts of successful planning are choosing the right scene or backdrop for your imagery and choosing the subjects that will visually interact within that scene.

You may need to consider elements as mundane as travel budgets and time of year as you map out your objectives and decide what aspects of your idea are practical and what is best left for another day. It sounds dry, but really it's pretty easy to come up with a good list of possible scenes and subjects with just an hour or two of brainstorming.

THE SCENE

Typically, the first step in creating your composite image is to define the setting. You need to determine the backdrop and general context of your final image. Very often the message your imagery communicates will be rooted in the background imagery you use. Before we go further, we'd like to make one point clear: Ultimately, composite image making is an art form. As such, there are no "rules" other than following the guidelines and schedule you set and the applicable laws related to the photographing or use of your source images. You can find more information about copyrights in Chapter 4, "Using Stock Images."

You may think the backdrop is going to be incidental to your final image, for whatever reason. That's fine, but it is still important to give your scene and context some careful thought as you begin the project.

Details Make the Difference

A successful composite image often starts with a unique viewpoint into the world you're creating. Will the point of view you want to communicate exist in the parts of the world that are reasonably within your grasp?

Start with perspective. What if your vision is to look down onto a distant hillside or up to a maze of modern building tops on a futuristic skyline, but your local geography is mostly flat and suburban? Can you legally negotiate your way to the roof of that new apartment building overlooking the nearby forest preserve lands? Are there stock illustrations you can blend with an existing big-city skyline that is an hour or two's drive from your home? Photography in this context is often about discovering opportunities and working with the locals.

Timing is key. What is the weather like from season to season at your proposed location? Are you counting on foliage or certain environmental elements being part of the scene, and are those elements typically present during the time of year you are able to travel? Understanding your regional geography and how the seasons can impact the photographic environment is important.

It's fine to choose a blaze of autumn colors as part of your scene, but if you live in a region dominated by conifers and frequent rains in the fall, it's better to choose a more practical option (unless you have the time and budget to travel) to get the shots you want (**Figure 3.1**).

Time of day is also of great importance. If you're planning a blue water scene, a few hours can make the difference between a beach covered with tan bodies, towels, and volleyballs … and a beach with an empty lifeguard stand and a lone beachcomber, set against the tumbling surf. As you consider the scenarios that can affect your chosen location, ask yourself which ones are best suited to your artistic vision.

Figure 3.1 Know your surroundings when choosing a setting for your composite.

Make a note of it. We have found that keeping a few simple notes as you travel and as you commute for your daily work can be invaluable. How many times as photographers or creative professionals have we driven by a truly unique or interesting scene (with no time to spare) and said, "I have to come back here" … only to forget about it because we didn't make a note of it? Be prepared to jot down a few notes so you can make it back for those photographs!

A variety of tools are available to photographers that aid in our quest to keep the important ideas we have and places we see stored away for quick retrieval. GPS is now an affordable technology for most people and is quite useful for marking the exact "location of inspiration." There are also freely available tools like Google Earth, which is a great research tool and can help you keep track of important locations.

When keeping notes, write your comments so that they will make sense to you later. Overdoing the shorthand can result in a collection of notes that have little context later or that don't enable you to recall what it was that inspired or interested you in the first place.

Scouting the Options

It is common for photographers to search the areas nearest to where they live when choosing photographic locations. This can hamstring your ability to generate a compelling composite image. Don't limit the quality of your final artwork just to save an hour or two. Launch your laptop's browser, pull out the atlas, and circle a few good spots. Take time to explore your local area over a long weekend! As with any photographic endeavors, a little scouting can go a long way. By scouting new locations, you may find inspiration for your composite artwork.

Orders from headquarters. Your profession can often influence the locations you choose to scout and photograph. Whether you're a photographer, a computer engineer, or an architect, factors such as the number of vacation days you have, the places you typically travel to on business, and other work-related issues will have a big impact. Make the most of your opportunities!

If you often travel to Arizona on business but your ideal photographic location is in Badlands, South Dakota (left), it might pay off to add an extra day to your next business trip to the Southwest. Would the red rocks of Sedona (**Figure 3.2**) or the mountains of Flagstaff, Arizona, serve you as well or almost as well as the Badlands? Sometimes a small compromise can go a long way toward making your final composite more attainable, without putting a crimp on quality.

Figure 3.2 Keep photographic alternatives in mind when choosing a location.

Maybe you're looking for that classic '50s neighborhood, complete with an old general store. Bear in mind as you go looking for it that you may discover that fabled street in not one but two locations. With a little extra scouting and an array of angles and focal lengths to choose from, there's no reason you can't blend the local malt shop storefront and your favorite street full of classic homes the next town over into a single backdrop.

The bottom line is that the most successful scenes work not because they're from a famous place but rather because they're from a place that lends itself to your vision. Keep your eyes and options open, including the possibility of piecing your background scenery together using the same techniques we will cover in later chapters.

Travel Now, Travel Later

Ultimately, you can take one of two paths when location photography is a must. The first is to plan for the short term. Knowing which weekends or days you will have free (or which days you will be traveling), pick a location that is within relatively easy reach, and make the best of that situation. We have found this is often the route people will choose for pragmatic reasons.

The other approach is longer-term. You can choose a location that will be absolutely perfect for the final image you want to create and then plan far in advance to ensure that you get there at the right time of year with enough days to capture the types of scenes you need. Your shooting days may be months away in some cases, but if it means you will have the time and budget available to travel and capture the perfect scene, you may find the wait to be worthwhile.

NOTE Typically this option is only viable for those who make their living in the photographic arts.

When you take the long-term approach, researching your location is vital to a successful photographic trip. You need to know what the weather is likely to do at any given time of year and be prepared for that. Hypothermia is a great way to ruin a trip! You should also pay attention to seasonal considerations. Airfare and rental car rates can change dramatically from month to month. If your location happens to be in a foreign country, it is also a wise idea to study up on the local people and the laws governing photography there (**Figure 3.3**).

Figure 3.3 Know the local laws that govern photography when traveling abroad.

In the rear with the gear. Another consideration when traveling is to figure out the type of camera equipment you will need and how easy it will be to travel with that equipment, based on your mode of transport. Once you have arrived by air, land, or sea, will you be able to carry this gear with you on foot? If not, do you have a spouse or friend who can travel with you and help you get your gear from point A to point B?

Your permit, please. Although you may be targeting a beautiful and isolated area, sometimes these areas can be very popular and often require a permit to be purchased weeks or months in advance. Some good examples are popular backcountry locations in national parks such as Yosemite or Banff (**Figure 3.4**). If there is a campsite in your future that is a brisk walk from the marquee destination at a big park, assume you will need to book that site the same as you would an airline ticket or hotel. Ignoring this reality could end in big disappointment when you arrive at the park.

Figure 3.4 Popular sites like Banff National Park may require permits.

GPS. Whether you are scouting a future trip or photographing your chosen scene, a mobile GPS can be an invaluable tool. These devices not only serve as a means of keeping track of important locations but also can help you navigate your way back to "base camp" in backcountry or forested locations. They also aid navigation while driving, just like automotive GPS systems do.

Handheld personal GPS units designed for trekking and camping (especially the higher-end models from Garmin) are very accurate and can reliably pick up satellite signals in remote locations such as deep canyons or other mountainous areas. They can even work well in urban environments when shooting photographs among tall buildings.

When you find the perfect location and vantage point, you can make a precise record of where you are standing—within a few feet in most cases—so that you don't waste time when you return trying to remember exactly where you stood.

Travel by Wire: Stock Imagery

If shooting your own pictures is not of interest to you or is cost-prohibitive because of travel or equipment expenses, you may want to consider stock imagery as an option. Online stock agencies have tremendous image (and even video) collections in many cases, and they usually have very reasonable rates. Many of the images in this chapter were chosen from iStockphoto to give you an idea of the quality and variation of what you can find there.

NOTE Depending on the agency and file type, a very unique and high-quality stock image can cost as much as a plane ticket, so don't count on stock imagery to be your cost savior in every situation.

Both approaches to acquiring a compelling images have their benefits and drawbacks. Your own images will convey your personal artistic style and vision, but sometimes there is no substitute for a high-resolution stock image of Iguaçu Falls, the Kremlin (**Figure 3.5**), or some other dramatic location that most people simply cannot access. Although it is true that you can easily change the character of a photographed location using Photoshop, there are limits to what should be attempted in this regard. Stay true to your original vision; use backdrop imagery that won't require "major surgery" to look right.

Figure 3.5 Sometimes scale is everything.

The drawback is that some stock images can have a generic or ordinary look to them. Ultimately, you have to decide which characteristics will benefit your images most and whether those are worth paying a premium. There are specific strategies you should consider when acquiring your source images from a stock agency, and Chapter 4 covers stock images in more detail, including important licensing considerations.

One final possibility is to get permission from friends or family to use some of their choice photographs as part of your composite. Keep in mind that it's always best to discuss any commercial ramifications up front and that you may need model releases for any photographs that contain people who can be easily identified before you can use your composite commercially or display it publicly. Seek legal advice from an attorney on this point if you are unsure.

The Subject

The subject of your composite image and artwork is where the real creativity comes into play. Simply taking two dissimilar subjects and blending them together in Photoshop because you can is not really what this book is about. The goal is to leverage Photoshop as a tool for creating artworks that you and only you can envision based on your life experiences.

More questions than answers. Before you begin, you need to ask yourself the right questions in order to wind up with a positive result. What is your goal? Who is this work for? Sometimes only the artist sees the final art. Other times great art starts as a work-for-hire. It could even be a gift for a loved one. The point is to know your audience. Just as musicians, authors, and moviemakers have identified their target audience (**Figure 3.6**), you must do the same if your project is to be a success.

Figure 3.6 Know your audience.

You have to know your audience before you can create something that will affect them emotionally or intellectually. For those in the graphic design world, most likely a business client is your audience (in other words, you create what they're asking you to create). For the rest of us, the "who" is not as clear-cut, but the process of thinking it through ahead of time is a necessary step if we are to make something worthy of their attention and, potentially, their business as well.

Good intentions. Do you want to create a scene that causes the viewers to suspend disbelief as they view a subject placed in a scene that is completely unexpected or impossible—yet looks completely real? Or, do you want to take a more subtle approach, seamlessly blending subject and scene in such a way that the viewers have to stop and consider what they're seeing and whether it is real or not? Both of these approaches, and every variation in between, can be a valid and worthwhile endeavor.

As long as the art you are creating means something to you on a personal level, and as long as it is executed with forethought and attention to detail, you are likely to create a successful work of digital art. Remember, there are no formulas. Give yourself plenty of options, and explore them before you begin the project.

As with painters or illustrators working on a new concept, sometimes it is best to quickly sketch many possible subjects and scenes on paper or with your digital stylus. Getting a rough 3D visualization of what your finished composite might look like can be enough for you to see right away that it can't work—or that it is the perfect idea. Avoid limiting yourself early in the process; experiment with different types of unrelated objects, even if they are not as familiar to you as your usual concepts (**Figure 3.7**). As you work with the different shapes, colors, and moods involved with different subjects, you may discover new avenues of inspiration you did not originally consider.

Figure 3.7 Experiment with a range of subjects.

Maybe a wild animal or an infant's eyes can be the start of your vision. And don't assume that the subject is always an object in the scene. Perhaps your subject *is* the scene, with elements of your other shots blended in to create a surreal and impossible landscape. Turn things around. Look at a subject or scene from an unexpected angle or perspective, and see whether you can find common threads where you can bring things together.

A reptile, you say? At first glance, an alligator and a rolling hillside landscape might not appear to have anything in common unless you look closer. What if you were a millimeter tall, standing on the back of that alligator? Perhaps the terrain before you now appears as dark hills made of stone, covered in moss and algae. Perhaps a melon has nothing to do with astronomy until you consider its geometric shape relative to the shape of the earth and realize that the artwork you need for the environmental conference might have a solution (**Figure 3.8**).

These are simple examples, but they drive home an important point: We must see things in new ways if we're to make art from the everyday scenes and subjects we are bombarded with on television, on the Internet, and from practically everywhere else we look. The best part is that seeing things in a new way is very easy to do; all it takes is a little daydreaming and 15 minutes of spare time. You can find the time while having your coffee on the train ride into work, during a short break from an important meeting, or on a rainy weekend afternoon.

Figure 3.8 Look at things in new ways when evaluating potential source materials. You may find that dissimilar subjects have more in common than you think.

Ideas are all around; you just have to take a moment to let them seep into your imagination! As your project concept evolves, keep your sketches and plans handy, and review them periodically.

So close, yet so far away. Another key point to keep in mind when evaluating potential subjects is to choose something to which you have access. You need to be able to acquire the subject imagery in a reasonable amount of time and within your budget, either via a stock agency or from your own photography. If you are the photographer, the subject imagery needs to be something you can capture from multiple angles, possibly with different lighting arrangements.

Other considerations. Whenever possible, make note of the relative scale for the scene and subject, as well as the presence of lens effects. When photographing the scene for your composite, do you plan to use a polarizing filter to remove some glare from a reflective surface in the image? Will you need to repeat this type of glare with your subject? How much distortion will there be because of the size and type of lens? Could other environmental factors throw a certain light or look onto your chosen subject?

Don't let the details get away from you. Ultimately, they are what will sell the illusion of your final image. For example, when working on composite images that are intended to mimic reality, the placement of shadows and specular highlights is critical. If not handled correctly, they can be telltale signs of digital enhancement. These and many related lighting topics are covered in more detail in Chapter 5, "Capturing the Scene and Subject."

OTHER CONSIDERATIONS

When creating a composite image, you'll want to include certain elements in your planning beyond just choosing the right scene and subject or the right context. Complexity, color, and light can make or break your final image, and that is the focus for the final part of our discussion of subject and scene.

Complexity

The level of complexity within any of the scenes or subjects you choose to photograph (or acquire from a stock gallery) is a vital consideration. Take landscape photographs as an example: The more contours, trees, and ground-plane objects within your scene, the more they will potentially overwhelm the other elements you blend into the scene, depending on their relative scale (scale and related issues are discussed in detail in Chapter 10, "Compositing Source Materials").

Keep it simple? Dealing with complexity in a scene is a big part of the compositing process. It can have a dramatic impact on time requirements and, potentially, budget requirements as well. Precisely masking the boundary of a grove of trees or complex terrain can take a lot of time and effort. Photoshop CS4 does offer new functionality, including the ability to generate color range based masks for adjustment layers, as well as an advanced masking panel that can make this type of task simpler. However, in some situations a third-party masking or matting tool is still a good investment, if it can save time.

It's not uncommon to create a precision mask using software such as Mask Pro from onOne Software (**Figure 3.9**). Sometimes you may even need to photograph a particular subject with a solid-color backdrop and "extract" the subject precisely using "green-screen" software such as Primatte from Digital Anarchy. The good news is that the results you pull from matting software can be directly applied to video and motion graphics projects as well, thanks to the close integration between Photoshop CS4 Extended and Adobe After Effects CS4.

Figure 3.9 The Mask Pro
Interface

The upside is that when a complex scene is layered and masked correctly, it can be used to more realistically obscure or direct focus to specific image elements, thereby making them a more convincing part of the scene. For example, a precisely masked tree can be used to overhang part of a subject, providing the illusion that the subject is between the horizon and the tree. Chapter 10 also covers the details of masking and other techniques for obscuring unwanted pixels.

Color and Luminosity

A common mistake when attempting to blend unique image elements into a scene is ignoring the realities of their color or apparent brightness, or both. As much as possible, you should plan to acquire and integrate images that fall within a similar range of hues, saturation, and lighting conditions. All three of these factors are often dictated by the visual environment in which a photo is taken. And although it's true that you will be able to make some changes in Adobe Camera Raw (ACR) and Photoshop to make the integration work (that's a big part of what this book is about), as much as possible you should start with source images that are already in the same ballpark in terms of lighting, color, and other important factors.

Color harmony. If your scene contains a range of muted yellows and beiges, dark greens, and a bit of reddish rock, attempting to integrate a bright orange or purple image element into that scene is not likely to turn out well. Conversely, if your scene depicts the Shanghai skyline at night (**Figure 3.10**), your best bet is to blend image elements that contain more saturated, bright hues (even "neon-like" colors), rather than subdued or darker colors of natural environments, which would get lost among so many stronger colors and bright lights.

Figure 3.10 The context of your composite will dictate the hues, saturation, and character of lighting that you will need from your source images.

Even though it may seem as if two things would go great together when you first think of them, keep their visual color context in mind as you make your choices. If you have two subjects you feel strongly must be used but their colors don't blend well or complement one another in the context you are planning, you'll find some alternatives in Chapter 7, "Processing Raw Source Files," and Chapter 8, "Enhancing Source Images." For example, the Color Balance adjustment in Photoshop (Image > Adjustments > Color Balance) can help make the colors of the images more consistent. The Hue, Saturation & Luminance panel in ACR and tools such as the Match Color adjustment (Image > Adjustments > Match Color) can also help you produce a seamless composite photo.

Again, planning properly can save you headaches later. If from the outset you choose scenes and subjects that can plausibly be integrated into a single scene with modest color tweaks rather than wholesale color shifts, you should find yourself in a better place when the project is finished. That's not to say it is impossible to work with source images from dissimilar environments, only that you should keep this concept in mind as you progress. The less you have to force things to fit together visually, the higher quality your final result will be.

Follow the light. You can think of *luminosity* as the apparent brightness of an image element, as determined by each viewer. In other words, unlike luminance, which is a measured quantity, luminosity is a more subjective assessment of the lighting within an image. Even when you get the colors right, you must ensure that the luminosity in your scene is believable as a whole and serves the purpose of drawing the viewer into the scene.

It may even be necessary to create the appearance that areas of luminosity are "interacting" with one another using the Lighting Effects filter in Photoshop (Filters > Render > Lighting Effects), shown in **Figure 3.11**. How you make things happen (in the camera or in Photoshop) will depend on the characteristics of the surfaces being photographed and other variables such as the time of day. Do these surfaces reflect light in similar ways? Does one light source overwhelm the others?

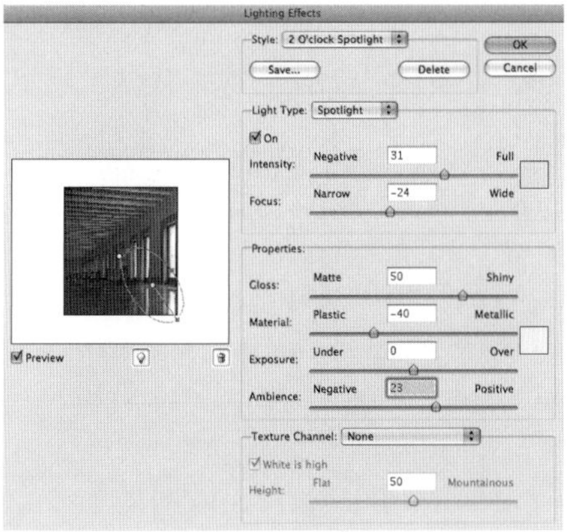

Figure 3.11 The Lighting Effects filter in Photoshop can help you manipulate your image's luminosity.

These are issues you must consider as you photograph the component parts of your composite image. We'll discuss working with photographic light in more detail in Chapter 5. We'll discuss the tools used to create and manipulate light in Photoshop in Chapters 7 through 10.

The bottom line. Everything starts with the quality of the photography (or the original source illustration); without good source material, you will have a much harder time putting together a compelling composite image. It pays to think through your project ahead of time and plan accordingly so that you give yourself the best chance to succeed when you begin working with Photoshop.

CHAPTER

mages

RIGHT SHOTS

ots you need may not be possible, either
use of other constraints that you can't work
s part of your composite has plenty of benefits.
ew hang-ups if you're not careful when choos-
of due diligence, you can avoid problems by
strictions and other terms of use that govern
s stock agencies.

ionplace online, which is great for photog-
igencies carry a wide variety of styles and
ze in a particular theme or look. Many carry
aphs and illustrations, also offering animations
oices are so varied that it is important to stay
for the composite image and keep things orga-

That You Need

Before diving into a sea of online catalogs, you should know what you want
from a stock agency. Many suppliers may have an image that will work for
you, but the agencies probably differ in terms of service, image formats,
and licensing. The web interface can also differ significantly from agency to
agency. For this reason, you need to do a little research and figure out which
one will work best for your purposes.

NOTE We are not attorneys, and therefore you should not consider anything you read in this book to be legal advice. Our goal is simply to help you become more familiar with the process of choosing and using stock images. If you need legal advice with respect to any of the topics discussed in this book, we strongly recommend you consult an attorney who specializes in copyright laws and licensing of artistic content.

Stock agencies are typically organized around themes and collections, but they also rely heavily on keyword systems. Notes that you have taken throughout your projects can be very useful at this stage! More information on this topic is available in the "Keyword Search Strategies" section later in the chapter.

Typically, the workflow for using stock agencies consists of a few key tasks:

1. Choose the type of image you need.

2. Find keywords that describe the image characteristics.

3. Search online agency catalogs using those keywords.

4. Review the licensing terms and restrictions, as well as cost.

5. Download and begin using the images that fit your purposes and budget.

In our experience, using online stock agencies is a straightforward process. Since you should already know what kinds of images you want to use (and we've dedicated a sidebar to using keywords), it's important that we spend some time in this chapter focusing on searching for the right image and keeping track of those you decide to purchase.

Searching and Organizing

Most stock sites have a mechanism, called a *lightbox*, for keeping track of images. This is simply a collection of images that you want to consider for an eventual purchase, grouped together and accessible from your stock account home page. While browsing through a catalog or search results, you can make note of which images you may need by assigning them to your lightbox. This is usually accomplished by clicking a small graphical button found near the preview on the image's product page.

Typically you can create and save more than one lightbox for a given agency once you have set up your account (which is usually free). Most users will create a different lightbox for each major category of content, such as the background textures shown in **Figure 4.1** or other topics such as portraits or landscapes. The advantage to this is that you can store collections indefinitely and return to them as time permits to make your purchasing decisions. You can also compare images within a collection to find just the right picture.

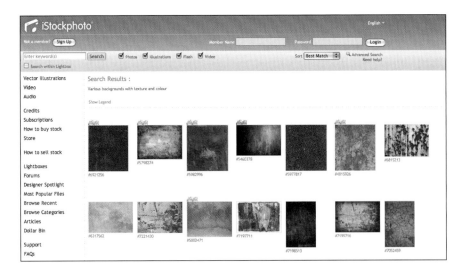

Figure 4.1 Custom light-boxes help you to manage the online stock images that interest you.

Besides lightboxes, some sites allow you to save search queries that you use often so that you don't have to reenter them each time you use the site. Finding the exact combination of keywords to generate the best search results can be tricky. Once you've found that combination, it is handy to revisit that search from time to time to see what additions a site has made.

Building on this idea of saving favorite search terms, many photographers and editors find they like a particular photographer or provider. Knowing which photographers shoot which styles can help reduce search time and is a good way to find inspiration by checking on updates from these sources. Some agencies even offer notification systems that let you know when new content is available from a given provider or in a specific category.

Over time, you may develop your own favorite list of shooters and agencies. Rob Haggart has a great list of agencies organized by category on his blog, A Photo Editor, at http://aphotoeditor.com/. Although the list is not exhaustive, it is extensive and therefore worth a look (**Figure 4.2**).

Figure 4.2 The stock agency list maintained by Rob Haggart is a great place to start your search for the right stock images.

Keyword Search Strategies

What good is a world full of digital stock images if you can't find the ones you need? The secret to effective cataloging is a good keyword system. Most online stock providers want you to use their services and will go to great lengths to provide flexible search options.

Start as general as possible in your keyword selection to see how many images you get. If you know you need a new sky for your background, using *sky* is a good start but will likely yield hundreds (or maybe thousands) of images. Once you see there are enough images to choose from, you can add modifier keywords to narrow the selection.

For example, if you need a sky with white clouds, just add *white clouds* to your original *sky* search query. If you still have too many results to browse easily, think about what other elements you need in your scene. Add keywords to describe those elements to narrow down your search results to more manageable levels.

The difficulty with relying on keywords, however, is that the words you choose to describe your ideal picture may not be the words the stock agency or photographer chose to describe the same subject. To help remedy semantic mismatches, many agencies use standardized keyword lists that are accepted by many photographers, designers, and agencies. This can help everyone to communicate, though the systems are not perfect because no single system is yet universally accepted as a true standard.

A quick web search returns many different keyword master lists, including software that is designed to help stock photographers automatically apply the most effective keywords. Using this type of software has the added benefit of reducing spelling errors, which are abundant on the Internet.

Even with these master lists and software helpers, keyword searches still have limitations. For example, it is difficult to find descriptions of lighting techniques or shadow direction in a given image, though some agencies do use these techniques as keywords. Using keywords for color, shape, and general mood is also a good idea in theory but has mixed results in practice. The bottom line is that you may have to make more than one search (or search more than one agency) to find a specific kind of image.

LICENSING AND RESTRICTIONS

Misconceptions abound about using stock images in derivative works. Since compositing is often about creating derivative artwork (see the sidebar "Derivative Works and the Internet"), it's appropriate to spend some time on this subject. The laws can be tough to interpret, so again, we strongly recommend you consult a qualified attorney who specializes in copyright law before making any decisions that you are not 100 percent sure about. This is particularly true if you intend to sell or distribute your composite images.

Works of art typically fall under the category of "intellectual property," and the copyright laws governing this property can vary from country to country. The United States agreed in 1989 to become part of the international union of countries that recognize and support the copyright stipulations of the Berne Convention. This convention states (generally) that there is an implied copyright to works of art from the moment of inception, regardless of whether a copyright notice appears on the work or in conjunction with it.

Derivative Works and the Internet

For more information on intellectual property laws, start by performing a web search on the Berne Convention of 1886, which outlines general principles of copyright. The Berne Union is the group of countries that signed the general agreement, which includes the United States. In the United States, the Digital Millennium Copyright Act of 1998 deals with electronic intellectual property and is based on treaties developed by the World Intellectual Property Organization. You may also want to check the latest edition of *Professional Business Practices in Photography,* from the American Society of Media Photographers (ASMP), for additional information and advice on this and related topics.

Digital photographs are no different. The copyright exists and is legally recognized from the moment the image is captured in your camera. To help move this process forward, some manufacturers, such as Nikon and Canon, are building cameras that have the option of imprinting a copyright directly onto your digital files from the moment they are recorded. This is done with the help of a metadata technology called Exchangeable Image File Format (EXIF) data.

NOTE Metadata is also discussed in Chapter 6, "Organizing and Evaluating Images."

A technology known as Extensible Metadata Platform (XMP) was designed by Adobe for use in a range of creative applications, and also works with EXIF data. It is built into products like Bridge and Photoshop CS4, as well as some third-party products. For example, using Photoshop's File Information panel (choose File > File Info), you can gain access to the full range of your image's EXIF data and other metadata (**Figure 4.3**).

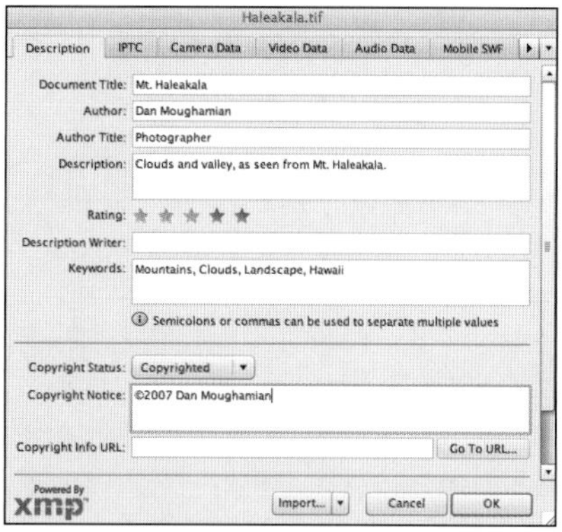

Figure 4.3 Exchangeable Image File Format (EXIF) data dialog box

Copy control. Moreover, the copyright holder has quite a bit of control in how their images may be used. With respect to stock agencies, this control is manifested as licenses for acceptable use. These licenses vary from source to source, so it is important to understand the licensing language for a given agency before you download and use its images. This is particularly true of images intended for commercial use.

The general idea of licensing is that you pay a consideration or fee to the copyright holder for some use to which you both agree. A *consideration* may be monetary, or it may simply be a credit or citation that is visible on your work. Use can be limited by date, number of reproductions in a given medium, or even publication type. In some cases, a license may also restrict the context for an image or derivative work. For the most part, stock images are licensed so that they can be used for numerous purposes and by many individuals.

The bottom line. Within a given stock agency website, licenses can vary from collection to collection and even from image to image within a specific collection. For every image you plan to use, review the associated licensing and terms of use carefully; make note of any restrictions. *Remember—paying for a license is not the same as owning an image!* You are purchasing the right to use the image in specific ways, without any claim of ownership and without holding the actual copyright.

The copyright holder, which may be the photographer or the agency itself, ultimately controls all usage rights until the image becomes part of the public domain (discussed later in this chapter) or until the copyright is sold to another individual or entity.

Payment methods. There are two common payment models for photography: per-use and general licensing. Under *per-use* models, the price for an image is based on how it will be used, which typically relates to how many people are expected to see it. For low-volume locations or appearances, say a small town's local paper or a website that has little traffic, this can be an attractive option.

A common variation on the per-use model is to pay *royalties*. This is an ongoing consideration paid every time an image is used after the initial appearance.

For example, when a photographer sells an image to a magazine, the magazine's circulation (which provides an estimate of the number of times the photo will be reproduced), along with other important facts such as whether the image will be used on the cover or in an advertisement, is used to determine the pricing for the image. In the case of a cover image or feature article image that will appear only one time, in one issue, usually a fixed fee is requested, because a close approximation of the number of reproductions is known in advance.

However, things become fuzzier when an image is to be used for an advertisement, because it is not always clear from the outset how many times (that is, in how many issues or places within an issue) that image will be used. This is a case where royalty payments can ensure both that the publisher doesn't pay for more than it needs and that the photographer is compensated for every usage in the magazine on an ongoing basis. Typically royalty payments are sent to the photographer once a month or once a quarter, based on the image's usage level during that time period.

The *general licensing* model is considered a one-time pay model. It is usually promoted as royalty-free. Royalty-free does not mean an image is free for use, though. Instead, it implies that once a fee is paid for an image, use of that image is unrestricted within the limits of the license. In practice, this relates to the number of times the image appears in the context of a given work or project. Additional projects usually require additional licenses. Paying once for an image does not automatically mean it can be used over and over in different works.

A third payment method that is used by some of the more popular agencies like iStock is the *subscription* model. Instead of paying per image, you can purchase a specified number of credits (sometimes called *points*) per day for use over a specified period (usually 3, 6, or 12 months). For example, you could purchase a subscription that would allow you to use up to 30 credits per day, for 3 months, at a cost of roughly $900. Most images of medium or high resolution typically cost between 5 and 15 credits each, so that gives you an idea of how many images that $900 would buy you.

Many subscription-based sites also let you pay for a specified number of pay-as-you-go credits. If it makes sense for you, you can purchase 30 credits (to be used at any time during the course of 12 months) for roughly $40, depending on the stock provider and any incentive programs it may have. **Figure 4.4** shows a simple example.

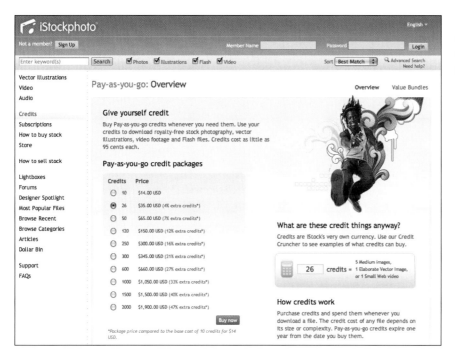

Figure 4.4 Pay-as-you-go models are often a cost-effective way of purchasing stock images over time.

It's important to remember that licensing also comes into play with respect to subscription pricing. Unlimited licenses typically require you to pay the equivalent of an extra 50 to 100 credits per image. So, carefully consider your intended distribution and uses when purchasing subscriptions, and evaluate how many images you are likely to need for your upcoming project(s). Typically it's wisest to pay as you go unless you are working on a large number of compositing and media projects that require large numbers of stock images.

Free Sites and Fair Use

In recent years, a variety of free licensing options have become available, giving artists more latitude in choosing how their images are used by others.

Creative Commons. One very popular version is framed by the nonprofit organization Creative Commons. The Creative Commons organization has structured several licenses to allow for a variety of uses and is quite a boon to popular photo-sharing sites and their contributors. The Yahoo-owned Flickr.com, for example, allows photographers to choose from several licenses for distribution and protection of their images, thus giving buyers more options as well.

As with for-pay models, free images can be rights-restricted by the copyright holder. Effectively, this means you still have to pay attention to the allowable uses for any images you purchase, regardless of the payment model being used.

Fair usage. Fair use can be a complex subject, and it has been the focus of many ongoing debates. Fair use revolves around the presumed right to use "found" images or works and create derivative works without paying the copyright holder. According to U.S. copyright law, fair use is restricted to using portions of a work ". . . for purposes such as commentary, criticism, news reporting, and scholarly reports." That quotation itself, for example, is considered fair use and comes from the U.S. Copyright Office website FAQ at www.copyright.gov/help/faq/faq-fairuse.html.

There are many interpretations of fair use, but we recommend that you avoid using images under these circumstances, if possible. When in doubt as to what constitutes fair use for a given image, talk to the copyright holders and find out. Don't make assumptions that you will be legally covered, even if you've seen a comparable image and concept used by another artist.

Public domain. Another alternative for acquiring content is to use images that are known to be in the public domain. According to the U.S. Copyright Term Extension Act of 1998, only works produced and published prior to January 1, 1923, and that have not had the owner's copyright legally extended, are considered public domain. The copyright holder may also choose to move a work into the public domain before the copyright expires, though this is somewhat uncommon.

Many old movies, as well as "public service" videos from organizations like NASA, also fall into the category of public domain (**Figure 4.5**). This means you can grab an individual frame from a public domain movie, and use it as part of your composite, the same as if it were a still.

Distinct from free-use licenses like those provided by Creative Commons, public domain images carry no restriction on use or reproduction and may be used across many mediums by all individuals who care to use them. There is no longer a copyright holder for these images, so use is truly unlimited. Here again, we recommend you not make assumptions about works that you believe may be in the public domain. Find out for sure whether the image you are considering is in the public domain before repurposing it for composite imagery or other uses.

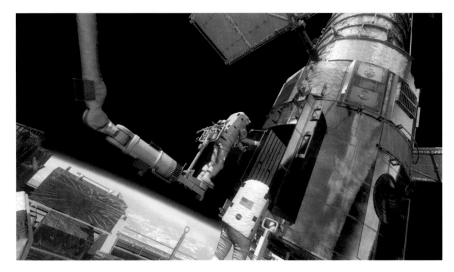

Figure 4.5 NASA provides most of its images and movies as part of the public domain, and requires only an acknowledgment of origin in most cases. Here a frame was pulled from a high-definition Hubble Space Telescope video.

Free stock? Many websites claim to offer stock images for free and with no usage restrictions. Although these may sound like a great alternative, the quality of work is generally not as high and the selection is not as good as with for-pay stock sites. However, they can be useful when testing new ideas or when you need a placeholder image. Another drawback to free sites is that they may not have robust keyword capabilities; in addition, they may not be accurately representing the copyright or terms of use of some of the images on their sites.

As with other situations in life, if a free stock site offers something that seems too good to be true, it probably is. When in doubt, go with a reputable stock agency so that you can be certain of the terms and who holds the copyright.

Types of Images Available

As noted earlier, many stock sites offer illustrations and computer-generated graphics in addition to photography, and several have high-resolution clips or stills from movies. The creative possibilities are virtually endless. For example, you can pull a single frame from a movie released in the early 1920s and build a modern scene around an historical character or famous actor.

Illustrations may also have a place in your repertoire; you can use them as guides for layout, as concept sketches, or even as art within your composite. Also, quite a number of 3D models are available that you can use as foundations for your composite imaging projects. With the new 3D capabilities in Photoshop CS4 Extended, not only can you match the lighting and color of your 2D scene and 3D model, but you can even paint directly onto the model! We'll cover 3D techniques in more detail in Chapter 9, "Creating 3D Content."

Capturing the Scene and Subject

This chapter focuses on the photographic elements in your composite images. Using the right photographic techniques can help you build a solid digital foundation for the Adobe Camera Raw and Adobe Photoshop CS4 processes covered later in the book. We cannot stress enough that although it's possible to correct many problems with Photoshop, you can avoid problems by photographing your source material with the final composite in mind. Ultimately this should improve the quality of your project and save time as well.

For some situations, you may need to use a photograph that was not shot with composite images in mind (for example, a stock image). This is fine and something we do all the time. The main point is that if you know ahead of time that you'll need certain kinds of shots, it's best to do a bit of planning and acquire the materials in advance if possible.

When photographing subjects for composite imagery, you should pay attention to several factors, including lighting direction and quality, focus depth, color, and camera noise, to name just a few. Let's take a look at some of these concepts as they apply to composite images.

WORKING WITH LIGHT

One of the first things viewers notice in composite images is consistency in the quality of light. Open a magazine with glamour photos, and you will see photographs with an ethereal quality; these shots are often lit with a mix of softboxes, reflectors, and strobe lights. Even images with a fill flash in the foreground and natural light in the background can draw attention to the contrast, especially when the color temperature differs. This can be desirable in situations where you want your subject to appear separated from its surroundings.

Lighting can be a difficult thing to control when integrating multiple images, as many subtle cues can tip the viewer off that something isn't quite right. The most common culprits include direction of light, diffuseness, reflection of off-camera objects, and color temperature.

Soft Light

Soft lighting tends to give the subjects or scene in your photograph a subtle, "glowing" appearance. Whether the soft light is created by ambient, atmospheric conditions (such as those seen in the mist at sunrise) or created in a studio with diffusers and flat lighting, soft light creates shadows with soft edges and transitions. This is what gives the image its glowing quality. What's actually happening is that the light scatters from many surfaces, bouncing in many directions and filling some shadow areas. This ultimately reduces the stark contrast along the periphery of your subjects.

Soft light also tends to lessen the effect of texture and can have an impact on perceived depth, while increasing saturation. Overcast days and diffuser panels can create wonderful soft effects and rich colors in your images when photographed properly. You can estimate the "softness" of a light by considering the size of the light source relative to the subject and the distance between the two. The larger and closer the light source, the more softly lit a photo tends to look (**Figure 5.1**).

Figure 5.1 The image on the left projects a different emotion than the image on the right. Directly lighting a subject from the side is a technique that produces a hard light rather than a softer look.

Human Visual Perception

Many psychologists believe humans treat vision as the primary means of understanding the world. This means your job as a compositor can be quite challenging. Throughout this book, look for hints on "selling" your image based on visual perception and, in some cases, visual bias. You can manipulate how a viewer perceives your image by understanding how that perception happens.

This book focuses largely on perspective and lighting as major contributors to perception, with color playing a part in both of these. However, *composition*—which you can think of as the spatial relationships between different parts of the photograph—carries a lot of weight in making images realistic. *Empathy*, the relationship the viewer feels to the work, can override other elements, especially if the viewer has a personal connection with one of the subjects depicted in the image. Though the focus of this book—with respect to photography—is on the mechanics of perspective, lighting, color, and composition, it's important to keep in mind any potential emotional reactions the viewer will have to the subjects you have chosen.

Inconsistent lighting is one of the most common problems encountered when evaluating a composite image. It's easy to miss small lighting details that ultimately might have an unintended effect on the viewer's perception. Fortunately, the proper photographic and Photoshop techniques can help you to avoid this problem. Some careful planning and digital processing can yield marvelous results with a modest amount of time and effort; for example, lighting cues can play an important role in defining depth and texture (**Figure 5.2**). By making small changes in shadow placement or contrast, you can enhance a subject or make it look entirely out of place.

Figure 5.2 Lighting cues can strongly influence human perception. The pumpkin on the right appears slightly farther away because of the low-contrast lighting.

Perspective is a bit more difficult to work with, because you can do only so much to change it once a subject or scene is photographed. If not handled correctly, perspective can have a detrimental effect, lingering in the back of the viewer's mind as "something not quite right." Most viewers will not immediately pick out small deviations with perspective, but almost all will "feel" there is a problem. There are some tricks to learn, but you can also use perspective to your advantage to build a sense of discord in your images or to misdirect a viewer's attention when you have a particular message to get across.

Hard Light

Hard light often creates the opposite effect of soft light for most subjects. Most notably, hard light produces a starker appearance where more fine details (that is, texture) may be noticeable on the surface of your subject. Hard light usually creates darker, sharper shadow regions as well, thus increasing image contrast. This increased definition in shadow boundaries offers the viewer a clearer sense of depth and relief, because the brain imposes a measurement on the length of the shadows.

Another characteristic of hard lighting is that the rays tend to be more parallel. This reduces the "confusion of light" around shadow boundaries. If you've directed a flashlight against a flat wall to create shadow puppets, you know that moving your hand closer to the wall creates sharper edges, while moving closer to the light softens edges. Assuming your camera and background surfaces are stationary, if your subject moves closer to the surface where the shadow is being cast or if the light (regardless of its type) moves closer to the subject, your shadows will tend to become harder edged (**Figure 5.3**).

Figure 5.3 Assuming a fixed distance between the shadow surface and the light source, the closer the subject is to the light source, the softer the shadow will be (right).

Controlling this quality of light in your photography is essential when trying to convey emotions or meaning. The softer a subject is lit, the more ethereal and calming the mood. Conversely, when a subject is lit with very stark, hard lighting, the mood produced is often an edgier or even shocking one, as seen in the hard light example in Figure 5.1. So, consider the emotion you are trying to elicit first and then what kind of light will help illustrate that emotion.

Don't be afraid to experiment. When shooting to match other images, the odds you will get just the right softness or hardness of light on the first setup attempt are slim. Chapter 8, "Enhancing Source Images," and Chapter 10, "Compositing Source Materials," both provide Photoshop techniques that can improve the consistency of light in your composite image.

Reflections

To distinguish between reflections and highlights (for our purposes), we'll call a *reflection* a virtual image that can be seen on some surface, such as a chrome hubcap or a window. A *highlight*, then, is a relatively bright area on a surface that does not reproduce a specific image. These definitions do not apply to 100 percent of photographic situations, but they will suffice for now.

Reflective objects in your source images can be difficult to deal with, often providing unintended clues about the environment around your subject. If you've ever tried taking a picture of a reflective object that doesn't involve the surrounding environment (**Figure 5.4**), you know that photographing this type of subject can prove challenging.

Figure 5.4 Keeping (reflected) background distractions out of photographs with reflective surfaces can be a challenge.

The use of windows as part of a composite image is one common scenario to consider. Some concepts may hinge on the use of reflections that appear in windows in order to complete the final illusion. Meanwhile, other window reflections may be little more than distractions. The latter cases may require that you remove the original reflection and replace it if the structure and framing around the window is important to the scene's integrity. The replacement can come from the same window (perhaps shot at the same time on a different day) or a completely new reflection, taken from an unrelated source and made to blend in using Photoshop. When replacing the reflection, the challenge is to figure out what angle you need to use to shoot the replacement reflection.

Consider two distinct cases: using the actual environment around the window and using an entirely new environment. For the first case, you may choose to shoot the reflection separately so that you can increase the detail of objects on the other side of the window or even pose your subject without the distraction of the environment potentially covering or interacting with your subject. Shooting the environment separately, by contrast, lets you choose your details or place your subject with less hassle, as shown in **Figure 5.5**.

Figure 5.5 Shooting the environment or your subject separately from the reflective environment gives you more control over placement in the final composite.

Figure 5.6
The final image, with the environment shot flipped on the vertical axis.

Now all that's left is to photograph the environment and layer the chosen shot into your images. Once you've taken the shot, you can rotate the image around the vertical axis to achieve the correct orientation for your reflection, as shown in **Figure 5.6**.

The second solution to replacing a window reflection is shooting an entirely different environment. The rules are mostly the same: Match up the angles and lighting, reverse the shot, and merge. Depending on the final image, you may have some flexibility in choosing your lighting and shadows. Remember that your reflection is going to have opposite shadows from left to right and complementary lighting from front to back.

Highlights

Paying attention to lighting also means paying attention to any highlights that exist or need to be placed in your images. Highlights can be specular or diffuse in nature, and depend on both the light source and the surface characteristics of your subjects. Here again, direction is important, but you shouldn't ignore the size and character of a highlight. Diffuse highlights are the softer, brighter areas of an image that imply a textured surface on an object, while specular highlights tend to be small, sharp points that easily overexpose to pure white and typically come from edges and very small curves on highly reflective surfaces.

The details in specular highlights can be difficult to maintain when not handled properly (**Figure 5.7**). This is often the case with shots of open water, where waves and ripples produce many specular highlights. Another common scenario occurs when photographing subjects in urban environments under bright sunlight, where specular reflections can often be seen on the sides of tall buildings and other structures in the distance. The lantern is something we'll want to use later in our image enhancement and image compositing examples, so we used ACR's Recovery slider to make sure the specular highlights were maintained, without loss of detail.

Figure 5.7 The image on the left is an example of specular highlights, while the image on the right illustrates diffuse highlights.

However, specular highlights are not always a negative. For example, you may want to draw the viewer's eye to a specific object in the scene with some specular highlights. The sunburst effect sometimes seen in animations or other imagery can be thought of as a specular reflection that actually occurs inside your camera lens. What really happens is that a reflection within the elements of the lens bounces off the various surfaces incompletely, creating a repeating pattern on the sensor. Thankfully, since it can be difficult to reliably reproduce the starburst effect in-camera, Photoshop provides a Lens Flare filter (**Figure 5.8**) that mimics the starburst effect created by different types of lenses.

Shadows and Texture

Where there is light, there often is a shadow. But shadows are more than simply darker regions of an image. They present unique challenges in photography, and for composite imaging, shadows can have great importance to the success of the image. One of the more challenging tasks in compositing two images together is the process of creating believable shadow regions in Photoshop, because they play off of other objects, textures, and contours in the scene.

Typically the way a scene is lit will determine the characteristics of its shadow regions. Lighting can also have a big impact on textures in your image. The perception of textures in an image is actually created by the contrast between very small, neighboring regions of lighter and darker photographic detail. Adjusting the angle, distance, and brightness of light can greatly affect the viewer's perception of texture in your images.

Figure 5.9 shows in a single scene how different the same type of texture can look when falling in shadow or under different types of light. Note the differences between the columns in the foreground versus the ones in the background and also the different look created on each of the three wall regions (in other words, the walls in the foreground, middle ground, and background). Later in the book we use similar columns to form the basis of a surreal landscape that could be used as a proof-of concept for 3D games or other design objectives.

Figure 5.8 The Lens Flare filter can be a useful substitute for capturing a starburst effect directly in your camera.

NOTE Chapter 10, "Compositing Source Materials," discusses techniques for creating shadows with Photoshop when there is not a suitable photographic alternative.

Figure 5.9 Light conditions can greatly impact perceived texture. This photo shows how very similar textures can take on a different appearance, depending on whether they are in dark shadows, warm sunlight, or lighter, diffuse shadow areas.

Figure 5.10 Time of day can greatly influence the look and effect that your shadow regions have on your composite image.

When you think about your composite images, consider how the lighting affects your shadows. Midday sun typically produces a darker, more contrasting shadow with a blue cast. As you near the golden hour of sunset, the color temperature of your shadow areas will look warmer, while the total difference between bright and dark regions diminishes quickly (**Figure 5.10**).

Early Afternoon Shadow

Early Evening Shadow

Shadows also provide useful information about the distance and direction of light sources in the scene. This is why many compositing artists will use Photoshop to place a shadow behind their subject sometimes; it's a great way to provide visual cues to the viewer. It also means that if you're not careful, the viewer will spot an incorrectly placed shadow (or one that is too large or small) very quickly. The most important thing is to find the precise direction and general elevation of the light source. Imagine a sphere surrounding the entire scene in your image: based on where the shadows fall, you should be able to guess quickly where the main light source is located (on the sphere).

Using similar visualization methods and a few standard photography tools, it is possible to control the look of the shadows in your images. Once the direction and general elevation of the lights are set, moving them farther away or closer to the subject should make it easy to control the hardness or softness of the shadow (as noted earlier). Diffusing the lights can also have an impact, so experiment until you have the look you want.

Drop in. There is also the question of creating drop shadows for subjects in your image that were not actually present when the background was photographed. You can create drop shadows in Photoshop in a number of ways, but two techniques are more common than most. The first is to use the Drop Shadow layer style, and the second is to copy your subject layer, create a fill, and then modify the shape and blending mode of the shadow as needed. Then use the Transform commands and the Move tool to adjust the shadow's placement.

EDGE CONTRAST

Virtually everything you photograph will have edges. First let's consider high- and low-contrast regions. For most situations, high-contrast edges are desirable when making masks or selections, because they are easy to see when using masking functions in compositing the final images. Low-contrast edges can be difficult to see and select properly. **Figure 5.11** shows the same subject photographed against two different backgrounds, one high-contrast, the other low-contrast.

Figure 5.11 The image on the left shows a subject with a well-defined edge contrast, which makes selections easier later in the process.

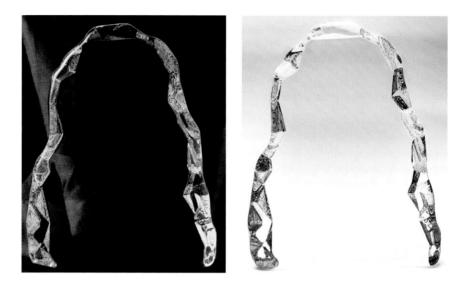

Opaque Edges

When photographing opaque subjects that you know will be broken into component parts for a composite, it's important to create well-defined edges. As noted earlier, the softer the edges, the more time-consuming it will be to select or mask the subject accurately. Generally, you can achieve good edge contrast through different combinations of light and color. This is usually easiest to achieve in a studio or other controlled environment. For example, directing a strobe light onto a contrasting backdrop color will provide high contrast with your subject for most subjects.

When shooting in the field (that is, in an uncontrolled environment), you may need to experiment with the position of the camera to get good results. Sometimes moving to a different vantage point can improve edge contrast, because the lighting effect on your subject will be different or because the subject will stand out more from the background (**Figure 5.12**). However, to make the most of this technique, it's usually best that you not photograph your subjects when the sun is directly overhead, because the quality of the light on your subject will not change much as you move from spot to spot. Edge contrast can also be improved in the studio by using *separation lighting*, which uses strobe lights placed at a 45-degree angle from the front of your subject and directly behind the subject. This is also sometimes called *rim lighting*.

Figure 5.12 Combining the effects of light and color can improve edge contrast.

Transparent Edges

Objects such as wineglasses and acrylic statues offer a unique challenge not only because of transparency but also because of the distortion at the edges. Edge definition on curved objects is a common problem, because these edges can blend into whatever background is behind them. One useful trick for clearly defining these edges is to use small, dark shims of paper held up with drafter's tack or clay (**Figure 5.13**). This allows the photographer to create a defined edge, making the masking process much easier.

To make the edges distinct, place a thin strip of contrasting paper near the edges of your object. You will have to mask or crop the paper out, but this will give your edge boundaries better definition. Using heavy construction paper, pipe cleaners, or similar materials will help you with complex curves like the ones you would find on a wineglass. You can bend the paper or pipe cleaners to more closely match your object's boundaries.

Figure 5.13 Placing a contrasting color on both sides of a transparent subject can be a big help in defining and isolating its edges.

DISTANCE FACTORS

Managing the viewer's perception of distance—which, fundamentally, is controlled by the relative scale of objects in your scene—is yet another variable in making successful composite images. However, merely resizing an object is usually not enough to get the job done. Perspective and atmospheric effects also play an important role. They are elements we see every day, so our brains are tuned to picking out these important visual cues.

One frequently overlooked photographic characteristic is the connection between saturation and distance. Traditional media artists use this feature frequently when showing distances, especially in landscapes. As the distance between the viewer and an object increases, there is more atmosphere through which light must pass. This translates into subjects or scenes that appear less saturated and lighter, and in many cases you will see a faint blue haze (shown in **Figure 5.14**) when a subject, such as a mountain range, is very distant from the camera. This is known as *aerial perspective*.

Figure 5.14 The farther away a subject is, often the less saturated its color will appear, and the more it will be perceived as having a "lightness" or slight haze.

PERSPECTIVE

Few things are more important to the creation of a successful composite scene than the precise use of perspective. The various components of your scene may need to appear as though they were all photographed together, from the same vantage point. Far beyond simply scaling an object to fit into the scene, perspective is something that cannot always be manipulated perfectly in Photoshop. Certainly, Vanishing Point, Lens Correction, some of the Transform tools, and the 3D capabilities can help you mimic the effects of perspective, but they may not always be enough.

The best bet for controlling perspective is to get the look you need straight from your camera. This requires the photographer to know quite a bit about the scene and the object's placement in the final image, but it's a big help when you can control the perspective for all composite elements ahead of time. **Figure 5.15** provides an example of changing perspective by using different focal lengths while keeping the object at the same relative proportion, thereby filling roughly the same amount of the image frame. In Chapter 8, "Enhancing Source Images," we will demonstrate how we corrected the perspective problems that occurred with this shot because of the wide-angle lens that was used.

Figure 5.15 As you move farther from a subject, you can use a longer focal length to fill roughly the same amount of frame that you would closer up but at a wide angle.

Farther Away, 38 mm   Closer Up, 31 mm

Note that nothing in the scene changed, but the camera moved closer and closer, using wider- and wider-angle focal lengths to maintain scale. Although the object doesn't actually get any bigger, our perception of it changes and can affect how the object will fit into a composite scene. You can use this effect in a number of ways, including making objects seem seriously out of proportion or very far away. By influencing the viewer's perception, you are able to maintain control over the sense of realism.

The perspective required for a given subject depends on the intent of the composite concept itself and who is supposed to be viewing the scene. A small child, for example, will have a different point of view than an adult, simply because of height. But if both a child and an adult are lying on the ground, the perspective might be exactly the same. So, the point of view helps *tell* the story, while perspective helps *sell* it. Referring to your scene notes, consider where the viewer is relative to the subject, along with any other viewer characteristics that might influence perception, such as height.

COMPOSITION AND SELECTIVE FOCUS

Once you have defined the perspective you want to use, you can guide the viewer's eyes to a particular area in your scene by using various camera techniques. The most common methods for guiding the viewer are to use compositional balance (also known as the *rule of thirds*) and depth of field (which is controlled by your camera's aperture setting) to help the eye move across the scene and find the focus transitions.

Compositional Balance

The rule of thirds is a widely discussed and popular method for breaking your image down (mentally) into nine equal-sized regions (in other words, three rows and three columns). Chances are good that you are already familiar with the concept, and you can find plenty of books and free articles online if you need to brush up on the basics of photographic composition. The main point is to keep the balance of your composition firmly in mind as you create the scenes and other elements of your composite.

Visual grid. If you are photographing a beautiful sunset with amazing cloud structure but with not much else going on visually (at ground level), don't split your shot into halves (using the horizon as the divider). Instead, capture a larger proportion of sky. Another important technique is to place items of importance at the intersection points of the grid lines that divide your image into nine parts. You can also use converging lines in the real world to quickly draw the viewer's eye to the termination point of those converging lines.

Focus control. The other common technique for drawing the viewer's eye to a certain spot is using focus control. As a rule, the human eye tends to gravitate toward those parts of an image that are relatively more in focus (and therefore that display relatively more details than other areas in the shot). You can accomplish focus control by setting the depth of field in your image via your camera's aperture control. For those unfamiliar with aperture, this value refers to the diameter of an opening (inside your lens) that allows light to pass through to the film or digital sensor. The larger the opening, the more light hits the sensor, and the more the details behind your in-camera focus point will soften.

NOTE Many digital SLR manufacturers sell optional focus screens for their high-end cameras that have a rule-of-thirds grid built into them so that you can see the lines and position your subject more precisely.

NOTE If you want to learn more about manual camera exposure than what your camera manual provides, consider acquiring a copy of *Understanding Exposure*, by Bryan Peterson (Amphoto Books), from your favorite retailer or library. It provides a solid foundation for working with manual camera exposure and understanding how aperture works.

Many professional photographers dictate focus by shooting in "full manual" mode to achieve the most control over their exposure. However, if you're not able or ready to shoot in full manual mode, shooting in aperture-priority mode and using your DSLR's depth of field preview is a good alternative. This method requires only that you control the aperture, and it allows you to see where the focus in your scene starts to fall off, before you take the picture. Regardless of which camera exposure mode you use, the depth of field preview on a DSLR allows you to find the best transition from focus to softness before you take the picture. This is especially true for scenes that cover a great distance (**Figure 5.16**).

Less can be more. Most days, any serious photographer works hard to create tack-sharp images. However, you may find it useful—in a limited number of scenarios—to photograph certain subjects so that they are slightly out of focus. This can simplify the placement of objects within a scene so they appear to naturally blend in with the rest of the image elements without much retouching. When retouching is your only option because of time constraints or other factors, Photoshop has a great feature called Lens Blur (discussed in Chapter 10) that you can use to control the focus points in your composite images by using layer masks or alpha channels.

Color considerations. Additional creative techniques exist for drawing the viewer's attention to a specific part of the image, such as the use of bright colors. For example, small regions of relatively bright yellows or reds can quickly draw a person's eye directly to that portion of the image. **Figure 5.17** shows how the localized use of color can draw the viewer in, without overwhelming the rest of the scene. Had the Mardi Gras mask and garland been photographed in a corporate lobby, chances are it would have overwhelmed the rest of the scene because most lobbies use a very muted color scheme with many whites, beiges, and light grays. In fact, here the white is just as much a draw as the saturated reds and purples, because it stands out so much.

Another thing to keep in mind is that—at any given saturation value—warm colors tend to be perceived as being closer to the viewer, while cooler colors tend to be perceived as being slightly farther away. Every person will perceive things a little differently, but if you want to use bright, saturated color (particularly warmer colors) to draw the viewer's eye, use it sparingly and make sure its position in the frame flows with the eye's natural scanning tendencies, which in Western cultures is usually from the bottom left to the top right.

NOTE Although it can produce good results, Lens Blur generally is not considered a replacement for the quality of blur (sometimes called *bokeh*) that is created with a digital SLR and professional lens. For this reason, important scenes or subjects may require that the selective blurring be handled in-camera rather than in Photoshop.

NOTE The human eye's scanning patterns can vary from one cultural region to the next, based on the way people are taught to read as children. For example, in many Asian cultures, words are not read from left to right but rather from right to left. Some are even written from bottom to top. These kinds of differences can affect how the human eye naturally scans visual information in a composite image, so, again, be aware of your audience when creating your composition.

Figure 5.16 Using your DSLR's aperture allows you to control focus and set the transition points between sharpness and blur in your images. Use your depth of field preview to see (through the lens) what the final image sharpness will look like before you shoot.

Figure 5.17 Areas of saturated color will draw the viewer's eye in an otherwise muted environment. Similarly, a small area of white can draw your eye in a "sea of color," as is found during Mardi Gras.

Tilt-Shift

A variation on the theme of depth of field is the use of tilt-shift lenses, shown in **Figure 5.18**. Standard lenses have a focal plane that is parallel to the film or sensor plane. Tilt-shift lenses are built to swing their lens elements so that the plane of focus can be changed to compensate for the distance from the subject to the lens. The classic use for tilt-shift (or swing) lenses is in architectural photography, where buildings suffer from keystone distortions.

Figure 5.18 The Nikkor PC-E 24 mm lens from Nikon

By changing the angle relationship between the lens and the image plane, not only is the focal plane adjusted, but the apparent perspective is also adjusted. When photographing a tall building from a short distance away, the top of the building appears to converge toward a *vanishing point*. This point, well-known to artists who work with perspective, is effectively pushed farther away to make lines along the angle of tilt appear more parallel. The effect is that the building now looks more like we expect buildings to look—straight and tall.

This is much the same as you would see with an adjustment to the Vertical Perspective slider in the Lens Correction filter (**Figure 5.19**), but the difference is that the tilt-shift lens will not require you to recrop your image afterward (from the transparent areas created when you make pronounced adjustments with the Lens Correction filter).

Figure 5.19 This image demonstrates why it's best to rely on a perspective correction lens, if it fits your budget, rather than defaulting to perspective corrections with the Lens Correction filter or other digital tools that will "cut away" parts of your image in order to straighten it.

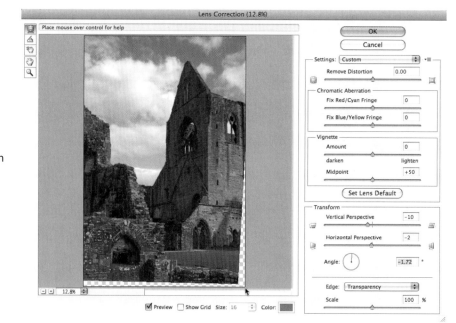

Lensbaby

Tilt-shift lenses are not cheap. As an example, Nikon's three PC-E lenses for its line of professional SLRs and DSLRs cost well over $1,500 apiece. The mechanical assemblies and optics involved are difficult to design and manufacture, thus driving the prices up to levels that only serious amateur and professional photographers would pay. But you can break the plane of focus without breaking the bank.

A few years ago, Craig Strong came up with a novel approach to modern photography … by taking it back 100 years! He invented a bellows-style lens called the Lensbaby (*www.lensbaby.com*). The idea is simple—put a lens in a flexible tube and mount it to a modern DSLR. The result is a truly manual lens in every sense of the word (**Figure 5.20**).

Focus and focal plane are both controlled by hand. You bend the lens and pull on the front of it to achieve the desired look. Although traditional lenses require that the zone of focus remain in the center of the frame, a Lensbaby allows you to place the focal zone on any part of the image you need, thus producing very creative effects (the many samples on the Lensbaby website are worth a look). Apertures are replaced by physically removing and changing the aperture plate in front of the lens.

Although these lenses are not true tilt-shift assemblies and would not be useful for critical architectural work in that capacity, they are wonderful creative tools. Working them into your compositing flow will take some time, because they present quite a few challenges in trying to match other images. However, with one of these beauties in your arsenal, you will be able to achieve some very unique perspectives and effects.

Figure 5.20 The Lensbaby is an affordable, manual alternative to a standard tilt-shift lens. The Control Freak model is shown here.

DIGITAL NOISE

For experienced photographers, digital noise is a fact of life. Depending on what type of camera you use and the types of images you are shooting, the process of managing noise in your composite images can range from something that takes a few minutes to something that requires several minutes per image. As with light quality, depth of field, and other photographic characteristics, there are ways of digitally working with noise in Photoshop (these are discussed with more detail in Chapter 7, "Processing Raw Source Files," and Chapter 8, "Enhancing Source Images").

When in doubt, avoid it. Despite all the techniques available to eliminate noise, the best solution is to avoid noise altogether. The less noise you start with in your source files, the cleaner and crisper your final composite will be.

The latest advancements in camera-based noise processing—such as those found in high-end digital SLR cameras like the Nikon D3 (**Figure 5.21**)—can save you a lot of time. It was only a few years ago that even the best digital SLRs produced obvious and distracting noise at settings as low as ISO 400. Today, although most consumer-grade cameras still struggle with noise performance beyond ISO 400, high-end DSLR cameras from Canon and Nikon in particular do a great job of keeping noise at bay up to about ISO 1600 in normal lighting conditions. Dark scenes can still suffer from some luminance (or monochromatic) noise beyond about ISO 800, but the noise tends to be finer grained and easier to control with the right "noise abatement" tools in Photoshop.

Figure 5.21 Cameras like the Nikon D3 Digital SLR can make your job easier (if you have the budget for it) because of their excellent high ISO noise performance.

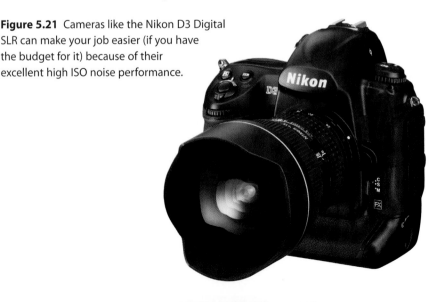

The latest professional DSLR cameras are relatively expensive, but they can help produce cleaner, virtually noise-free images from the start. Whether such investments make sense for you will depend on the camera you are considering, your budget, and other factors. The trade-off is generally time. The up-front expense for a superior camera may be larger, but working with older-generation cameras will mean more time spent mitigating noise in Photoshop unless you are photographing scenarios that do not involve lower-light, high-ISO settings.

Light it right. Assuming you have a more recent DSLR at your disposal, the next best thing you can do to avoid noise problems in your images is to light the subject properly. If you're photographing outdoors, add a couple of small light stands with clamps, along with a collapsible reflector/diffuser, to your travel kit. Fairly inexpensive, they can collapse to a compact size and be invaluable in the field. You may find that just a bit of reflected sunlight from a distance throws enough light into the darker or shadow areas of your subject to help the camera pick up those extra details cleanly.

One final option for reducing noise ahead of time, if you find that your camera and the available light just aren't cutting it, is to consider the coloration of the subject itself. Avoiding subjects with dark coloration will often save you a few headaches. Dark brown and dark blue tones in particular can sometimes generate more noise than their counterparts, so keep the color of your subject in mind as you are planning. If you know there is no way around photographing a darkly colored subject, then having a solid plan for how to light that subject becomes paramount. As you have gathered by now, many if not all of these photographic concerns are connected to one another and impact each other throughout the process. Plan ahead!

Triage. If you've taken steps to avoid camera noise but still have some noise to deal with in your images, you can use a variety of built-in and third-party tools with Photoshop to remedy the situation.

NOTE Keep in mind that virtually all noise reduction functions or plugins (regardless of who develops them) will tend to soften your image details when applied.

The first step you can take to remediate noise in your raw images is to use the Noise Reduction controls in the Detail panel in Adobe Camera Raw. This is discussed in detail in Chapter 7, "Processing Raw Source Files." In Photoshop, the Reduce Noise filter (Filter > Noise > Reduce Noise) can provide good results for images that have light to moderate amounts of noise. However, once out of Camera Raw, our preference is to use the third-party tool Noiseware, which is covered in Chapter 8.

COLOR CONSIDERATIONS

Another crucial element to getting your source images right is starting off with a consistent color character. The fewer color replacements or wholesale color shifts you use to make your source images in Photoshop, the better off you are likely to be. This is true not only from the standpoint of saving time but also in terms of maintaining image data integrity as much as possible during numerous edits.

For things to go smoothly, you need to keep several factors in mind, including the final mood or look of your image, the color of your subjects and the surrounding scenery (if any), and the color of the light at the time and location of your photographing those subjects. Considering the color of the light (or light temperature) is particularly important when photographing outdoors, where you are less likely to have complete control over your lighting scenario.

RGB Working Space and Document Profiles

No discussion of handling the color in your source images would be complete without mentioning the different color space options that are available. If you are taking all the shots yourself and doing all the Photoshop work, color managing your images (that is, managing their color profiles throughout the editing process as well as your RGB working space) should be a straightforward process.

However, when using many different sources or editing as part of a workgroup, managing your document color profiles can become tricky. Early in your workflow, you should consider which RGB working space to use and try to get everything into that space (ideally as part of a raw image conversion process) before you begin your Photoshop edits. Communication with other team members on this issue is key, and it may make sense for one person to handle the conversions and color settings on everyone's Mac or Windows machine.

For closed-loop workflows where you will be handling all the capture and editing requirements for your project *and* where the image is *not* likely to end up on a CMYK press, the ProPhoto RGB option offers by far the largest color space you can use and therefore will help eliminate the possibility of color banding as you edit your images.

For workflows that may require subsequent CMYK conversion *or* that bring together images from multiple sources, working in Adobe RGB 1998 can be a safer bet than ProPhoto RGB. Even if you get stuck with one or two source files in sRGB but have control over the rest, it's often better to convert those two sRGB images and use an Adobe RGB workflow, rather than working within the very limited colors of the sRGB gamut.

Mood swings. Keep the objectives we've talked about in mind as you plan your photography sessions. If you want your composite scenery to produce warm, ethereal qualities, shooting either scene or subject in bright sunlight won't help your cause. Based on the time of year and geographic location, decide when the golden hours (**Figure 5.22**) will start, and get there a little early. Take some test shots just before or after "prime time" so that you have a nice variety of tonal variations, from slightly cool to the very warm colors of sunset or sunrise.

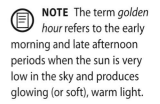

NOTE The term *golden hour* refers to the early morning and late afternoon periods when the sun is very low in the sky and produces glowing (or soft), warm light.

Figure 5.22 Photographing an outdoor scene during golden hours can improve the quality of ethereal composites, even though it is often possible to change the color character of an image with Photoshop.

Similarly, if you need to ensure that your subject is evenly lit with a specific color (or completely neutral) light so that you can make digital alterations more easily later, it's best to work in a studio environment. This allows you to precisely control the "flow" and color of the light falling onto your subject by using temperature dials, gels, or other means of color manipulation.

Cast away. The color of your subjects and scene can also play a big role in how much postproduction is ultimately required for your final image. Again, although it's easy enough to get your color temperature right when processing in Adobe Camera Raw, that may not be enough depending on the circumstances. Capture a portrait next to that big green tree, and you may be in for a surprise when you evaluate your images in Adobe Bridge. Even if you've used the correct white balance, it is likely your subject's clothes and skin tone will carry a greenish tinge. Most photographic subjects tend to take on color casts from other objects in the scene if those objects have a very saturated color and either are casting a shadow over the subject or are close enough to reflect some of their color onto the subject.

Real-world color. Sometimes you may want a surreal composite where the colors do not mimic the real world at all or have accents that would never appear in nature. However, even when you want "crazy color," it can be better to get that from your camera, rather than trying to turn a white rabbit red with Photoshop. Although it's easy enough (simple, in fact) to turn an orange basketball red using the Hue and Saturation tools, working with a subject that has fainter neutral tones requires a different approach. It's often better to throw a light with a red gel on that rabbit and capture it with color in place.

CAMERA LOCATION

Take 2. An important consideration when photographing your source material is to be sure you note the exact location and orientation of your camera. This is helpful when you have to take multiple shots of different subjects from the same vantage point but perhaps don't have the time to take all of them at one time. Or maybe you didn't really like the way the clouds looked that day so you want to go back and try again. If you have to return later, will you remember exactly where you were set up? If you're like most of us, the answer is no—not unless something is truly unforgettable about the exact spot where you placed your camera, which 99 percent of the time just isn't the case.

All-around absolute. It can also be helpful to know your camera's exact location if you're scouting panoramic locations. Sometimes it's most practical to make a quick trip to the general area where you will take your panoramic shots and snap many potential "anchor scenes" around which the rest of your panoramic image will be built. Perhaps you would like to photograph a scenic park or downtown cityscape, but first you want to evaluate 15 or 20 potential locations within those areas. Taking that many sets of panoramic images at one time would be very time-consuming or impossible, depending on your time limitations and the weather.

Instead, you can photograph each of those 15 or 20 locations with a single anchor scene, at the time of day you want, and then evaluate which one or two best suits your purposes. Once you've chosen the winning locations, obviously you have to go back and shoot the actual panoramic stills. The only way to be sure you're in the right spot is to either mark that spot (a somewhat unreliable venture unless it never rains or it's legal to spray-paint the street at your location) or use notes.

As you take your sample anchor shots, make detailed notes of where you are standing relative to other nearby objects, the elevation of your camera body, and any other factors that will help you return to your chosen spot. An example could be "Approximately 30 feet from the bent stop sign, on the left side of the storm drain, camera at eye level." Don't leave it to chance.

And although location details can be easier to remember in urban settings you are familiar with, an exact location is almost impossible to remember in natural settings unless there is a memorable-looking tree, boulder, or other landmark nearby that you can't mistake for another location. Will you remember the exact stretch of highway where you saw that colorful stand of trees or the exact area of the park where the hills were sloped just right to create the composite image you need?

Using GPS is also a very good idea when returning to locations in nature, rather than winging it or going by notes alone. GPS can even help you avoid getting lost if you don't find the general area at first (especially if a fair amount of time has passed since your last visit).

Equipment Considerations

Although there is no single correct way to light your scenes or single set of lights, backdrops, reflectors, or diffusers that will yield the best result in all situations, you can keep in mind these simple tips as you head out to capture your source images.

Use a tripod! This is one of the most commonly ignored rules of photography, and the consequences of not using a tripod to steady your camera are just as unpleasant for compositing projects as they are for fine-art photography. Sure, it's always possible to use Photoshop tricks to sharpen up your images a bit. But no amount of Photoshop trickery is going to make a soft image sharp; all you can hope for in that instance is "less blurry." Nothing beats a tack-sharp image straight from the camera!

If you're not fond of carrying extra weight around with you, Gitzo makes an excellent range of photographic tripods that—although more expensive than

Figure 5.23 A well-made center-ball tripod head can save you a lot of setup time when working with a tripod.

the competitors in most cases—are extremely sturdy and also very light. The use of carbon-fiber materials has made the steel-frame tripod (and the bulk and weight associated with them) virtually obsolete. So if you plan to do a lot of your own photography and don't yet own a high-quality tripod, get one!

Swivel-head. Speaking of tripods, a great way to make your life easier in the field as you adjust your camera orientation and angle is to invest in an Arca-Swiss (or equivalent) "ball head" (**Figure 5.23**). Essentially, this means your camera will be sitting atop a spherical support that rests inside the tripod head and that allows you to swivel your camera around (while the tripod remains stationary) with complete freedom. Again, although this type of tripod support may cost a little more, the time you save by not having to constantly fiddle with your camera orientation will make the investment more than worthwhile for any aspiring photographer or serious hobbyist.

Pack it in. For most field photography, a good photo backpack (we recommend you check out the Lowepro brand) can be a lifesaver. Not only can you stuff your favorite lenses, cameras, triggers, and other gizmos into a backpack, but you can also pack some other important gear such as a rain suit (hypothermia and photography don't mix—don't get caught out in the field with wet clothes!), compass, GPS device, and other important tag-alongs. Usually you'll have enough room in one of the side-pouches for some quick energy food and a small water bottle as well. The point is that a backpack will often give you more options than a traditional camera case or Pelican case that you might have in the studio. You can also strap your tripod right onto the side or back of the pack in many cases.

Diffuse and reflect. One of the handier tools to have at the ready is a collapsible, portable, handheld diffuser-reflector combo. The outer, reflective surface can be unzipped and removed quickly, exposing the diffuser material inside. The uses of a portable diffuser-reflector are almost countless, and it's relatively inexpensive, so it pays to have one close by that you can quickly retrieve if necessary.

Stand up. You might be asking yourself, "What if I'm photographing a scene by myself and there's no one to hold the diffuser or reflector?" Good question. The answer is, purchase a couple of simple, lightweight light stands with small clamps that can hold your flexible diffuser or reflector in place. Usually these are small enough that they can fit right in the back of your trunk and not cause too many headaches. Some photographers will even leave them in the trunk so that they're always available.

Speedlights. If you think there's a reasonable chance the location you're photographing won't have adequate lighting (natural or otherwise), it can be a good investment to purchase a couple of extra hot shoe-mounted flash units for your camera, with adapters that will allow them to rest on your light stands. In many cases, these flash units can be triggered wirelessly from your camera. For example, you can combine any of the high-end Nikon DSLRs and a set of SB-800 or SB-900 speedlights (**Figure 5.24**) to create an effective mobile lighting system that is far less expensive than even a modest battery-powered strobe kit.

Figure 5.24 Radio-controlled, hot shoe-mounted flash units can provide extra flexibility when lighting a scene in the field at a far lower cost than a dedicated strobe system.

Organizing and Evaluating Images

One of the most important things you can do to help keep your source images organized, and subsequently find them with minimal effort, is to leverage the power of keywords. The first part of this chapter covers some of the important keyword functionalities and other techniques (using Adobe Bridge CS4) that can help you stay efficient. The second part of the chapter deals with the prospect of managing multiple images on your screen, which is often a requirement when building composite images. Adobe Photoshop CS4 offers new and important capabilities in this regard.

BRIDGE WORKFLOW TIPS

Understanding the different keyword-related tools that Bridge offers is important. Applying keywords to your source images as you bring them into your computer from week to week (or day to day if you work with a commercial studio) can mean a lot of time saved once you begin to comb through all the different shots you might use as part of your project.

Since a comprehensive discussion of all the useful tools Bridge can offer to those involved in digital workflow is beyond the scope of this book, we recommend—for those who want to learn more about Bridge specifically—that you take a look at *Real World Camera Raw with Adobe Photoshop CS4*, by Bruce Fraser and Jeff Schewe (Peachpit Press). The authors have laid out some excellent general workflow principles that benefit not only photographers but also compositing artists. In Chapter 7, they describe the five primary stages that apply to most digital imaging workflows: image ingestion, image verification, preproduction, production, and postproduction.

What we cover here instead focuses on the most important tools and techniques you can use, in both Bridge and Photoshop, to stay organized throughout your compositing project.

The process of creating a composite often involves using images with dissimilar subject matter and compositions. Finding the right images in this scenario can require a significant amount of time as your project grows more complex. You may have to search an ever-growing number of image collections to find what you need. Fortunately, Bridge offers useful keyword and metadata capabilities that will help you save time and ultimately do a better job of evaluating images.

As with any Creative Suite workflow, you can manage the imaging process in different ways. The key is to set up a system that makes sense to you (and your workgroup if you're part of one) and then stick with it. As you work, the project will evolve, but as long as everyone on the team agrees on the overall process and understands how to best take advantage of the Bridge toolset, things should go smoothly, ensuring that you produce your work in a timely and efficient manner.

Tips for Metadata

As noted earlier, *preproduction* refers to the process of preparing your images for editing. For our purposes, we'll consider adding metadata (and keywords) as part of the preproduction process. The word *metadata* means "beyond information." This may seem a little counterintuitive, so think of it this way: Metadata is specialized information that has become useful in a specific context. Keywords, camera settings, and photographer information are all considered metadata and can be helpful in finding or describing digital images.

Photoshop and Bridge both have tools for handling metadata, and one of the more convenient tools is the metadata template, which can be created in Bridge by choosing Tools > Create Metadata Template.

Template power. You can open the Create Metadata Template dialog box (**Figure 6.1**) by choosing Tools > Metadata Template in Bridge. It allows you to input a wide variety of image and photographer information to be saved with your template. You can apply this information to your images from a number of locations—in the Photo Downloader dialog box (as noted in the next section), via the File Info command (found in the File menu of both Bridge and Photoshop), and via the Append Metadata or Replace Metadata commands (also found in the Tools menu in Bridge). This may not seem like a big deal, but if you shoot enough images over a period of time, having important information about the images saved with their metadata can save you a lot of head scratching later.

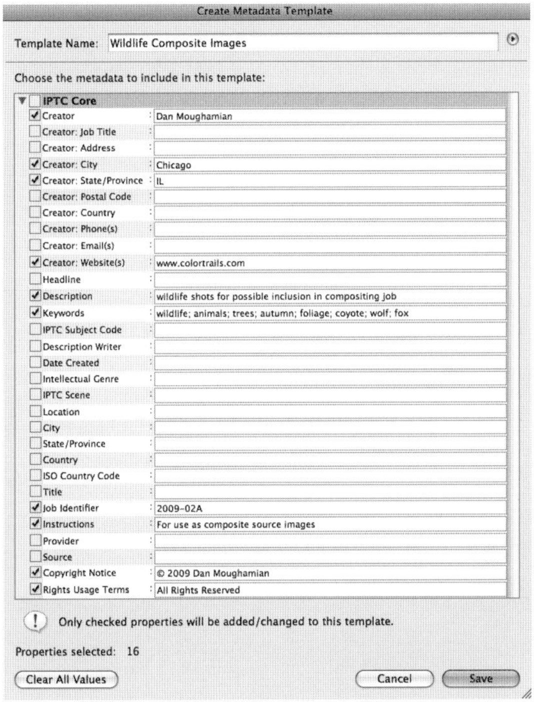

Figure 6.1 The Create Metadata Template dialog box is an indispensable tool for assigning important information to your images (in a single step) so they are easy to find later.

Take a few minutes to set up a template for each primary photographic context that you use (for example, landscapes shot at your favorite park or street images from a particular block in your favorite town).

The quickest way to get started with metadata templates is to define those bits of information that most often apply to your images and build your first template from that. You can edit metadata templates whenever needed, so it's not necessary to get things exactly right on the first attempt. No single template will apply to all the images you might use in a compositing project, unless your work follows a very consistent theme or subject. Once the general metadata template is applied, you can later use the Metadata panel in Bridge to add information specific to a particular image or set of images.

You can also (as mentioned earlier) append or replace metadata using different saved templates based on different project criteria. As the name implies, *appending* will leave all current metadata intact while adding project-specific information to it. Appending does not replace information that is already entered in a property field but adds only to fields that are empty. *Replacing* clears all previous data and enters new data. Similarly, you can use the File Info dialog box (by choosing File > File Info) to append or replace metadata of a specific image or selected images.

Two birds with one Bridge. One of the easiest ways to apply metadata in Bridge is by utilizing the Photo Downloader dialog box (**Figure 6.2**). You can access the Photo Downloader dialog box by opening Bridge and choosing File > Get Photos from Camera. To access the metadata functionality, click the Advanced Dialog button (which toggles to Standard Dialog when you're in Advanced mode). The extra functionality you see allows you to apply a metadata template to a specific range of images while they are being downloaded to your computer! This is another time-saver that you should consider if you have a large number of images to import. With just a few clicks, you can ensure that the images you are downloading will be easier to find when you search with the applicable criteria.

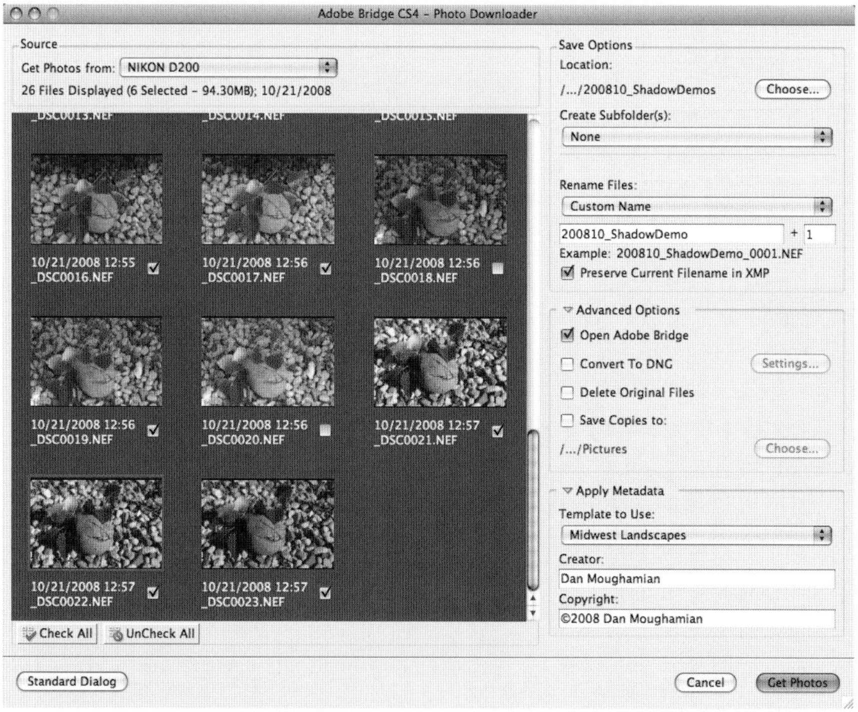

Figure 6.2 The Photo Downloader dialog box in Bridge can add metadata to your images as they are being saved to your hard drive.

Tips for Keywords

Adding keywords to images from Bridge is often the second step that many photographers will follow, once images have been "ingested" by their hard drive with basic metadata already applied. But regardless of when you choose to apply keywords, it's a good idea to *use your notes.*

Take note. During the planning process, you probably used a specific vocabulary to describe the scene or elements in the scene. These words make for good keywords as you create your master hierarchy in the Keywords panel, which is shown in **Figure 6.3**. That hierarchy should include the total range of topics, places, people, and things you photographed (or that are present in the stock images you have purchased).

Figure 6.3 The Keywords panel makes the process of creating an information hierarchy a relatively simple one, if a bit time-consuming for large and varied image collections.

Using the Keywords panel, you can start your hierarchy by adding several top-level, or *parent*, keywords to the panel. If you use your own system rather than importing a third-party hierarchy, you may want to follow the common hierarchy structure of People, Places, Events, and Things, or you can use universal photographic genres such as Portraits, Landscapes, Sports, Wildlife, and Products. The main point is that the hierarchy has to make sense to you and the people you work with regularly, so talk it through in the beginning if needed.

Grow your tree. Whichever system you use, it's important to set it up so that you can branch subjects out into different categories when necessary. For example, you may need to use the keyword *boat*, but that could refer to a model boat or a cruise liner in a nonhierarchical system. If you also happen to have many pictures of models or scenery in miniature, *model* may also be one of your higher-level keywords, so you could—in this scenario—create a new *boat* keyword within the *model* category. When you apply the *boat* keyword from that category, it will inherit the associated hierarchical values (in this case *model*). This would allow you to quickly narrow your search and distinguish between photographs of model boats and ocean liners.

You can also create keyword hierarchies by typing them directly into the Metadata panel's Keywords field. To take full advantage of your keyword hierarchy, use a delimiter character when applying keywords in this way. You can choose delimiter options in Bridge in the Keywords panel of Preferences (**Figure 6.4**). *Delimiters* are special characters that Bridge recognizes as implying a structure. Using the previous example with the pipe (|) as a delimiter, you could distinguish between *model | boat* and *boat | ocean liner* quite easily.

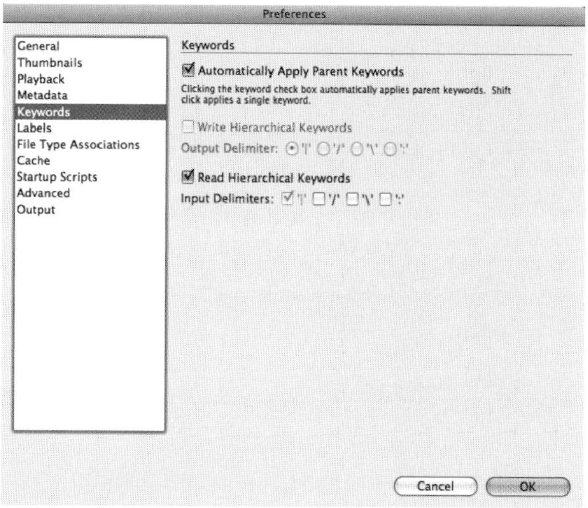

Figure 6.4 The Keywords panel of Preferences in Bridge

NOTE You can access your keywords in Bridge in several ways. The Keywords panel allows you to set up and populate keyword hierarchies, which you can then assign to images as you work. The Metadata panel also allows you to populate a Keywords field with delimited values, and the Filter panel allows you to sort images by any keywords that are present in the current folder of shots.

Choosing the Automatically Apply Parent Keywords option automatically assigns all the keywords in the existing folder hierarchy, whereas choosing to write out the structure makes the path a unique search string that you can save for later reference. The difference is that each word in the hierarchy will appear as a distinct search term when applying parent keywords. Once you have a good keyword scheme and start to expand your master keyword list, you can export your keywords as a text file for use in other programs (when creating your brainstorming spreadsheet, discussed in Chapter 2, for example) or just as a simple readout. This can make things easier when planning future projects, enabling you to refer to your entire keyword list at a glance when describing new shots or scenes.

Tips for Searching

Once you are ready to begin searching your entire collection of images (which in many cases will have been built up over months if not years), how do you go about finding the images you need? Assuming you've been vigilant about applying metadata and keywords to your images as you brought them into your workstation environment, Bridge has two general methods for finding images. The Filter panel (**Figure 6.5**) is by far the quickest and most intuitive in most situations. It allows you to select a range of images based on which keywords are applied to those images, at the exclusion of all others. You can then create a Bridge collection from the results in your Content panel (this process is described in more detail later in the chapter).

Figure 6.5 The Filter panel in Bridge makes finding images by keyword a very quick and simple process.

If, and, or greater than. If you need more complex filtering, you can use the Find dialog (**Figure 6.6**), which you can open by choosing Edit > Find (or by pressing Command+F [Control+F]). This command provides a robust dialog box where you can search not only by keyword but also by including or excluding additional image criteria. You can also apply Boolean logic to each type of criterion. For example, you could choose to include only those images whose ISO value (recorded in the image's EXIF metadata) "is less than or equal to" 800.

Figure 6.6 The Find dialog box allows you to quickly set up complex Boolean search criteria to assemble a group of targeted images from a specific folder.

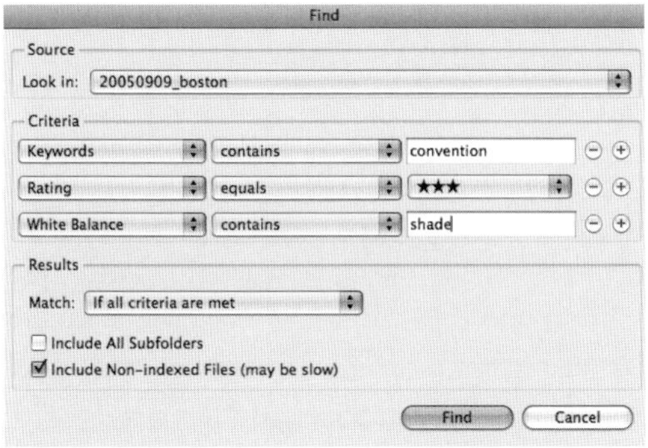

NOTE If you run a search on a large number of files that have not been indexed (the process by which Bridge initially "registers" your file into its database and generates an image thumbnail and preview), the search results can take a few minutes to fully populate.

The following are several of the more potentially important search criteria that are available. Combining these criteria with Boolean operators and specific values—and with the presence of specific keywords—can help you to efficiently search through thousands of files, producing the exact set of images you need for a project.

- File name
- Creation date
- File type
- Bit depth
- Color profile
- Copyright notice
- Description
- Label
- Rating
- Keywords
- Exposure values
- Focal length
- ISO

Also important to remember is that setting up a complex query takes only a few seconds using the Find dialog box, because it's quite simple to use. Besides establishing very specific criteria for inclusion in your Bridge search results, you can also limit your image search to any folder (including subfolders) on your computer or local network. This is how Bridge can help you find images across workgroups or in distributed locations, as well as on local drives.

Tips for Using Collections

One of the more promising improvements for Bridge involves the Collections panel. At their core, *collections* are groups of images that you want to associate with one another. You create them in one of two ways. First, you can click the New Collection button at the bottom-right portion of the Collections panel and then drag images onto the Collection icon from the Content panel (**Figure 6.7**).

Collections panel

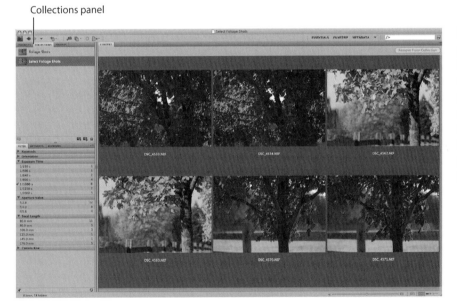

Figure 6.7 The Collections panel in Bridge allows you to gather specific kinds of images. Here a static collection was created by dragging thumbnails from the Content panel. This type of collection remains static until you add new or remove existing images.

The second method—called *smart collections*—is new in Bridge CS4 and allows you to create virtual collections of images and other media assets that are based on metadata criteria. To define your smart collection criteria, click the New Smart Collection button at the bottom of the Collections panel (the one with the gearlike icon). This opens the Smart Collection dialog box (**Figure 6.8**). The process of creating a smart collection is very much like creating a search query in the Find dialog box. Once your criteria are set, your collection will be updated in real time as you add more content to Bridge.

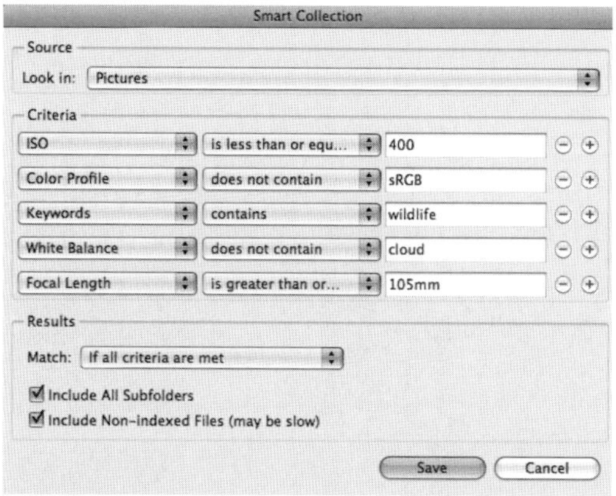

Figure 6.8 With the help of the Smart Collection dialog box, Bridge automatically gathers any ingested files that meet the metadata criteria you have specified.

For example, if you are a wildlife photographer looking to make a composite image for advertising your business, you can create a new smart collection that will stipulate that any photo shot during a specific season, using a particular ISO, and whose keywords contain *coyote*, *wolf*, or *fox*, be added to your collection results. Then, as you ingest more images and begin to add the applicable keywords to your shots, every time an image meets your smart collection criteria, it will be added to the smart collection automatically.

This means that once you decide what types of images you want to use, if you have already applied your metadata and keywords to your collection of media, you can simply create a smart collection, and it will not only act as the searching mechanism but also gather the files for you into a virtual folder without disrupting how your images are organized on the hard drive!

Tips for Evaluating and Comparing Images

There are also some useful tricks for accurately evaluating and comparing two or more images within Bridge. A common scenario when choosing images for compositing or other creative projects is selecting the best image from two or three similar compositions. Often these shots have been taken at the same time, at the same location, and from the same vantage point, perhaps with slightly different exposure values, depth of field, or lenses.

Side by side. One of the most useful features in Bridge is the ability to enlarge the Preview panel so that it occupies most of the user interface, except for the Content panel. Using this workspace setup, you can Shift-click a contiguous range of images from the Content panel, or you can select a group of noncontiguous images by Command-clicking (Control-clicking). As you do so, each image will be added to the Preview panel (**Figure 6.9**).

Figure 6.9 The Preview panel in Bridge allows you to enlarge and compare two or three similar images easily, providing far more detail than large thumbnails would.

Close-up. Another useful means of evaluating images (particularly small details and relative sharpness) is the Loupe tool, which previews a region of your image at 100 percent and is active when you see the magnifying glass icon over your image in the Preview panel. Once you've opened the loupe, you can move it around by clicking and dragging it to a new location, and you can zoom in beyond 100 percent using a mouse wheel or comparable control on your graphics tablet if you happen to use an Intuos3 from Wacom or other input device that supports loupe scrolling.

You can also compare the same region of multiple, similar compositions (in the Preview panel) by opening a loupe for each image and moving them to the same relative location (**Figure 6.10**).

Figure 6.10 The Loupe tool in Bridge can also work with multiple image previews to identify areas of superior detail or sharpness between shots with similar compositions.

PHOTOSHOP WORKFLOW TIPS

Since compositing is, by definition, the blending of multiple images into one, it makes sense to discuss some new ways to work with multiple images onscreen. Photoshop introduces some great workflow enhancements that make this task quite a bit easier and more flexible.

Managing Your Workspace

Photoshop provides some important new ways to arrange your workspace when you have multiple images open. The first time you launch Photoshop, you will find a new set of tools called the Application bar (or App bar) just below the standard menu bar at the top of the screen. Adobe has designed the App bar to help you manage all your documents and key viewing options. Although this can take up some valuable screen space for laptop users, any Photoshop user working on composite imagery with a large LCD screen should benefit greatly from the new App Bar and its viewing options.

The bar is now open. You can show or hide the App bar (**Figure 6.11**) by selecting or deselecting the Application Bar option at the bottom of the Window menu. Key to the App bar is the new Arrange Documents menu, which provides options for arranging all of your open documents into specific window layouts, as well as options for managing how each window is viewed.

Figure 6.11 The Application bar in Photoshop offers many options for simultaneously viewing multiple images.

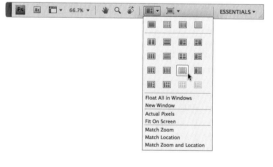

Put it on my tab. The Consolidate All feature utilizes a new technology called *tabbed documents* that allows you to place all your images—still maximized—into a single window but be a click away from any one of them. This is a great way to access several images at once but still focus on one at a time. You can tear off an image "tab" from its window by grabbing the tab and dragging it outside the bounds of the document. Then you can re-dock the image by dragging the title bar of the image back into the window where it was "torn" from and releasing the mouse button when you see a blue highlight.

Your number is up. Other options in the Arrange Documents menu include the familiar tiling options that let you choose from grid, vertical, and horizontal layouts. Below those choices, however, are the new N-up view options, which provide staggered layouts for specific numbers of images. With N-up viewing, you can rearrange your layouts by dragging images just as you would with the tabbed layout (as you drag an image over other image borders, the blue highlight will indicate where your image can be dropped, as shown in **Figure 6.12**).

NOTE By default, Photoshop has tabbed documents active. You can turn this feature off (if you prefer working with the legacy-style document windows) by choosing Preferences > Interface and deselecting Open All Documents as Tabs. When you do this, Consolidating All will convert the "floating" images to tabbed images.

Figure 6.12 The tabbed documents and N-up viewing options in Photoshop allow you to modify window arrangements by dragging an image to the border areas between images or between images and the traditional Photoshop UI elements.

Having the ability to view so many images at the same time might cause you to wonder just how useful the N-up feature is—but it's extremely useful. For example, you can still use the traditional Match Zoom and Location command (also in the Arrange Documents menu), but you can now apply it across a larger number of arranged documents. You can also match the rotation settings for all images. This is a great tool for comparing image content or quality and for precision retouching when preparing your images for compositing (**Figure 6.13**).

Figure 6.13 N-up views let you work on more documents side by side, without the screen clutter that would have been inevitable with prior versions.

NOTE Dragging and dropping layers from the Layers panel to another (hidden) document's tab is not yet supported. You also cannot drag and drop paths or channels from their respective panels onto another (hidden) document's tab.

To summarize, N-up views, combined with traditional Photoshop viewing and matching options, allow you to edit one image while comparing it with another. And you can drag layers from one image to another in N-up view just as you normally would—simply select the layer from the image canvas, drag it over the target document's tab, and release the mouse button. Holding down Shift while you do this centers the layer in the target document.

Using Layers and Layer Groups

Not much has changed in Photoshop with respect to handling layers and grouping those layers, but it's important for you to utilize these features often when working on composite images. Grouping layers is a fantastic way to keep your individual image components organized. Adjustment layers, smart objects, and image content can all be grouped in whatever fashion makes sense for your project.

For example, you may have applied several adjustment layers to a single pixel-based layer; by grouping those adjustments in a folder, with one click you can preview their cumulative effect on your target layer. You may also have small bits of cutout imagery that should be edited and viewed as a unit rather than as separate layers. Sometimes grouping these "bits" into folders helps keep them from falling through the proverbial cracks in your workflow.

To group a collection of layers, select them as you normally would, and drag them to the Folder icon at the bottom of the Layers panel (**Figure 6.14**). You can also drag and drop layers to change their order in the Layers panel hierarchy or to group them in another folder.

NOTE When grouping layers, be aware that order is important. A group can have a pass-through blend applied, which affects every layer in the group or only those that you have individually adjusted.

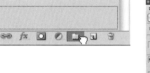

Figure 6.14 Grouping layers keeps things organized, which is vital when coordinating several elements. Anything that can be on a layer by itself can go into a group, including adjustment layers and smart objects.

Processing Raw Source Files

It is often a good idea to use raw (or DNG) photographic files as the starting point for your composite images. The tools provided by Adobe Camera Raw (ACR), when combined with a well-exposed raw image, offer unrivaled editing flexibility. When processed properly, DNG and raw files can result in enhanced tone, range, detail, and color in your final composite.

Although today's Digital SLRs can produce beautiful JPEG files that you can edit with ACR, JPEGs are still fundamentally 8-bit files with a compression scheme applied. They also are captured to a color space (sRGB) that is somewhat inferior to other color spaces you can apply natively when outputting a raw image from ACR (such as Adobe RGB or ProPhoto RGB). Some cameras also enable you to capture your images as TIFF files (which, unlike JPEGs, are not compressed); however, these files are usually much larger than an equivalent raw file and offer no added benefit. For this reason we almost always capture our source images in raw format and process them with ACR to get things rolling.

This chapter covers the most important aspects of working in ACR to create the best source material for composite images, while maintaining image data integrity as much as possible. Chapter 8 discusses the task of enhancing (or retouching) your processed raw files in Photoshop CS4. Then in Chapter 10 we cover the techniques for bringing all of your source materials together, to form a new composite image. We decided to go this route rather than grouping all of these topics together, so that you can get a better sense of how the process is broken down, and if need be, go directly to the chapter that most relates to your situation.

ENHANCING COLOR AND TONE

TIP If you need to share raw source files, use the Adobe DNG Converter application that is bundled with ACR. Using DNG versions of your raw files ensures compatibility with other versions of ACR that others may be using, as well as third-party programs that are not compatible with your camera format. For more information on DNG, visit: http://www.adobe.com/products/photoshop/cameraraw.html.

TIP To open your processed raw file as a copy in Photoshop, hold down the Option (Alt) key, and the Open Image button will change to Open Copy. Holding down Shift-Command (Shift-Control) will open your image as a smart object in Photoshop.

NOTE Going forward, we will cover the different processes and steps that we use when building our composite images. However, as with graphic design and other Photoshop workflows, there are often different ways to arrive at the same result. It is less important that you follow our sequence of techniques exactly than it is to understand how each technique can improve your photos and composite images.

The most important part of processing raw images is getting the color and tonality right. This is a point of confusion for some, because "right" is often taken to mean the most neutral white balance or overall color temperature, and a nice, evenly lit exposure. This mindset is driven by the principles taught in traditional photography classes. Although neutral colors, and even lighting, may be preferable in some composite images, keep in mind that ultimately you are trying to achieve a specific vision, not make every region of color or tonality perfectly balanced or "neutral."

Your vision likely is associated with a unique mood or setting that may not equate to perfectly neutral white balance and bright imagery throughout your source files. More likely, some images will need to be warmer or cooler, lighter or darker. Does the part of the image you intend to use for the composite fall under sunlight or shadow? Is it part of the foreground or the background? Is it best shown as a sharper, grainy image, or soft and smoothed out? These are the types of questions you should ask yourself as you begin to process your source files.

You may even want to take advantage of the ability in ACR to open a specific set of changes as a copy, so that you can try different variations and moods with the same source file. Always keep your final vision in mind as you work in ACR.

Global Color Corrections

Before we talk about the specific techniques you can use to optimize the color in your source files, it's important that you start with a good foundation. We will assume for the remainder of the book that you have some familiarity with basic color management concepts, like calibrating your monitor and using a monitor hood if you work under difficult lighting conditions.

Set the thermostat. The first thing we do with our source files is set their color temperature in a way that will help them blend in with their final composite surroundings. The warmness or coolness of an object can have a big impact on the mood your composite image creates, so keep this in mind as you work. It's true you are likely to need additional corrections in Photoshop, but the closer you can get to the correct color temperature in ACR, the better off you'll be. This will provide more leeway to push the composite image's layer data with Curves, Color Balance, and other Photoshop color and tone tools.

It's also likely that for most of the source images you process, you will use only one region or part of that file. As you move the Temperature slider in the Basic panel in ACR, keep an eye on the region of the image you are targeting for the composite (**Figure 7.1**). As long as that portion of the photo provides the color character you need without introducing bands or other undesirable effects, don't concern yourself if the rest of your image looks a little off-kilter—that effect is likely to be cut out or masked away later.

Figure 7.1 Use the Temperature slider to set the overall color mood of your target area (in this case, the driveway). Don't worry about the rest of the image if you know it won't be used.

Cooler Temperature   Warmer Temperature

Near or far? Another issue to consider when making global color corrections is whether your composite image must provide the illusion of great distance. The distance from subject to viewer makes a difference in terms of the color and saturation adjustments you might need to make. As discussed in Chapter 5, "Capturing the Scene and Subject," the farther away an object is in the real world, the less saturated its colors tend to appear to the naked eye. Keep in mind also the blue haze that is often associated with this type of image.

The bottom line is that subjects in the final image that are intended to be perceived as "far away" from the viewer often benefit from a moderate Vibrance reduction (**Figure 7.2**), as well as small reductions in Saturation in some cases. These simple changes enhance the illusion that the image region you are targeting is farther away than it actually was in the original photograph.

Conversely, if your subject is "front and center" in your composite, its Vibrance value, and to a lesser degree the Saturation setting, will likely need to be increased. The need for an increase in relative saturation will depend

TIP Strictly speaking, ACR's Clarity slider (grouped with Vibrance and Saturation) is not a color correction tool. However, it can enhance the illusion of greater or lesser distance. Increasing Clarity gives the appearance of sharpened mid-tones. The crisper an object's details, the closer it's perceived to be, all else being equal. Conversely, reducing Clarity will give objects more of a far-off look in shots like Figure 7.2.

on how strong the source image's hues are to start, and whether you want them to stand out relative to the color of the surrounding source elements in your composite. Generally speaking, the more saturated something becomes, the closer to the viewer it will appear to be.

Figure 7.2 The goal here was to make the peninsula appear even more distant, so the Vibrance was reduced by a moderate amount, and the Saturation was reduced slightly.

This example shows a source file that we use later in the chapter. Since we want to use this image as a "distant background," we had to reduce the color saturation and vibrancy a bit. Later we will re-introduce some color into the foreground and soften the background details (enhancing the perception of great distance) by creating localized edits with the Adjustment Brush. We handle Vibrance and Saturation in the Basic panel because there is not yet a Vibrance setting for the Adjustment Brush feature. And, while more corrections are needed in Photoshop before this image is ready, we always take the image as far as we can in ACR so there is less work later.

TIP It is useful to make note of any pronounced tonal or color shifts you apply to a specific image in ACR. This will help you make smarter decisions later when performing additional color or tonal edits in Photoshop.

Keep in mind that the Vibrance slider can do the best job of increasing or decreasing an area's color saturation without clipping the colors. This is true especially of skin tones and earth tones. Try Vibrance first, and if you don't get the result you want, use minor corrections to the Saturation value to finish the look. If you make a saturation correction first, pushing the Vibrance slider to a large degree can introduce clipping, because the effects on a given color region are combined when the two sliders are used together.

Global Tonal Corrections

Another key step in setting up your source images for inclusion in your compositing project is modifying the tonality of your source imagery so that it matches the context it will have in the final composite. As you do so, consider final elements such as shadows, glowing effects, or additional light sources you might want to create with the help of Photoshop—and the general direction of lighting for a given image. What you do in ACR can make those changes an easier task or a headache. We apply most global tonal corrections for raw source images in the friendly confines of the Basic panel (**Figure 7.3**).

Figure 7.3 The Basic panel in ACR. The Exposure, Recovery, and Fill Light sliders are the best place to start when you need to lighten your source image. The Exposure, Blacks, and Brightness sliders will often help when darkening areas of an image.

The corrections you create at this stage are just a starting point. You are likely to need additional tonal corrections in ACR, additional changes in Photoshop, or both. The idea is to get as close as you can to a final product with ACR so that you have more room to push tonal values with Curves, Shadow and Highlight, and other Photoshop tools, several of which are discussed in later chapters.

Lightening Source Imagery

When lightening the tones in your scene or subject, the Exposure, Recovery, and Fill Light sliders are often a good place to start. The Recovery slider is an indispensable tool that allows you to bring back lost highlight details in the brightest portions of your image, as a result of slight overexposure in the camera or a moderate increase in ACR's Exposure value.

Exposure. Typically we start our tonal corrections with the Exposure slider, which tends to have an equally pronounced effect on all tones in your image. To make sure we don't go overboard, we first turn on the shadow and highlight clipping previews, and then slowly move the Exposure slider until the tones in our image look right (**Figure 7.4**). Keep the other parts of the composite in mind as you make your tonal edits, especially if you are setting the global tonality for a backdrop image that the rest of your images will be set into later.

If the highlight clipping preview starts to show large regions of solid color over your image's target area, bring the Exposure slider back a little bit, and try your luck with the Fill Light slider or the Brightness slider. Keep in mind that the Brightness slider may also cause clipping in these scenarios, as it will affect all but the brightest and darkest 10 percent (approximately) of tones in your image.

Figure 7.4 The ACR clipping previews can help you make a tonal correction that doesn't dramatically alter the distribution of tonal data in your file. This will provide more flexibility when editing tones in Photoshop later in the process.

Image with Highlight Clipping Preview On

Image with Highlight Clipping Preview Off

Modest alterations with the Exposure slider are generally best. Pushing the slider beyond a value of +1 or –1 can result in an output file that has little latitude for further tonal corrections when layered into the composite image. It is also important to understand that the Exposure slider's values do not literally correlate to camera stops. They are at best approximations of what a one-stop increase or decrease in camera exposure would look like.

Recovery. Lightening source images often causes the brightest details to become pure white. The Recovery slider helps restore some of those details (**Figure 7.5**), though it can't work miracles. Any overexposure in the original file makes recovering highlight detail less likely.

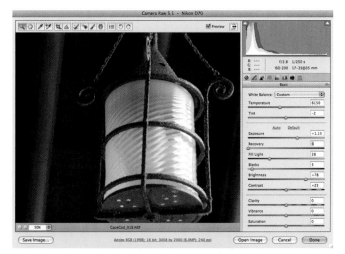

Image with Exposure Correction Only

Figure 7.5 The Recovery slider can help reclaim lost highlight details.

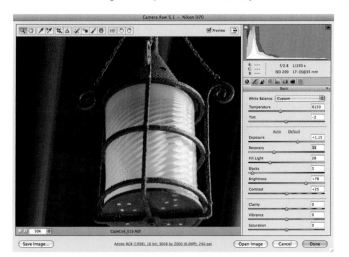

Image with Exposure Correction and Recovery

Another trick you can use when trying to recover lost highlight detail is to pull back the Contrast slider slightly. This will flatten the tonal range of the image a bit and in some cases bring back lost highlight or shadow details. It doesn't always work, but it's worth a shot if it can provide a little more detail.

Fill Light. The Fill Light slider simulates a fill flash on your camera, brightening the darker tones or shadowy areas in your image. Typically we use only modest amounts of Fill Light unless we have some foreground areas that are still too dark even after an Exposure increase. You may have to apply additional Recovery edits if you significantly increase Fill Light after your initial Exposure and Recovery edits.

Darkening Source Imagery

The controls you will first use for darkening source material are the Exposure (described in the previous section), Brightness, and Blacks sliders. As with the sliders used for lightening an image globally, these sliders also benefit from the use of the (Shadow) Clipping Preview. Make sure it's turned on before you start to darken parts of your image, so you can see where the darker details are turning to pure black.

Brightness. The Brightness slider operates in much the same fashion as the Mid-tone Input slider in the Photoshop Levels dialog box. It is designed to make the entire scene brighter or darker, without having a pronounced effect on the very brightest and darkest details in the image. For situations where you want to maintain the original look of your brightest and darkest image details, the Brightness slider might be a better option than the Exposure slider.

Blacks. If you want to make the darkest regions in your image a little bit darker to increase contrast, try moving the Blacks slider a modest amount—anything past 6 or 7, and you are likely to lose most of your shadow details, as shown in **Figure 7.6**. The Blacks slider can also be used as a makeshift equivalent of the Recovery slider, where lost shadow details are concerned. If the image you are editing already seems to have lost some shadow details at ACR's default Blacks setting, you can pull this slider back a couple of points, as it may reveal some additional shadow detail, though this is far from a sure thing.

Image with Slight Correction to Black Levels

Figure 7.6 The Blacks slider can help increase contrast by pushing the darkest details to pure black, but you should use it sparingly.

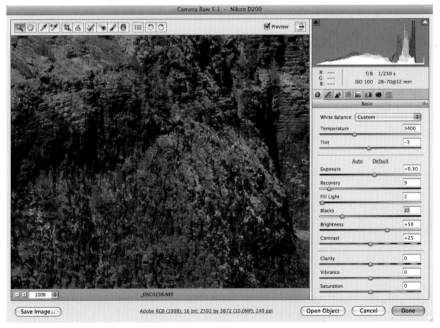

Image with Too Strong a Blacks Correction

Localized Color and Tone Corrections

ACR 5.2 provides three new tools that greatly enhance its ability to target corrections to specific areas in an image. The Targeted Adjustment tool, the Adjustment Brush, and the Graduated Filter, all discussed here, are worth investigating, as is the HSL panel. All of these tools can enhance your workflow.

Take 3. One of our favorite tools for making color-targeted modifications to source imagery is the HSL panel (**Figure 7.7**). This tool is especially useful when you have your general color temperature and overall Vibrance levels set, but need to shift one or more colors within the target region. The HSL panel allows you to target specific color regions in the source file so that you can modify them to be a different hue, saturation, or luminance without impacting other colors.

For example, you may need to blend in a woman in a red dress with a fire engine from another image, but the two reds don't match closely enough. HSL is the tool to use to address that problem right from the start, if you have raw source images. Unfortunately, there is not yet an HSL Adjustment Layer in Photoshop, but in the meantime, the HSL panel in ACR (and also the Targeted Adjustment tool, which is our next topic) do a fantastic job.

Keep color relationships in mind when working with hue, saturation, and luminance (HSL). Subjects that contain colors in adjacent regions of the color wheel (**Figure 7.8**) tend to react to changes in slider values for each of their component colors. For example, spring vegetation will tend to react to movements of both the Yellows and Greens sliders for each HSL component. Similarly, earth tones and some skin tones typically react to the Reds, Yellows, and Oranges sliders, and scenes with ocean and sky will react to Cyans, Blues, and sometimes even Purples!

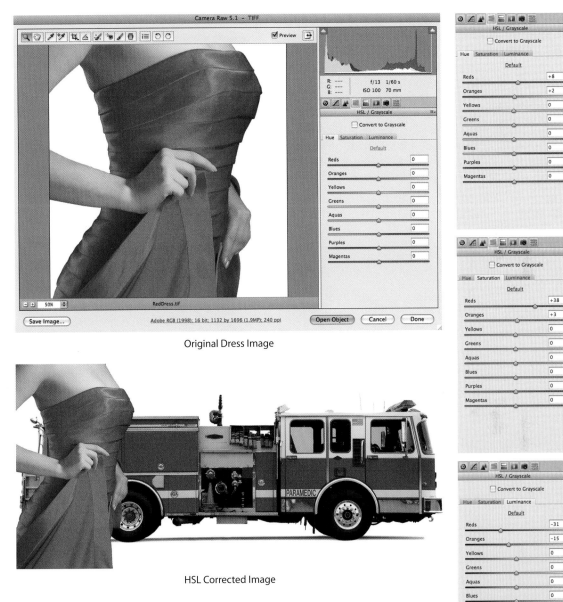

Original Dress Image

HSL Corrected Image

Figure 7.7 The HSL panel can be a tremendously useful asset when shifting the hue or saturation of a particular color range so that it matches the colors in another image.

HSL Settings Applied
to the Dress

Figure 7.8 The Itten color wheel is useful as a visual guidepost when working with HSL. Note that there is not a one-to-one relationship between the colors used and that you don't have to use this specific color wheel as long as the alternative shows the primary colors and their complements.

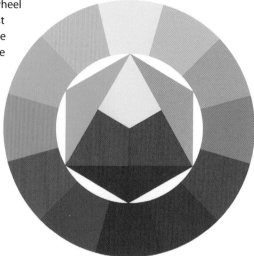

Click and shift. When ACR 5.2 was released shortly after Photoshop CS4, users were greeted with a surprise addition: the Targeted Adjustment tool (**Figure 7.9a**). This tool is tied closely to the functionality of the HSL panel (and also the Parametric Curves). To use the Targeted Adjustment tool, select it from the toolbar and choose the mode you need (Curves, Hue, Saturation, or Luminance) from the pop-up menu. Then click directly on the part of the image you wish to modify, and drag until you see the result you want!

Figure 7.9a The Targeted Adjustment tool and its related HSL controls help you isolate color and tonal corrections to specific regions of color.

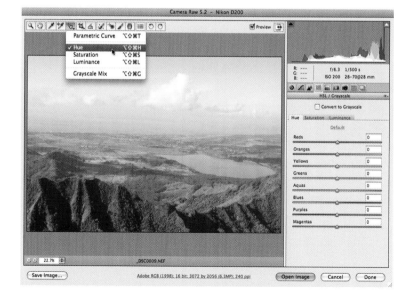

The new Curves dialog in Photoshop (covered in the next chapter) has a similar control mechanism and the results can be fantastic. For the example in **Figure 7.9b**, we needed to shift the color and luminance of the blue sky and tweak the color and saturation of other areas in the shot. The changes took less than a minute to apply and the results were exactly what we wanted. We think this tool will become an instant favorite among die-hard Photoshop users; you should get familiar with it and integrate it into your workflow.

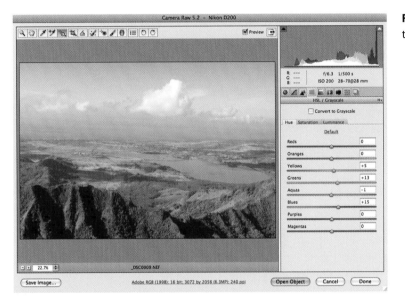

Figure 7.9b The final result after using the Targeted Adjustment tool

Think globally, brush locally. The new Adjustment Brush allows you to make corrections to specific regions of an image using the same kind of brush strokes you might apply to an image in Photoshop! With this tool, you can brush localized color and tone corrections directly onto the raw image, as you would in Adobe Photoshop Lightroom 2 or Photoshop. As you brush over an area, a *selection mask* is created, showing you where the corrections will have an effect. Once you begin to move the sliders—which work in the same way as their counterparts in the Basic panel—corrections are applied only to the mask regions. The brushed adjustments for this example are shown in **Figures 7.9c through 7.9g**.

For example, it may be necessary in your raw processing to make an irregular-shaped area in the image brighter or darker, a different or more saturated color, or both. You can now accomplish this task directly in ACR, saving yourself time later in Photoshop and again providing more "headroom" for altering image data. You can also apply different settings to more than one region in a single image by creating a new mask region.

Figure 7.9c and **d** Using the new Adjustment Brush, you can create a selection mask to apply localized color and tone corrections directly onto an image.

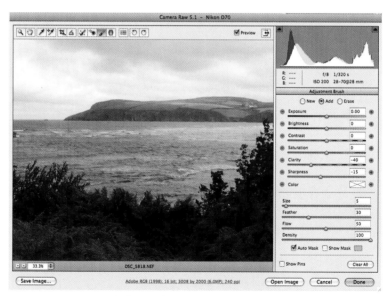

Background Area Masked

Background Area Corrected, Mask Off

Using the example of a windy ocean bay from Figure 7.2, we needed to make further adjustments to provide the depth cues for the final composite. Namely, the background needed to be slightly blurred, while the foreground sharpness was increased a bit. The foreground also needed more color, as did the ocean regions. So we had three regions—some of them slightly overlapping—that required different corrections. We created multiple mask correction regions (using the New button) so that we could use unique settings for the same sliders, in each correction region.

Foreground Area Masked

Figure 7.9e and **f** Create multiple mask correction regions to make different corrections in more than one region of an image.

Foreground Area Corrected

The Pins feature allows you to quickly jump back and forth between mask regions so they don't get lost. Using the Auto-mask option on both solid and irregularly shaped regions makes the masking accurate and simple, though a bit slower with complex details.

Figure 7.9g Corrections made using the Adjustment Brush and Pins feature

Ocean Area Masked, with Pins Visible

Graduated Filter. Another new but perhaps slightly more awkward localized correction tool is the Graduated Filter tool. This tool was designed so that you can modify a region of the image to have progressively more or less of a specific color or tonal correction, without affecting the remainder of the image. The Graduated Filter tool allows you to draw a "beam" (similar to the one in Lightroom 2 but not as easy to maneuver) over the target region, with the green end indicating the start of the full correction values and the red end placed at the point in the region where you want the correction to stop (**Figure 7.10**).

You can also try the Graduated Filter tool on image regions that contain a shadow or another area that needs a progressive change from lighter to darker or from less saturated to more saturated, such as a midday blue sky. Whether you ultimately choose to make this type of correction in ACR or in Photoshop depends a lot on how intuitive you find the Graduated Filter tool to be. Moving the "I-beam" around can occasionally be an exercise in frustration, despite its effectiveness once positioned correctly with settings applied.

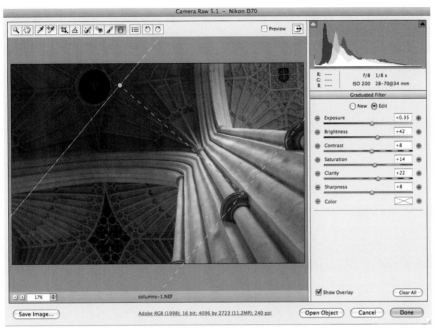

Graduated Filter Correction, Preview Off

Figure 7.10 The Graduated Filter tool in ACR and its associated sliders

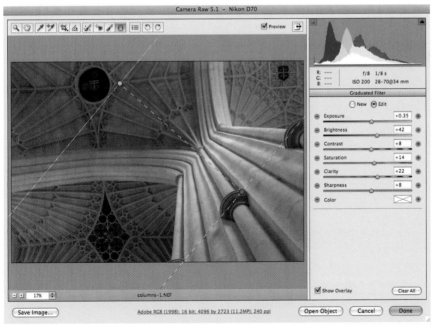

Graduated Filter Correction, Preview On

CONTROLLING CAMERA NOISE

One of the most overlooked strong points of ACR is its ability to handle noise and sharpening duties. This wasn't always true; versions of ACR prior to the one that came with Photoshop CS3 were equipped with some noise and sharpening functionalities, but they were not as powerful as what currently is available. Once you've finished with your color and tonal corrections on your composite source images, we strongly recommend that you zoom to 100 percent (or more) and jump over to the Detail panel. Use the Hand tool to move around your image and look for any sign of color noise or luminance noise….

Noise abatement. The first step we take in ACR noise reduction is to remove any hint of color noise. Unlike luminance noise that can—in a few circumstances—have a visual character somewhat like film grain (which can be desirable), color noise is almost always a nuisance. Once you've found a region of color noise, move the Color Noise slider at the bottom of the Detail panel until the color splotches are almost completely gone (**Figure 7.11**).

Figure 7.11 Color noise from your camera can degrade the final quality of your composite.

Region of Color Noise Viewed at 100 Percent

Same Region with Color Noise Removal Applied

Next, follow the same process for identifying and removing the luminance noise, if you find that it is distracting (**Figure 7.12**). Occasionally a little "graininess" is useful, depending on the look you want to achieve. For many daylight shots we remove roughly 50 percent of the luminance noise in our source images, unless we have a compelling reason to remove more. The reason is that removing large amounts of both color noise and luminance noise can make your image noticeably softer. This too can be a judgment call, depending on the look you are striving for, but typically it's not something any compositing artist desires.

Figure 7.12 Luminance noise from your camera can degrade the final quality of your composite, or it can provide a hint of graininess if that is your goal.

Region of Luminance Noise (with Color Noise Removed) at 100 Percent

Region with Luminance Noise Removal Applied

CONTROLLING SHARPNESS

The Sharpening controls in ACR have reached a point in recent years where it's almost foolish not to employ them—with some moderation—before outputting all of your raw files into Photoshop (**Figure 7.13**). For each of the ACR Sharpening controls, an extremely useful grayscale mask preview allows you to see exactly how much your image is being sharpened and where. At a minimum, you will want to reap the benefits of some judicious sharpening any time you use the noise reduction tools in the Detail panel, to offset any softness they introduce.

Figure 7.13 The ACR Sharpening controls in the Detail panel

Amount. The Amount slider controls the intensity of the sharpness correction being applied to your image. You can push this slider quite a ways before you start to introduce artifacts or haloes into your image, and in the latter case you can control the haloes to great degree with the Radius slider. The ACR Sharpening tools can do a remarkably good job compared with the Unsharp Mask filter and other "old-school" sharpening tricks.

NOTE To see the effects of the various Sharpening (and Noise Reduction) tools in the Detail panel in ACR, you must view your image at 100 percent magnification or greater.

The first step in sharpening is to move the slider to a value of about 40 or 50 to see what kind of improvements (or problems) appear as a result. Try to locate a region of the image that is representative of the whole; usually a region with a mix of detail and smooth texture will work best. You can then make your remaining Sharpening slider corrections with this region visible.

Radius. As with other Sharpening tools, the Radius slider allows you to control the size of the sharpening region around the affected pixels. Hold down the Alt (Option) key as you move this slider to call up a grayscale mask that shows you exactly where the haloes start and stop (**Figure 7.14**).

Figure 7.14 Holding down the Alt (Option) key while moving the Radius slider can make a big difference when controlling sharpening haloes.

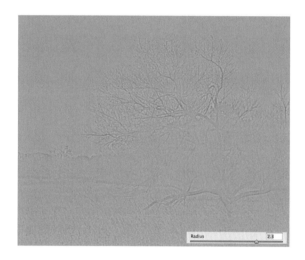

Detail. This slider allows you to control the amount of sharpening that is applied to heavily textured or detailed areas. Sometimes it can be desirable to avoid sharpening areas with distinctive textures, because it can change the character of the image. Again, hold down the Alt (Option) key to get a grayscale preview of the details being sharpened as you move the slider (**Figure 7.15**).

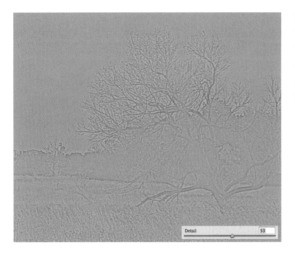

Figure 7.15 Holding down the Alt (Option) key while moving the Detail slider can help you avoid over-sharpening textured regions in your image.

Masking. The Masking slider works in the same way as the Radius and Detail sliders, except this setting reduces the amount of sharpening applied to regions of the image that have little or no texture (**Figure 7.16**).

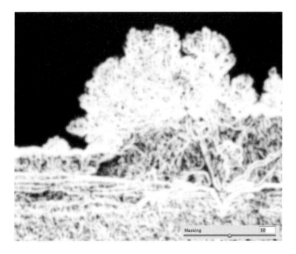

Figure 7.16 Holding down the Alt (Option) key while moving the Masking slider can help ensure that areas with little detail or texture are not sharpened (avoiding the creation of unwanted artifacts).

HANDLING MULTIPLE CORRECTIONS

Synchronicity. If you find yourself in a situation where you need to correct multiple raw files with very similar or identical global settings, the Synchronize function in ACR can make your workflow much more efficient without diminished accuracy or quality.

The first step is to open Bridge CS4, then highlight and open all of the raw files that require the same corrections (**Figure 7.17**).

Figure 7.17 You can start the process of correcting multiple source images at one time by selecting a range of images in Adobe Bridge CS4 and opening them into ACR.

TIP If you are using the Spot Removal Brush for retouching, make sure you want the same correction applied to every image in your group, at the same location. Otherwise, synchronizing Spot Removal across images can cause unintended edits.

Once the images are open in ACR (the thumbnails will appear along the left edge of the window), click the Select All button. Next, click the Synchronize button and you are greeted with a dialog box that allows you to click and choose exactly which ACR corrections to include in the "grouped correction" (**Figure 7.18**). You can even include corrections from the Spot Removal Brush, to get rid of any lens dust or water spots that appear in the same spot on all of your images!

A common scenario in compositing—where you need to apply the same corrections to many images—would be when you are creating a panoramic image from many shots (creating panoramic images is discussed in Chapter 10, "Compositing Source Materials"). As long as the lighting in your scene is even or close to it, you should be able to save a lot of time by making many of the same corrections from the Basic panel and HSL panel, for example, to all of the source images at once. After you've made your choices in the Synchronize panel, you can apply your edits with the ACR controls as you normally would. Highlight any single image to make further changes to that shot alone.

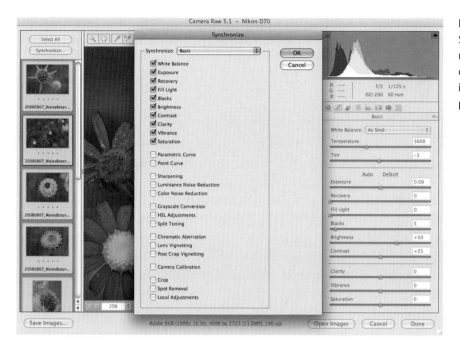

Figure 7.18 The Synchronize function in ACR makes it a great tool for correcting multiple source images that were shot for a panoramic composite.

MANAGING OUTPUT

ACR workflow options are vital to the success of any compositing work-flow that starts with raw source images (**Figure 7.19**). The most important thing you can do is make sure you output each image that you're going to be manipulating in Photoshop as a 16-bit file. This will give you more data to work with and is one of the key benefits of shooting raw files, which, unlike JPEGs, are often captured at 10, 12, or even 14 bits in some cases. The more data in your files that you have to work with, the better.

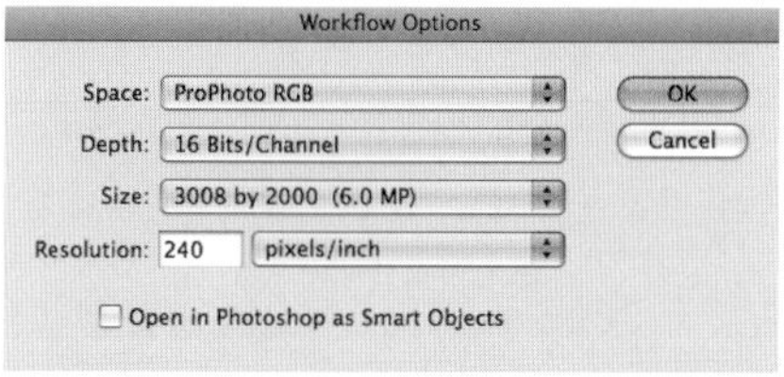

Figure 7.19 Using the Workflow Options dialog box in ACR is vital to getting maximum value from your source images.

Another important decision is choosing the right color space, usually by selecting either the Adobe RGB 1998 or ProPhoto RGB option. The latter in particular is a huge color space that ensures there is less clipping, banding, or other unwanted effects as your images are edited in Photoshop. Adobe RGB is a better choice if there's a chance you will be passing your processed source files to other artists or companies that may have Adobe RGB as part of their standard workflow and RGB editing space. We try not to use sRGB as an output option unless we're processing JPEG files out of the camera and/or have a Web-focused workflow for a specific project.

If you want to make your image larger or smaller than your original camera source's native format, the Size options in the ACR Workflow Options dialog box do a comparable job to the Bicubic Smoother and Bicubic Sharper options in the Image menu in Photoshop. The one caveat is that if you choose to enlarge the image outside of ACR, you will likely need to perform that enlargement in multiple steps, so for that situation, using ACR's enlargement options will be more efficient and produce as good or better results. For more information on resizing images, check out *Real World Photoshop CS4 for Photographers*, by Conrad Chavez and David Blatner (Peachpit Press).

CHAPTER EIGHT

Enhancing Source Images

Once you have processed your raw source images in ACR (or have acquired stock images), the next step is to ready them for compositing using various retouching techniques. This chapter focuses on removing defects and distractions from your image and on making further enhancements to tone and color. Important topics covered include working with layers, handling smart objects, selecting and masking images, using the improved color and tonal correction tools in Adobe Photoshop CS4, managing perspective correction, using the Transform commands, and developing workflow efficiency.

Ultimately, the goal is to ensure that your source images blend smoothly with the other images, illustrations, or 3D content you will include as part of your final composite. This could be a simple matter of matching light intensity and direction, or it could involve more complex tasks such as setting up the illusion of distance and perspective.

COMPOSITING WORKFLOW

As you begin modifying source images, it's important to manage your workflow and documents carefully and efficiently. It's not enough to know the 1-2-3s of how a particular task is accomplished; you need to stay organized and keep your images flexible. Although some editing sessions are slam-dunk situations, we often perform initial edits for an image and then come back later to apply more changes as the composite concept evolves. If you don't keep this in mind, rather than just adding a few changes to an image, you may find yourself needing to redo an entire layer and its specific look from scratch.

Identifying Problem Areas

As Photoshop users, many of us tend to correct anything that doesn't look perfect or ideal in the mind's eye. The more problems Photoshop can quickly and accurately solve, the more we are inclined to use those features because we can, rather than evaluating first whether we *need* to use them. Sometimes a little imperfection and asymmetry can make the final composite more compelling.

Imperfect or distracting? This is the question you should ask yourself as you evaluate each image that will be integrated into the composite. To some degree, the answer will be subjective (in other words, one person's imperfection is another's distraction), but keeping the context of each composite piece in mind will help you spend time only where you need to do so.

Are you creating a jungle-like atmosphere or other wilderness scene, which, in the real world, contains obvious asymmetry and disorder? If so, then removing every stump or rock in your source image is probably not a good idea (**Figure 8.1**). If, on the other hand, you are creating a composite involving sports cars and stereos, then chances are the quality of your final image will benefit from fixing every little detail and smoothing every "rough edge." Context is everything!

Figure 8.1 How much you need to clear your image of small imperfections will depend on the context of your image. This shot benefits from the complexity.

So, what constitutes a distraction? The more the shape, placement, or color of an object in the scene could potentially pull the viewer's eye away from your intended point of focus, the more you should consider removing or modifying it. For our hypothetical wilderness scene, we found a good balance between leaving certain imperfections intact and removing unnecessary details that would potentially distract the viewer (**Figure 8.2**).

Figure 8.2 The original image (left) contained distracting elements (like dead brush) that were replaced with foliage from other areas (right), making it easier to place other images in the scene.

The same thought process holds true for people who are placed in composites. If you want to show kids at play in your composite, cleaning every freckle or ice cream smudge off their faces or smoothing out their hair might not produce the effect you want, even though as portrait-retouching artists this might be our first instinct. For people shots, keep track of what truly needs fixing as you evaluate each image. The new Notes panel in Photoshop is integrated with the Annotation tool, which is now more useful because you can see the full image when viewing your notes. Only the note icon is present on the document (**Figure 8.3**).

Figure 8.3 The Notes panel in Photoshop is a good way to keep track of the retouching tasks needed for each image.

Retaining Image Flexibility

Image flexibility may sound like a new concept, but it has nothing to do with keeping your images limber. Rather, it's a reminder that, whenever possible, you should work in 16-bit mode, using layers, layer masks, smart objects, and alpha channels as part of your imaging workflow. We discuss these concepts in more detail throughout the chapter, and they will provide the flexibility you need to make iterative changes to specific parts of your document without starting over.

No other asset is likely to be more valuable and in short supply than your time. Having to recorrect or rebuild parts of an image (which could take an hour or more in many scenarios) because you flattened your document too early in the editing process or used destructive editing options such as the Eraser tool is a mistake you're likely to make only once, but it can be a costly and frustrating one.

16 bits or 8 bits? One of the more commonly overlooked benefits of Photoshop is the ability to edit in 16-bit mode when using source files generated from raw captures. Without realizing it, users will often work in 8-bit mode even though they have better options. Although this can speed up certain operations (since Photoshop has half as many data bits to modify), you give up flexibility in terms of defining the colors and tonality in your image. If you've ever watched what happens to your histogram after making a big shift in levels or hue and saturation when working in 8-bit mode, you know that the data can get stretched or compressed quite a bit.

Figure 8.4 Working in 16-bit mode provides added flexibility when editing.

Except for simple projects that start out as 8-bit source files, we recommend working in 16-bit mode. This allows you to push the color and tonal data further when making creative decisions, without creating situations that involve color banding or clipped tonal values. **Figure 8.4** shows a simple comparison, where the same edits were applied in Photoshop to two versions of the same image—one output from ACR as 8-bit, one as 16-bit.

8-bit Image with Edits Applied

16-bit Image with Edits Applied

For some projects, you may need to consider using High Dynamic Range (HDR) images, which contain 32 bits of data. While HDR is an important topic with relevance to compositing, it is a complex one that warrants study in its own right. If you'd like to learn more about HDR imaging, we recommend you pick up a book on the topic, such as *The Complete Guide to High Dynamic Range Digital Photography*, by Ferrell McCollough (Lark Books).

Adjust and conquer. It is difficult to overstate the importance of using adjustment layers (and the new Adjustments panel, shown in **Figure 8.5**) as part of your compositing workflow. The Adjustments panel contains a non-modal version of the following settings from the Image Adjustments menu: Brightness/Contrast, Levels, Curves, Exposure, Vibrance, Hue & Saturation, Color Balance, Black & White, Photo Filter, Channel Mixer, Invert, Posterize, Threshold, Gradient Map, and Selective Color.

Figure 8.5 The new Adjustments panel makes it easier to leverage the power of adjustment layers to provide localized color and tonal changes to specific layers, because you can make and view changes on the fly.

Adjustment layers allow you to make various kinds of color and tonal corrections while your original pixel data remains unaltered. If you need to retrace your steps and modify your initial edits, double-click the individual adjustment layer icons to open their settings in the Adjustments panel. This is far simpler (and provides better results) than attempting to modify an image where the previous adjustments were applied directly to the pixels and then saved as part of the document. The Adjustments panel also allows you to access the current adjustment's settings nonmodally so you can make changes on the fly.

NOTE Choosing the Apply Layer Mask option will permanently alter the pixels in that layer or image. For this reason, leaving the mask intact as long as possible is usually a good idea.

Mask power. Chances are good that you will need to isolate many of your edits to specific regions of each image you enhance. One way to achieve this is by leveraging the power of layer masks and the new Masks panel (**Figure 8.6**), which are covered in more detail later in this chapter and in Chapter 10, "Compositing Source Materials." Like adjustment layers, layer masks have a nondestructive effect on image pixels. When used on adjustment layers, masks prevent the masked regions of the image from being adjusted. When used on pixel-based layers, masks allow any underlying content to show through. For this example, only the yellow flowers will receive a Vibrance adjustment.

Figure 8.6 The new Masks panel makes creating complex layer masks a more accurate and efficient process, enabling you to quickly isolate adjustment layers and other pixel-based edits to very localized regions of your image.

TIP To create selections from Pen tool paths, right-click (Control-click) on a closed path and choose Make Selection. From there you can choose anti-aliasing and other options; then convert the path into an active selection by clicking OK.

Alpha dog. There are few things more certain in the world of compositing than the fact that you will have to make some complex selections—often using a combination of selection tools and edge refinement commands. For example, one popular way to select irregularly shaped objects is to make a couple of quick passes with the Lasso tool and then use the Refine Edge command to smooth out the overall contour of the selection. Others will use the Pen tool almost exclusively for complex selections, even if it takes a bit longer, because of the precision that tool offers.

You can make complex selections in many ways, but the characteristic the selections all have in common is that they are often time-consuming beasts. The last thing you want is to waste time making that same selection over and over, each time you revisit a particular part of the image. Alpha channels (**Figure 8.7**) can save you time by allowing you to store complex selections as grayscale data. Alpha channels are also essential to the functioning of certain commands and filters, such as Content Aware Scaling (CAS) and the Lens Blur filter. We cover the use of alpha channels and the related filters and commands in Chapter 10.

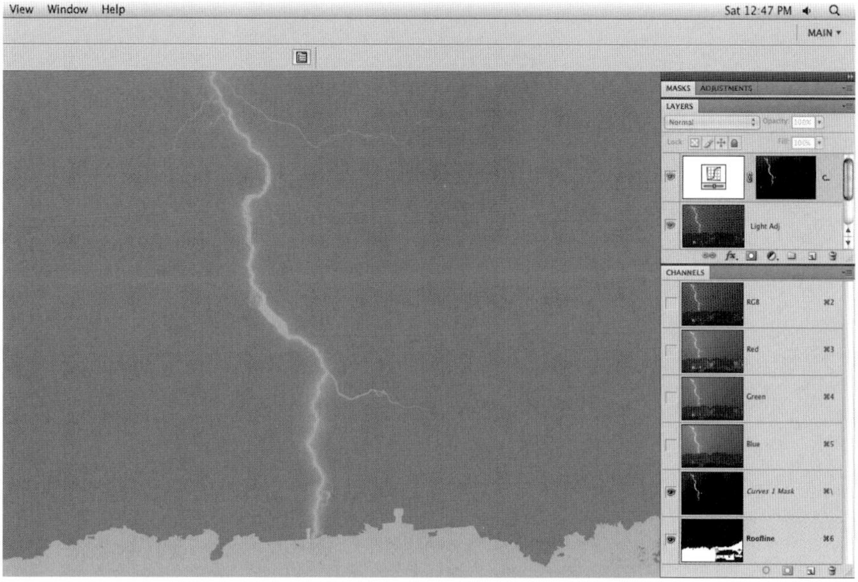

Figure 8.7 Alpha channels are a must for storing complex selections that you may need to use again later, and also for applying certain image effects, such as Content Aware Scaling and the Lens Blur filter.

Smart objects. One of the newer innovations in Photoshop, which has become even more useful in Photoshop CS4, is the smart object layer. Smart object layers now support the ability to nondestructively transform your layers and (finally!) also have the ability to be linked to their layer masks so that you can move your smart object around the canvas without losing its masked appearance. For example, you may realize at some point that an image requires corrections using the Perspective and Skew Transform commands. Photoshop now allows you to convert your layer to a smart object, transform it as you normally would, and then reinvoke the same commands later to recover the individual transform grids and control handles as you last left them (**Figure 8.8**). We discuss these techniques in more detail later in the chapter.

This means if your transform doesn't look perfect the first time you apply it, you can simply open the command and modify things from where you left off rather than starting over! Not only does this give you the flexibility of keeping your original layer data intact, but it can save you time as well. This example shows the tower we introduced in a previous chapter, with initial Perspective edits applied, via a smart object. Later in this chapter we use the Lens Correction filter to perform final perspective tweaks.

Figure 8.8 Smart objects now support both layer mask linking and the ability to use Transform commands (including Warp) nondestructively. This is a big advantage for compositing artists over previous versions of Photoshop.

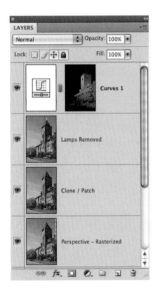

Figure 8.9 Breaking your composite images down into multiple layers and working on those regions of the image in isolation can result in both higher-quality edits and fewer situations where you have to redo an entire area of the image from scratch because you applied the wrong effect or correction.

Layer IQ. Whenever possible, use the tried-and-true method of breaking your image down into layers. Layering ensures that your edits are targeted, giving you more creative freedom to try a range of retouching and styling options that might otherwise negatively impact the rest of the image. There are many schools of thought on how to layer your image, but the methods we prefer are to create layers based on the types of edits that are needed, or to create them based on the region being edited.

The key to successfully working with layers is to make sure you build up each image layer upon the most recent completed edits (**Figure 8.9**). For example, when retouching a portrait, photographers will often duplicate their background and rename it after the part of the portrait they will retouch first (this is the "content region" method noted earlier). For example, they may start with the person's hair or facial complexion. Once that region has been edited, the photographer or postproduction person will duplicate the initial edit layer so that the changes carry forward. From there the duplicate is renamed (to match the next region), and then the second group of edits is applied. This process is repeated with each new image region until the entire portrait is retouched.

Another benefit to "content region" layering is that it provides an opportunity to isolate your image adjustments. Using adjustment layers, you can modify the colors and tones in a specific region of the image with the adjustment layer's mask, or by using the "clip to layer" button, found at the bottom of the Adjustments panel (see Figure 8.17).

Color Critical

The process of matching printed colors to those you see on a computer monitor is called *color management* and is the cause of many a wrinkle and gray hair! If you'd like to know more about color management, several good books are available on the topic.

The two we recommend most frequently are *Real World Color Management, Second Edition*, by Bruce Fraser, Chris Murphy, and Fred Bunting (Peachpit Press) and *Color Management for Photographers: Hands on Techniques for Photoshop Users*, by Andrew Rodney (Focal Press).

Be warned: If you want to really learn color management, you can't do it halfway and expect good results. However, it's something that is extremely important (if a little mind-numbing at times), so we recommend at some point that you familiarize yourself with the core concepts and techniques for managing color across devices in your workflow.

For scenic images or product shots, it can make sense to break your layer structure down by the type of edits the image needs rather than by region. For example, you could first duplicate the background and use the new layer as the basis for your noise reduction edits. You could then duplicate the noise reduction layer and apply cloning and patching across the entire image. As with the other layering method, you would repeat this process until all of the edits are complete.

You may decide you need some combination of these two layering techniques. Do whatever is most comfortable for you. As long as you're layering things in a systematic way, you are ensuring that you don't waste time reediting significant portions of the image, should something go wrong.

The downside of having many pixel-based (including smart object) layers is that they make your files much larger (particularly if the source images were shot at sizes beyond 7 or 8 megapixels). This in turn can slow the process—especially on older computer hardware—of opening and saving files or applying certain filters such as Lens Correction or Lens Blur. For this reason, how you handle layering can also depend on the complexity of your concept.

Reference works. One final workflow tip that can help you achieve a great result is to make sure you keep any reference images open so you can make the types of edits you need more precisely. For example, you may have found in your planning and research a couple of stock images that are styled in the same way you would like to style parts of your composite. Having those stock images open (even if collapsed to the Mac OS X Dock or the Windows Taskbar) can be invaluable for making comparisons as you edit.

Even keeping a magazine open on your desk can be helpful, although the process of mimicking that magazine in a digital medium can be tricky, because your monitor is a medium of transmitted light (additive color), while printed materials use reflected light (subtractive color).

TIP For more information on additive and subtractive color models, check out *Real World Color Management, Second Edition* (see the "Color Critical" sidebar).

MAKING IMAGE CORRECTIONS

Once you have a handle on how to keep organized and flexible with your images, you can begin editing and stylizing your raw-processed or stock images so they are more easily pieced together during the final stages of the compositing process. The key to producing good images is understanding the general sequence for the major edit types (noise reduction, retouching, and sharpening) and knowing Photoshop's tools and the situations for which they are best suited.

Reducing Noise

If processing your raw images in ACR did not remove enough of the noise, it's important to address this issue early in the Photoshop retouching process. Leaving camera noise untouched until late in the editing process means that any changes to image tonality, color, or sharpening will likely amplify the noise, making it more obvious and harder to eliminate. When our source material needs noise reduction, we typically use a third-party plug-in called Noiseware Professional. Noiseware excels at removing color noise from dimly lit scenes and shots with dark backgrounds or textures.

The user interface (**Figure 8.10**) is quite intuitive even though there are many controls and options. Noiseware's results are often superior to what can be achieved with Photoshop's Reduce Noise filter, though Noiseware is a bit more complicated to learn. Although it's an extra expense, the modest investments in time and money are worth it if you find that many of your images suffer from noise issues.

Detail View (Active)

Frequency View

Tonal Range View

Color Range View

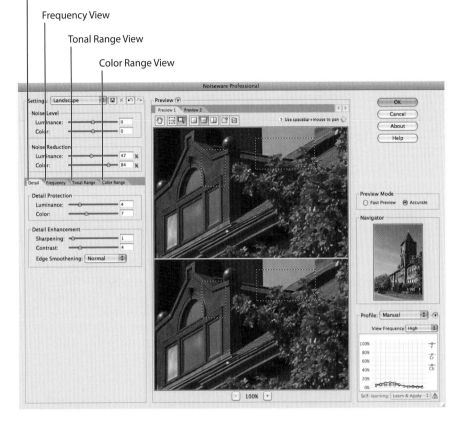

Figure 8.10 Noiseware allows you to address—in an intuitive way—the different characteristics and locations where camera noise appears in your images.

The trick to setting up Noiseware is to create a baseline correction using one of the presets from the Settings menu. This menu includes several common photographic scenarios, including portraits, landscapes, and night shots. Once you choose your preset, help Noiseware apply its algorithms more accurately by adjusting the Noise Level sliders. From that point, we usually use the settings found under the Detail, Frequency, Tonal Range, and Color Range tabs to fine-tune our image (**Figure 8.11**).

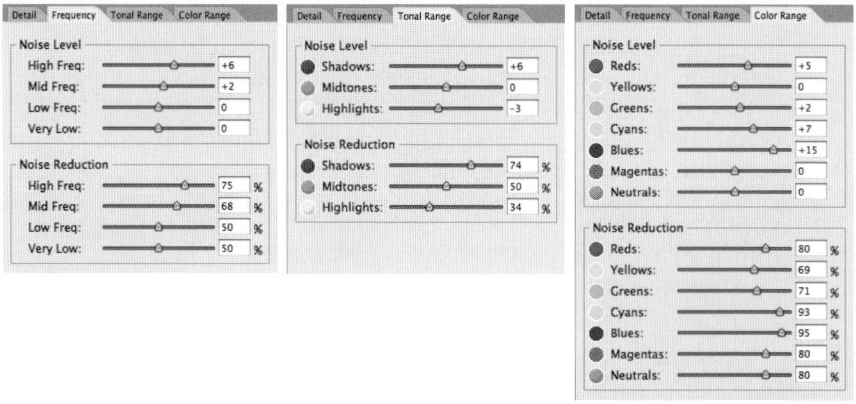

Figure 8.11 Noiseware's Color Range sliders (far right) operate on a similar principle to the HSL panel in Adobe Camera Raw, allowing you to manage noise in each color region of the image without affecting the sharpness of other color regions.

NOTE All noise reduction software, no matter how polished, will tend to soften your image details, especially if larger amounts of reduction are applied. Keep this trade-off in mind as you use Noiseware or other popular noise reduction tools, such as Noise Ninja or Nik Sharpener Pro.

We usually get the best results when we include the Color Range tab in our corrections, which operates in a manner very similar to the HSL panel in ACR.

If different areas of the image require fine-tuning—as indicated from a large preview that you can use to compare the same image region with different settings applied—you can delve into the Detail, Frequency, Tonal Range, and Color Range sliders to reduce specific kinds of noise or noise in specific image regions.

We can usually apply precise corrections by using the Color Range tab (shown on the right in Figure 8.11), which operates similarly to the HSL panel in ACR. Instead of removing color or luminance noise from the entire image, this function allows you to remove noise from only specific color ranges within the image. This is quite helpful, because many cameras tend to produce noise in some color areas but not others. Keep in mind that as you work with Noiseware, you may need to experiment with different settings to achieve the best results with your image.

Modifying Tonal Values

You can alter the tonality of your images in many ways, but the best tool to use when preparing them for composites is the Curves adjustment. The most powerful tonal correction tool in Photoshop, it is probably the most inscrutable as well. However, Photoshop CS4 has added two features that make Curves even more powerful yet at the same time much easier to use. The first of these is the new Adjustments panel, which provides a nonmodal means of accessing all adjustment layer controls in a single panel, including Curves.

This means you can have each image adjustment open while you make and preview your changes, without obscuring large regions of the image.

The second improvement is part of the new Curves dialog box (and the Adjustments panel when Curves is active). It may not seem like a big deal at first sight, but near the top left of the Curves panel is a button with a hand and arrow icon. If you click this button and then move the cursor over a specific tonal area, clicking again places a point on the tonal curve. You can then drag upward to boost the tonal values, or drag downward to reduce them. This feature will help you to work more efficiently with Curves and achieve more precise edits (**Figure 8.12**).

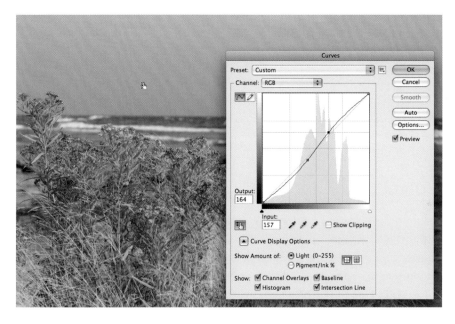

Figure 8.12 The Curves adjustment is much improved in Photoshop CS4 with the addition of an on-document control.

As with other workflows, the Curves adjustment helps ensure that specific areas of an image will seamlessly blend in with other images. You can also use it to create specific lighting effects that you want in the final composite. **Figure 8.13** shows a typical situation in which Curves helped make the tonal qualities of two images appear more similar so that less fine-tuning is needed later. The original fish exposure looks okay on its own, but it's much darker and lower-contrast than the pier. We again used the new on-document Curves control to boost the brightness of the fish, and make other tweaks to the piers and water in the other source image.

For simpler tonal corrections, you can use the Levels adjustment to save yourself a bit of time, but when you need to localize your tonal corrections to specific parts of the image, there is no substitute for Curves.

Figure 8.13 Sometimes images that appear adequate on their own will need additional Curves correction to become part of a convincing composite image.

Original Exposure   Target Environment   Curves-Adjusted Exposure

Correcting Color

 NOTE We cover the techniques for creating realistic shadows using the Drop Shadow layer effect and transformed fill layers in Chapter 10, "Compositing Source Materials."

A common task when compositing is modifying your source images' color so they blend together smoothly. You can do this with a variety of tools in Photoshop, and sometimes you will need to experiment with two or three adjustment layers to get the right results. Again, there is no formula here, only a collection of useful techniques that you can use at different times to enhance the color of your images. However, we use some adjustments more often than others.

Color Balance. Evaluation is again the key: Take a look at your source images, and note the variations in hue (for similar colors) across a range of tones. If you're working with natural scenery from multiple shots, how do the blues in the sky and greens in the foliage match up? Chances are good that no matter what type of scenes or subjects you've photographed, the hues will not match up precisely, and areas that are meant to blend together will probably need some minor color adjustments. Color Balance allows you to modify the hues in an image, based on which parts of the tonal range they fall within.

Color Balance targets its corrections using the three major tonal ranges in an image—highlights, mid-tones, and shadows—and uses three color "axes" to define the corrections being made (**Figure 8.14**). You can make any one (or all) of these tonal regions: more cyan/red, more magenta/green, or more blue/yellow. You can also mix and match these slider values either to reduce color casts created in-camera or to stylize the image. As noted earlier, we recommend using adjustment layers when editing image colors. This is nondestructive and allows your adjustments to be isolated to specific areas, either by applying a layer mask or by clipping the adjustment to the layer immediately beneath it.

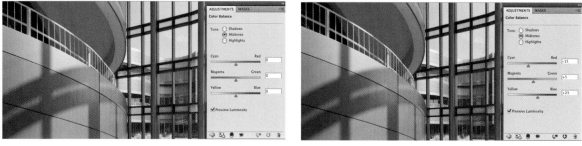

Original Colors

Color Cast Removed

Figure 8.14 The Color Balance adjustment allows you to target color changes to the highlights, mid-tones, and shadow regions of your image.

Vibrance. Just as the Vibrance slider in ACR can provide subtler and more realistic-looking shifts to your image saturation, the new Vibrance adjustment in Photoshop CS4 similarly allows you to push the warmer tones in your image up a bit without clipping them (**Figure 8.15**). At the same time, a standard Saturation slider is available as part of the same adjustment so that you can mix and match them as needed to stylize your image.

Figure 8.15 The Vibrance adjustment allows you to quickly and smoothly modify your saturation values for the entire image.

Photo Filter adjustments. Sometimes you just need to make an image a bit warmer or cooler or throw a particular color cast across part of the image. You can quickly accomplish this using the Photo Filter adjustment. This adjustment uses simple Color Picker and slider controls to create an image-wide adjustment. The most common uses are to make outdoor images a bit warmer (especially those shot in midday sun) or images shot under incandescent light a bit cooler, but you can choose any color hue as the basis of your edits (**Figure 8.16**).

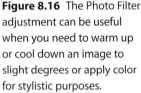

Figure 8.16 The Photo Filter adjustment can be useful when you need to warm up or cool down an image to slight degrees or apply color for stylistic purposes.

You can also leverage the Levels and Curves commands to make the entire image (or parts of the image) more red, green, or blue, assuming you're editing in RGB mode. However, using a combination of the Color Balance and Photo Filter adjustments often provides more creative flexibility and accurate results.

Making Layer-Based Edits

Clip and group. As your adjustment layers build up, layer management becomes a critical aspect of the editing process, because you will need to isolate specific adjustments to specific layers and see those adjustments as a whole collection rather than as individual corrections. The new Adjustments panel allows you to "clip" or isolate specific adjustments to specific layers by clicking the "clip to layer" button. We also group all adjustment layers that apply to an image or specific layer so that we can toggle them on and off as a unit to see the total effect (**Figure 8.17**). This provides a more accurate reflection of what is happening to your image when compared with turning each layer's visibility on or off individually. It's also a time-saver because fewer preview clicks are required to achieve the final result.

Layer Group   Clipped Layer

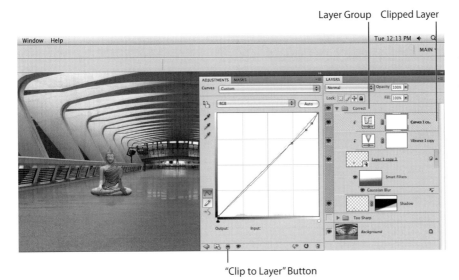

"Clip to Layer" Button

Figure 8.17 Clipping your adjustment layers and grouping them so that you can view their cumulative effect is important for making precise and efficient edits.

Masked adjustments. One of the most valuable capabilities of any adjustment layer is the ability to utilize a layer mask as a means of isolating edits to a specific region of the image. Using our earlier Photo Filter example, you may decide that only one portion of an image needs to be a little warmer or cooler and then gradually fade to no correction at all. The best way to do this is by using a combination of layer masks and the Gradient tool.

Every adjustment layer is created with an empty layer mask by default. To create the gradient mask, select the mask itself, press G (or Shift-G if the Paint Bucket tool appears instead of the Gradient), and then select the "black-to-white" gradient in the Options bar. Drag a gradient across the image so that the white areas begin where you want 100 percent of the adjustment to show through. You may need to experiment with different gradient angles. As you draw out a new gradient, the prior attempt will be replaced.

For **Figure 8.18**, we used the Gradient tool and layer mask to gradually make the sky less and less warm until nontargeted regions of the image appear unaltered. You can use this technique with any adjustment layer; it is a great way to exert a lot of creative control over your source images. We also brush our masked regions with white, shades of gray, and black to control the look of our adjustments if the gradient alone isn't sufficient.

Figure 8.18 Using your adjustment layers' built-in grayscale mask and the Gradient tool (or Brush tool) allows you to visually isolate your adjustments in precise ways.

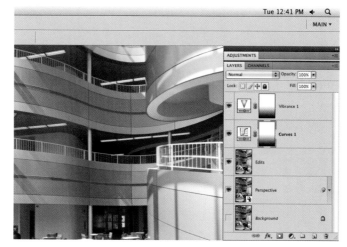

Be selective. Virtually all compositing projects require that you make complex, oddly shaped selections in order to isolate parts of an image so that you can apply various effects, such as cloning in a specific area, applying a filter, or performing another task. One of the best ways to save yourself some grief (and time) is to make sure you're using the right selection tool for the job at hand. Sometimes Photoshop users will build up skills with a particular tool (such as the Lasso) and begin to rely on that too heavily, making all selections with it rather than only where it makes sense.

TIP Holding down the Alt (Option) key while the Polygon Lasso is active and making a selection will switch on the fly to the Lasso tool so that you can draw portions of your selection freehand.

If you need to quickly isolate a road sign, for example, you could use the Lasso or Pen tool or even the Color Range selection command in some cases, but typically the fastest way to precisely select any geometric object is to use the Polygon Lasso tool (**Figure 8.19**). Similarly, if you have a situation where part of your selection is geometric and another part is more irregular shaped, the Pen tool provides the most flexibility in making a relatively quick and accurate selection. To turn the paths you create with the Pen tool into selections, simply Control-click (right-click) the path and choose Make Selection from the context menu. You can also choose to apply antialias settings to the selection if you need to soften its contours a bit.

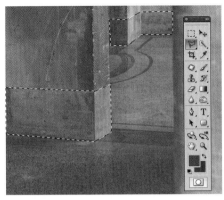

The Polygon Lasso tool is invaluable for quick geometric selections.

The Pen tool works well for subjects that have both geometric and irregular contours.

Figure 8.19 A key part of working through your image enhancements and compositing efficiently is choosing the right selection tool for the job and familiarizing yourself enough with all of them so that you are equally comfortable no matter which tool is needed.

Complex or irregular shapes may require the Color Range tool in combination with other tools.

Another important consideration when making your selections is whether you may need to reuse that same selection later, if you decide that part of your image needs further work or styling. If you decide to reuse the selection, you don't want to remake it each time, as noted earlier. Take advantage of alpha channels as a means of storing your most used or most time-consuming selections with your document (**Figure 8.20**). We discuss selections and alpha channels in more detail in Chapter 10.

TIP You can also convert complex selections into layer masks by clicking the Add Layer Mask button in the Layers panel.

Figure 8.20 Alpha channels are indispensable for compositing artists. Here we have saved the lantern's complex selection as an alpha channel for reuse later in the compositing process.

TIP Although perspective correction lenses may not be an option for you, keep perspective correction in mind when photographing your scenes and subjects. Give yourself a little bit of extra room around the edges of your subject to account for the "cropping effect" that often occurs with strong perspective corrections.

Transformational. Another important part of improving your source images is to correct the perspective lines that may have become distorted by your camera lens. This is particularly true of those shots taken with wide-angle lenses. Note that although you can avoid perspective issues with a special perspective correction lens such as the one discussed in Chapter 5, "Capturing the Scene and Subject," these lenses often cost close to $2,000. This makes them an impractical option for many artists or photographers who cannot recoup that expense with photography services.

Perspective correction can be accomplished using the Lens Correction filter (**Figure 8.21**) or the Transform commands, which you can find in the Edit menu. Which ones you use (or whether you need to use them in combination) will depend greatly on the types of distortions found in your images and what you ultimately intend for the viewer. We often find that for the best effect you will need to use a combination of both tools.

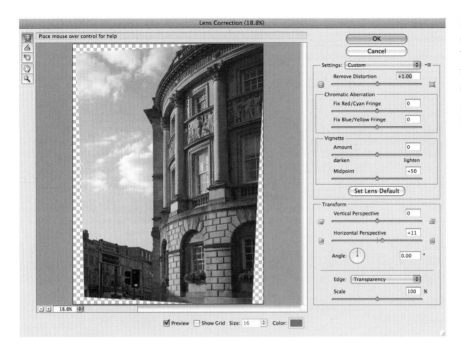

Figure 8.21 The Lens Correction filter and the Transform commands (in the Edit menu) are the tools of choice when correcting perspective lines in your images.

Typically, if you have simple keystone distortions (caused by tilting a wide-angle lens up or down or to the left or right, relative to your subject), you can quickly correct them using the Lens Correction filter. Keystone distortions are easily identified by the keystone-like effect seen on vertical lines in your image. You can improve this condition by using the Horizontal Perspective and Vertical Perspective correction sliders, often in tandem with slight modifications to the default Angle value. You can also correct for barrel distortions using the Remove Distortion slider at the top. For images that appear to bow outward, you can drag this slider to the right until the shot has more of a natural, "flat" appearance (or until it matches the look of the other images with which it will be composited).

Sometimes you also need to use the Transform commands in the Edit menu to put the finishing touches on your Lens Correction edits (**Figure 8.22**). To access these commands, choose Edit > Transform, and choose among Perspective, Distort, and Skew (usually some combination of these three commands, plus a minor Lens Correction, will do the trick).

TIP You can apply both the Lens Correction filter and Transform commands via a smart filter/object layer by first creating a duplicate of the target layer, choosing Convert for Smart Filters from the Filters menu, and then opening the Lens Correction filter or Transform commands. Afterward, you will be able to reaccess your filter settings and transform handles at any time.

Figure 8.22 You can combine the smart object Transform commands with results from the Lens Correction filter to precisely correct perspective lines and lens distortions.

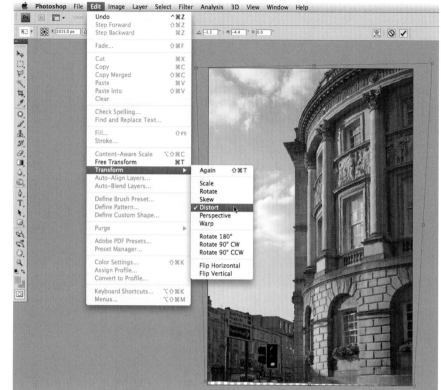

TIP You can also use the Warp command to make minor perspective corrections, particularly in cases where there are minor barrel distortions.

Warpitude. Photoshop is loved not only for its ability to correct problems but also (of course) because of the creative things you can do with your images, and this is no less true in the world of compositing. One great example of this is the ability to use the Warp command to layer one object on top of another, giving the appearance of one layer being "affixed" to its companion layer.

For **Figure 8.23**, we wanted to unite the crest and the cooling tower (just for fun). Prior to placing the crest as a smart object, we toned down its colors in ACR and made other adjustments so that it would blend in better. Once we placed the object, we used the Warp transform handles to push and pull the corners of the crest until it started to look like part of the tower. Finally, we added the shadow on the tower. We cover creating shadows in Chapter 10.

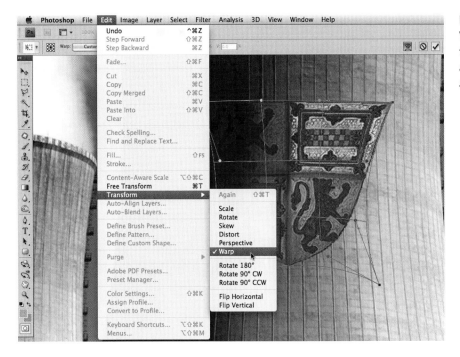

Figure 8.23 The Transform > Warp command is a fantastic tool for giving the appearance of two subjects being affixed to one another.

Liquifaction. The Liquify filter is another Photoshop tool that allows for tremendous possibilities, both in retouching portraits and when applying unusual or creative effects to targeted areas of your composite image. You can think of the Liquify filter as something that can turn all or selected regions of your image into a piece of clay, allowing you to "smush" and distort the pixels in ways that you cannot with the traditional brush tools.

The possibilities are limitless, ranging from the tried-and-true "bulging eye-balls" to adding "heat waves" to restructuring the shape of someone's cheekbones and jawline (**Figure 8.24**). The key to working with the Liquify filter is to keep your mesh visible, use masks when possible (just as you would with layer masks in a standard workflow), and experiment with the help of the Reconstruct tool. This feature allows you to try different tools with specific brush size and pressure settings and then quickly undo things if you don't like the look you've created, without resetting the entire range of changes you've made or closing the dialog box and reopening it from scratch.

Forward Warp Tool
Reconstruct Tool

Effect Tools

Masking Tools

Tool (brush)
Options

Mask Options

Mesh Options

Figure 8.24 The Liquify filter offers a large array of creative options for applying special effects to your composite imagery.

Gallery power. Finally, though we use them only on more creative projects that allow for more of a graphic arts look, you can use the wide array of creative filters in Photoshop (which you can preview by choosing Filters > Filter Gallery) to enhance the look of your source images. The Filter Gallery (**Figure 8.25**) contains only the items from the Artistic, Brush Strokes, Distort, Sketch, Stylize, and Texture Filter menu sections and operates only in 8-bit mode. For that reason, when creating images with more of a free-form or illustrative look, it can make sense to perform all your edits in 8-bit mode.

Figure 8.25 The Filter Gallery can be a useful creative tool for working on images that are using illustrative styles rather than photographic ones. You must be in 8-bit mode to use the Filter Gallery.

The downfalls discussed earlier in terms of color banding and tonal clipping when pushing the tone curve or working with hue and saturation, for example, may also be less noticeable when you're applying creative filters to your images, because you are not trying to maintain a photographic look with these filters. Keep in mind also as you use the gallery that you can combine multiple filters in a single session to create image stylings that are not possible with any one filter. This puts a virtually limitless combination of creative possibilities at your disposal, particularly when you start combining layer blend modes with filter effects (**Figure 8.26**).

As you might have guessed, you can use the Convert for Smart Filters command prior to opening the Filter Gallery and applying the effects to your image. Since most of the creative filters in Photoshop require experimentation to find the right look in a given situation, we recommend always converting your target layer to smart filters before using the gallery. This lets you fine-tune all your filter adjustments as you go, instead of starting over each time you apply a filter to a layer . . . and deciding the look isn't quite right.

Smart Filter and Blend Opacity
Dialog Box

Figure 8.26 A huge number of visual effects are possible when combining the effects of layer blend modes with the creative filters in Photoshop as part of a smart filter setup. Although it may take some time to get the right look, you will find the results are well worth it!

Modified Creative Effects

Creating 3D Content

Creating 3D content is not something artists and photographers tradition-ally consider when working within Adobe Photoshop. Even when tools like Vanishing Point (and later the ability to import basic 3D objects) appeared, many users viewed the capability as being too specialized for a typical graphic design or compositing workflow. However, the new features in Photoshop CS4 Extended make the world of 3D postprocessing more approachable for graphics professionals, photographers, and other creative professionals.

We could fill this entire book (a series of books, actually) with information on how to build and leverage creative 3D workflows, but ultimately our objective is to help you become more familiar with what 3D is all about and how the new 3D functionality in Photoshop helps create more compelling composite images.

A typical workflow involving 3D images used to require the artist to render a scene and then edit the flattened, 2D result in Photoshop. Now the tables have been turned, rotated, and scaled. Photoshop CS3 Extended intro-duced basic 3D functionality, but Photoshop CS4 Extended makes the third dimension a truly viable option for Photoshop compositing artists.

3D FUNDAMENTALS

NOTE Throughout the remainder of the chapter, any reference to "Photoshop" refers to Photoshop CS4 Extended. The standard Photoshop CS4 does not include the 3D functionality discussed in this chapter.

TIP 3D rendering performance depends heavily on your GPU. You can find more information from Adobe about OpenGL and GPUs at www.adobe.com/go/kb405745 and www.adobe.com/go/kb404898.

Working with 3D content offers many benefits. Although learning the fundamentals of 3D workflow and design is a challenge, once you know the basics you can quickly use a mix of 3D models and 2D imagery (as backgrounds or textures) to build a scene inside Photoshop or your favored 3D application. One advantage to this is that you can quickly simulate a large array of lighting conditions, camera perspectives, and other photographic techniques that would take days of work in the field. Photoshop includes many improvements to 3D workflow, such as a more powerful rendering engine and the ability to create and manipulate various kinds of lights and materials.

Keep in mind that the 3D functionality in Photoshop is not meant to replace stand-alone 3D applications. Instead, Photoshop serves as a means of making 3D workflow more efficient and providing more creative options for artists and designers. Even so, the new 3D capabilities allow you to do much more directly in Photoshop than was previously possible. Ideally, this reduces time spent moving between applications making lighting or scene modifications and opens up new paths for producing more compelling artwork.

If you are new to the world of designing in three dimensions, this section provides an overview of 3D design fundamentals as they apply to Photoshop and other applications. If you are familiar with 3D workflow, you can jump ahead to the next section, which covers the new 3D capabilities that Photoshop offers.

Polygons. Most 3D models are made from many smaller, 2D polygons that are grouped together "edge to edge" to create the illusion that an object has volume and depth. The size, shape, and number of the polygons determine the level of detail in your model. It is not uncommon for even relatively simple models to have many thousands of polygons. The smaller the polygons (and the larger the polygon count), the more accurate and detailed your model will be.

You can't do much to modify the properties of individual polygons in Photoshop (you will need a 3D application such as Strata or Cinema 4D for that), but you can affect the total polygon *count*. For a scene that is very detailed, expect a high polygon count. Having more polygons ultimately demands more memory and processor power; depending on how many viewports you have open, some areas on your model may not be visible onscreen. Some programs also give you the option of leaving hidden polygons unrendered as you work, which can save a lot of time.

Basic Terminology

Although it's not possible to cover every important 3D concept in this book, you can use this sidebar as a simple glossary for understanding fundamental 3D concepts. Most of these terms relate to any 3D program you might need to use, not just Photoshop.

Aerial perspective. This is the atmospheric effect of distance on an image. This includes haze, light falloff, and loss of detail and saturation with increased distance.

Depth map. This is a translation of an image's gray values into distance from a plane or surface. Typically white is the highest possible value (or altitude from the surface) and black is the lowest possible value, with intermediate gray values representing the distances between black and white.

Ground plane. This is the visual aid used by all 3D programs and Photoshop to provide a horizon reference and the ability to accurately judge vertical movement of a model.

Linear perspective. This is a simple perspective using converging lines to define the horizon and vanishing point. The Vanishing Point filter in Photoshop uses algorithms based on this perspective to generate its results.

Material. This is the general term given to all the textures, opacity, and other surface characteristics that define the appearance of a mesh in a 3D shape layer.

Mesh. This is a collection of adjoining polygons that define the shape or surface contours of a 3D model, including landscapes. For Photoshop, a model may consist of one or many meshes, which are often viewed as a wireframe-like structure. Because of a higher polygon count than a 3D shape layer, meshes in Photoshop often take longer to create, modify, and render.

Modeler. This is software that generates the illusion of a complex shape (such as a person) in three dimensions by combining numerous 3D primitives, and then using various shape modification tools to smooth the boundaries between them so that they look like a single, continuous shape. These representations of real-world or imagined objects are called *models*.

Object movement vs. camera movement. The 3D camera tools in Photoshop move the viewer "around" the object, while the object itself stays put relative to the document grid. Conversely, the 3D object tools move the actual object around the document grid, while the camera (or viewer) stays in place.

Primitive. This is a simple geometric shape with depth and volume. Made from small, 2D polygons, primitives are used as the building blocks for more complex shapes. Common examples include cubes, spheres, pyramids, cones, and cylinders.

continues on next page

Basic Terminology *(continued)*

Rendering. This is the process that gives a model a realistic appearance or, at a minimum, a smooth, continuous surface so that you can evaluate its shape, mold and edit your model, and apply textures to it. There are different "levels" of rendering quality; typically lower-quality (that is, low-resolution) renders are used when working on a scene or model, and high-resolution renders are used only at the end of the process because they can take quite a long time to finish.

Rotation. This is the ability to rotate a model, object, or camera around a specific axis.

Texture. In Photoshop, this is one of the component surface characteristics that defines the appearance of a material.

Viewport. This is the name often given to special windows inside a 3D program that display your model from different points of view (for example, a Top view or Front view). It is often possible (and useful) to have multiple viewports open at the same time when modeling. **Figure 9.1** shows a rendered version of a wireframe model using multiple viewports in Maxon Cinema 4D.

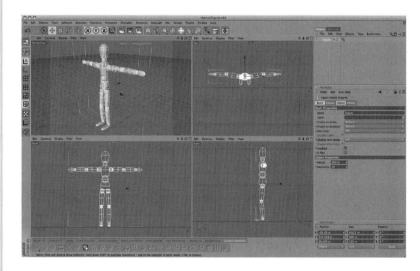

Figure 9.1 Viewports allow you to see models from multiple vantage points in 3D space.

continues on next page

Basic Terminology *(continued)*

Wireframe model. This is the most basic way to view any 3D model, showing only the outlines of the polygons that are used to create it. That is, a wireframe model has no surface characteristics; it is like a digital skeleton of the object you are creating (**Figure 9.2**).

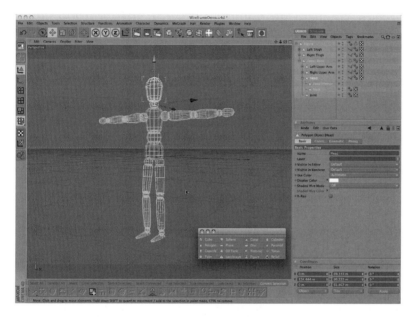

Figure 9.2 Wireframe model of a human-like shape. The model consists of many primitive shapes, which in turn are made from many small polygons connected together.

X axis. This is the horizontal reference axis in 3D space. Moving an object along this axis in a document will move it from left to right relative to the model's Front view.

Y axis. This is the vertical reference axis in 3D space. Moving an object along this axis in a document will move it from top to bottom relative to the model's Front view.

Z axis. This is the depth axis in 3D space. Moving an object along this axis in a document gives the illusion of moving from front to back relative to the model's Front view. That is, it will appear to move closer to or farther away from the person viewing it by becoming respectively larger or smaller in scale as you move it.

Materials. Working with 3D involves not only building and positioning models but also controlling the surface characteristics of your model (**Figure 9.3**). Once you've built your model, you must add materials—to cover the lines and fill the gaps in the wireframe view of your model. These materials interact with light and the simulated environment to give the model a realistic appearance.

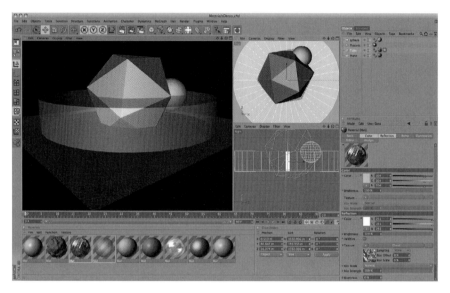

Figure 9.3 These materials were created in just a few minutes using Cinema 4D's Materials panel (bottom-left) and the Attributes panel (bottom-right). Each sphere in the Materials panel provides a preview for a different custom material.

 NOTE The terms *texture* and *material* are sometimes used interchangeably, but in Photoshop a material is actually a collection of textures that are applied to one of the surfaces in your model or 3D shape layer.

Each material typically serves a unique purpose and can be combined in different ways with other materials to create a specific look. For example, to create a 3D model that appears to have human skin, you would need to define a specific material for each skin characteristic. Materials would need to be defined for the skin's color, reflectivity, translucency, texture, and even contours (sometimes called a *bump map*), which are created by hair follicles, muscle tone, and the like. Similarly, if your model needed other human traits such as hair or sweat, you would need to generate materials for those as well. It is not unusual for a model to have dozens of materials defined for any surface type.

Lighting. Once you have defined your materials and applied them to specific regions of your model, you need to create a surrounding environment with which they can interact. As with photography, the most important part of any successful 3D design is the lighting. Lights are needed to define how the model is lit (obviously), as well as to define additional properties. As you might expect, 3D lights have many editable properties, such as color, focus, falloff, and the ability to cast shadows, based on the characteristics and position of your models.

However, lighting properties can come from multiple sources, not just from the lights you create. Some materials have properties that define whether they glow, reflect, or even self-illuminate! Lights can even be placed inside a model in some cases to create unique visual effects. The sobering part of all this creative freedom is that each characteristic of 3D light, each material, and each model has to be defined and controlled in software. Most 3D programs have many buttons, sliders, and menus to learn and keep track of! The new 3D panel in Photoshop (discussed later in the chapter and shown in **Figure 9.4**) is fortunately easier to learn but nonetheless a good example of the complexity behind 3D content.

Environment. The final building block of any 3D scene is its environment. A 3D model by itself is usually not very interesting, until you place it into a specific environment or context. An environment can contain a variety of lights, atmospheric effects, materials, and other items (sometimes unseen) that interact with the surface characteristics of your model to create the desired effect, such as a sparkle, a reflected color, or other "looks." For many situations, an actual 2D photograph is used to create the "setting" for a 3D model, with 3D lights added into the mix to illuminate the model in ways that are consistent with the photo.

Many professional 3D applications—including Cinema 4D, profiled later in the chapter—let you simulate realistic 3D environments, including atmospheric effects and natural features such as clouds, bare earth, fluids, and foliage. Other programs are dedicated specifically to this purpose and can "grow" a terrain by using so-called organic terrain generators. 3D artists often use specialized applications, rather than a single program, to perform a specific task in their 3D workflow. This is facilitated through the use of common 3D file formats that allow the model and scene data to be exchanged between programs. These formats are discussed later in the chapter.

Rendering. As you work in a 3D program to create your content with models and environments, the view on the screen will usually be a low-resolution preview. Most 3D-capable programs provide preview options to ignore features such as shadows or complex material interactions so that your computer can quickly approximate the model's appearance as you modify its shape and material properties. If you were to use the "final render

Figure 9.4 The new 3D panel in Photoshop allows you to manipulate a variety of texture and lighting properties for imported models and 3D shape layers.

quality" settings each time you previewed your model, the design process could take a very long time! For this reason, high-resolution render settings are typically used only at the end of the 3D content creation process.

Rendering takes your models, lights, materials, and environment in their current state and performs complex calculations on the entire scene to produce its final appearance. This means all the lights, materials, and other entities are interacting with each other visually, as they do in the real world. It also means any rough edges or "jaggies" are smoothed out completely. Most 3D programs offer several "quality levels" for the rendering process, allowing you to decide how detailed you want each render to be, based on where you are in the creative process. The highest-quality render settings take the longest but produce the most striking results when the image is exported to a flattened format.

As with scene generation, several programs are dedicated entirely to rendering, providing many creative options during this phase of image creation. Photoshop also has its own set of render options discussed later in the chapter (**Figure 9.5**).

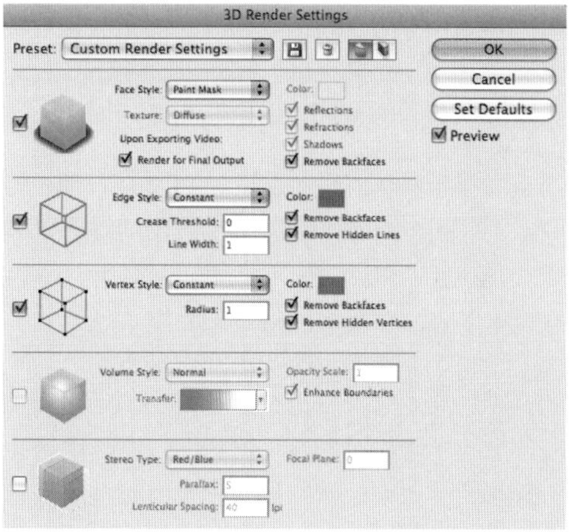

Figure 9.5 Photoshop CS4 Extended provides a new Render Settings dialog that offers options for defining the quality and style of your rendered objects or shapes.

Abilities and limitations. You can use Photoshop to import 3D models from other applications, edit model textures in a variety of ways, and create a basic lighting setup. You can also build primitive 3D shapes from 2D image files and position your shapes and models (or the cameras viewing them) in different ways. The latter is discussed in the next section.

For now, Photoshop does not allow you to directly modify the shape or arrangement of the primitives that make up your imported model, or edit any of the 3D properties beyond the ones provided in the 3D panel. This is best left to professional 3D applications, because most have a large array of shape modification tools that are not available in 2D image editors like Photoshop.

3D in Photoshop

This section of the chapter covers the important tools and options that Photoshop uses to create and manipulate 3D content, including models imported from other applications. While this is not an exhaustive discussion of how every feature works, we hope to provide you with a good foundation for experimenting with these new creative options.

Basic 3D Tools

Photoshop provides several new tools for working with 3D content. They are broken into two groups: 3D tools and 3D camera tools.

Moving 3D objects. The 3D tools are designed for moving 3D objects across the canvas in different ways (**Figure 9.6**). This group includes 3D Rotate, 3D Roll, 3D Pan/Drag, 3D Slide, and 3D Scale. For the most part, these do what their names suggest: The 3D Rotate tool allows you to freely rotate an object around its own X and Y axes; the 3D Roll tool rotates the object about an axis that is parallel to the screen; the 3D Pan tool moves the object along its X and Y axes only; the 3D Slide tool lets you move the object along its X or Z axis; and the 3D Scale tool changes the object's size without relocating it.

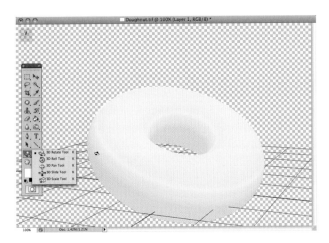

Figure 9.6
Photoshop's 3D tools allow you to manipulate your 3D content on the document canvas.

To use one of the 3D tools, select it, and then click and drag on the canvas near your 3D object (be it a shape layer, mesh, or model) to perform the desired action. When a layer with 3D content is active and any of the 3D tools are selected, the options bar provides additional settings for modifying the individual X, Y, and Z axis values for each tool (**Figure 9.7**). These allow you to precisely position your 3D object relative to the background image or document grid, based on the type of movement the tool provides. When you move an object around with the different tools, this is called a *custom position*.

Figure 9.7 Photoshop's 3D tool options, as seen from the Options bar

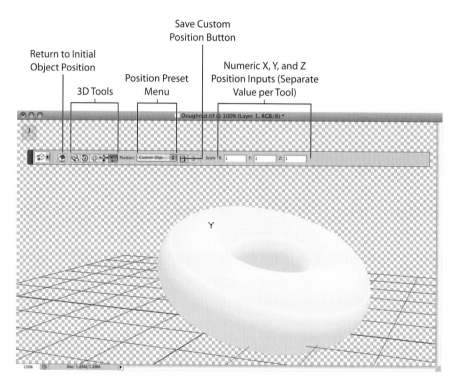

You can save any custom position by clicking the disk icon and saving it as you would any other preset. You can also choose a preset position (such as Left, Right, Top, or Bottom) from the pop-up menu. The house-like icon, Return to Initial Object Position, resets your object position to wherever it was when the document was last saved.

Keep in mind that the object tools move the actual model around the canvas (relative to the document grid), while the positions of the lights and cameras remain static. This means that shadows, light intensity, and a few other characteristics can change as the object is moved in different directions. For this reason, even if you think you have your lights set up just right, moving your 3D object around on the canvas may require you to make additional changes to lighting afterward (**Figure 9.8**).

Figure 9.8 Moving a 3D object changes its position relative to lights and other scene elements, and thus can affect the object's appearance.

Moving cameras. The 3D camera tools provide options mostly identical to the 3D tools but cause only the camera to move around your 3D object, giving the appearance that the entire scene has shifted position, even though nothing but the camera has moved (**Figure 9.9**).

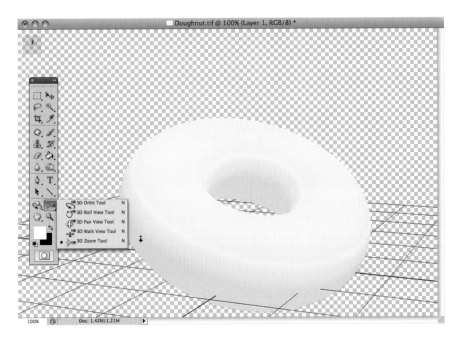

Figure 9.9 The Photoshop 3D Camera tools

Turn on the Ground Plane option in the 3D panel pop-up menu (discussed in the next section), and the difference between each of the corresponding tools' effects on the document becomes obvious. For example, using the 3D Rotate tool and the 3D Camera Rotate tool may appear at first to have the same effect, until you activate the Ground Plane visibility. Then you see that when using the camera tools, all 3D objects and lights retain their positions relative to one another and to the document grid as the camera moves around them. You can use the 3D camera tools when everything is positioned properly on the document but you want to see what the scene looks like from new angles.

NOTE When you render a scene, both the object and camera position are taken into account! There is no "default render view" in Photoshop.

One 3D camera tool doesn't have an equivalent—the 3D Zoom tool. It behaves similarly to a zoom lens on your DSLR. You can zoom in or out on a 3D object, which has the same effect as scaling, but the lighting and other scene elements are retained. **Figure 9.10** shows the difference between zooming in on an object and scaling the object so that it fills the identical amount of frame.

Zoomed In

Scaled

Figure 9.10 The 3D Zoom tool controls the camera like a zoom lens on your DSLR. Zooming in will appear to make the object larger, though there is no effect on lighting or other material interactions.

Using the 3D camera tools, you can also employ extra settings in the options bar that are nearly identical to the ones discussed in the 3D tools section. You can independently set X, Y, and Z axis values for each camera tool to create a custom view, use the pop-up menu for view presets, return your camera to its original position, or save the custom position as a new camera view preset.

The 3D Panel

The main hub for working with 3D content in Photoshop is the new 3D panel. **Figure 9.11** shows the default view for the panel, which filters all the 3D content in a layer as parts of a scene. Though nothing is actually being filtered in the default view, it's important to understand that each of the view types is considered a *filtered view*. The 3D panel allows you to modify multiple properties of your 3D objects, including light settings, the colors and material properties of any surface on your 3D object, and the positions of your meshes.

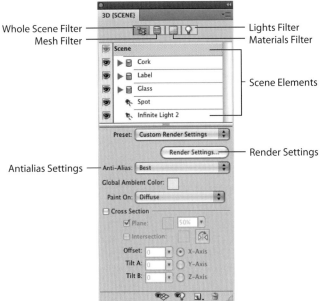

Figure 9.11 The new 3D panel in Photoshop is where most creative 3D edits are applied.

Filter by: Whole Scene. The Filter by: Whole Scene view shows the entire stack of elements that makes up your 3D layer or model. Though it refers to the "whole scene," it shows only those elements from the current layer. Other 3D layers do not appear unless they are selected in the Layers panel. It is possible to combine several 3D objects into the same layer if you need to, using the layer merge features in Photoshop. Although this filter mode works well for simple models or shapes, we generally recommend using the individual filter modes described later in this section to target specific portions of the model or 3D shape more quickly.

Filter by: Meshes. The tools provided in the Filter by: Meshes view work according to the same principles as the 3D tools described earlier and are used to position and rotate the individual meshes (polygons) that make up your Photoshop-generated 3D shape (**Figure 9.12**). When working with models created in other programs, Photoshop treats the entire object as a single mesh, rather than as a collection of mesh objects. You can also set whether the mesh catches and casts shadows, which can be important when integrating a model or 3D shape with other elements in your scene.

Figure 9.12 The Filter by: Meshes view in the 3D panel offers tools for positioning and rotating the meshes in your 3D shapes or your imported model. It also allows you to define whether your object will catch or cast shadows.

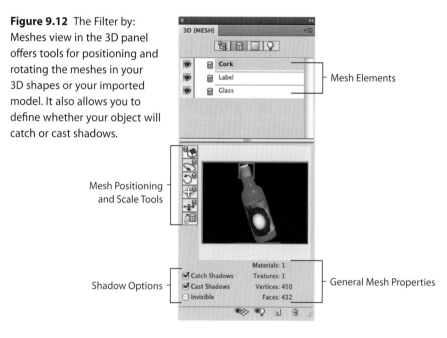

Filter by: Materials. The Filter by: Materials view gives you tools for creating and adjusting surface textures (**Figure 9.13**). If you have generated a 3D shape in Photoshop, each side (or mesh) can leverage these material properties individually. More than any other set of 3D functions in Photoshop, these material properties have a big effect on how your 3D content will look and interact with other parts of the scene, whether 2D or 3D. Material properties allow you to control everything from reflectiveness to opacity to the color of self-illumination. We discuss the different material options in more detail later in the chapter.

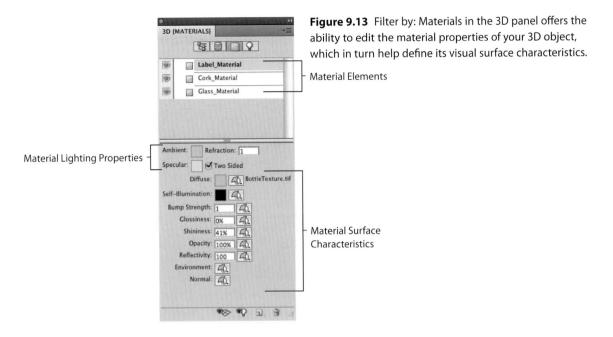

Figure 9.13 Filter by: Materials in the 3D panel offers the ability to edit the material properties of your 3D object, which in turn help define its visual surface characteristics.

Filter by: Lights. The 3D lights that illuminate your 3D object are controlled directly from the Filter by: Lights view. Each model starts with a default set of three "infinite lights," which can be turned on or off. The Lights controls (**Figure 9.14**) let you create new lights—infinite, spot, or point—as well as control some aspects of each light individually. *Point lights* emit light in all directions, similar to a lightbulb. *Infinite lights* behave like sunlight, giving off light as if from a plane. *Spot lights* have a cone-shaped light beam, which can be made wider or narrower, and you can also adjust the hot spot and falloff of spot lights.

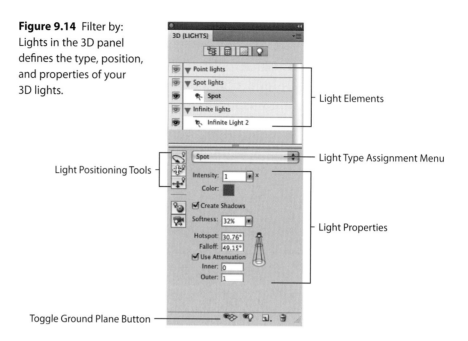

Figure 9.14 Filter by: Lights in the 3D panel defines the type, position, and properties of your 3D lights.

All the lights can be placed at the current camera position, and spot and infinite lights can be aimed at the origin from their current positions. To better see lights in your scene, you can use the "Toggle lights" icon at the bottom of the 3D panel, which turns on or off the light guides. Also at the bottom of the 3D panel, you can create or delete new lights and toggle the Ground Plane indicator to help with orientation. Understanding these options is key to defining the appearance of your model, so don't overlook them.

The 3D Axis

One of the challenges of working in three dimensions is making precise movements when manipulating your 3D objects. To make this task more intuitive, the Photoshop team has included an object/camera control called the 3D Axis. To use it, choose one of the 3D tools; you should see the 3D Axis appear in the upper left of your workspace (the 3D Axis requires a GPU that supports OpenGL 2). By mousing over the different axes, you'll see temporary *rings* and control *blocks*. Manipulating these controls allows you to rotate, scale, or move your object in one direction at a time. If you haven't worked with 3D before, trust us: The 3D Axis is a big time-saver!

You can see the control surfaces on the 3D Axis in **Figure 9.15**. Keep in mind that the 3D Axis stays aligned with the object's local orientation. That is, when you rotate the object, the 3D Axis represents that object's original orientation regardless of how many times you've modified or saved the document. When you go back to your file in the future, the 3D Axis will still show you the object's original orientation.

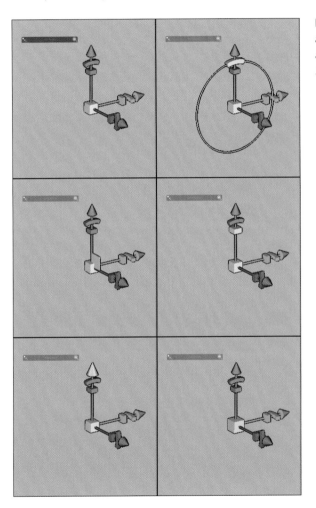

Figure 9.15 The 3D Axis allows you to position and orient your model or 3D shape layer.

The 3D Axis also lets you scale your object, either relative to one plane (or axis) only or relative to all axes at the same time. It does not allow you to scale in an arbitrary direction, meaning you cannot define a random axis along which to distort your object. You can approximate this by scaling along individual axes independently, but this does not always give you the same look. For example, you cannot stretch a cube along opposite corners, leaving all other corners in place. You will need to use a 3D modeling program for that task.

3Dconnexion SpaceNavigator

One of the trickier aspects of working with 3D is controlling your model in virtual 3D space. The folks from 3Dconnexion (http://3dconnexion.com), a division of Logitech, offer a handful of outstanding computer peripherals designed to make 3D workflows more efficient. One of the easiest products to use (and most affordable) is SpaceNavigator (**Figure 9.16**).

Figure 9.16 3Dconnexion SpaceNavigator makes moving through virtual 3D space an easier task in supported applications.

This small but weighty device gives you an intuitive way to control your models through the use of a pressure-sensitive grip mechanism. The lightly textured grip has a limited range of physical motion, which means you won't be dragging the thing all over your desk to move models around. It can move your 3D objects in four directions, allowing you to zoom, rotate, and pan your model or camera with total flexibility. It works much like a gaming joystick but adds twisting and sliding to the mix.

It does take some getting used to for mouse or trackball users, but if you are going to work with 3D more than a few hours per month, a specialized 3D controller is a necessity. SpaceNavigator is a slam-dunk choice for many 3D pros and is compatible with Photoshop, so you may want to look at the video demo on its website to see whether this product would be a useful investment for your workflow purposes.

CREATING 3D CONTENT IN PHOTOSHOP

Photoshop now has new options for creating 3D shapes from scratch, using photographs or empty 2D documents as the source (**Figure 9.17**). To create a 3D shape such as a pyramid, create a new document (or open an existing photo), and then choose 3D > New Shape from Layer > Pyramid. Photoshop then transforms your 2D layer into a 3D shape.

NOTE The larger your document dimensions and resolution, the longer Photoshop will take to generate your shape.

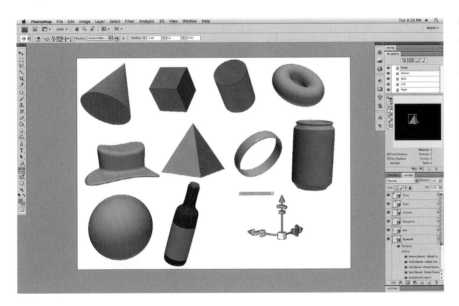

Figure 9.17 Photoshop has several options for creating basic 3D shapes from 2D image layers and backgrounds. Although it's possible to reposition the sides (or material) of a 3D shape layer, complex 3D shape edits are best handled by a dedicated 3D program.

Once your shape is created, use the 3D panel to modify the texture and lighting properties affecting each side of the object (a pyramid in this case), and use the aforementioned 3D and camera tools to manipulate the pyramid itself or your view of the pyramid. The process is the same for any type of 3D shape you want to create in Photoshop, and you can create multiple shapes in a single document by following the steps noted earlier but by using a separate color or image layer for each shape you want to create.

It is important to understand that when Photoshop maps your layer pixels onto one of its predefined 3D shapes, the manner in which the pixels are mapped is a fixed operation you cannot control. For this reason, we usually experiment with different images or shapes to find the right visual effect. For multisided images, you can control which images are placed on which sides of the 3D object by starting with an empty 2D image. Create your 3D shape, and then select a Diffuse texture for each material, as shown in **Figure 9.18**. For this example we used a macro shot of a flower for our wine bottle's label, assigning a photo of the flower to the Label material's Diffuse texture.

Figure 9.18
The Filter by: Materials view in the 3D panel allows you to define the surface characteristics of your 3D objects by defining the textures they use.

NOTE When you create a 3D shape layer from an empty document, any meshes that make up your layer will be given placeholder materials by default, usually each with its own color so that you can identify it more easily when moving the meshes around from the 3D panel.

TIP Another way to speed your 3D workflow is to click Remove Backfaces or Remove Hidden Lines, both found in the Render Settings dialog box. This frees up processor and GPU resources by not rendering any sides or seams of your polygons that cannot be seen from the active camera view. Many 3D programs have a similar feature that allows you to turn off "hidden polygons."

The original shot for this texture was 6 megapixels, but we bumped it down to roughly 500 × 300, which worked quite well because the size of the original image the 3D shape was generated from was 800 × 600 at 90 ppi. As you might expect, the larger your texture dimensions, the harder Photoshop has to work to generate previews and perform other 3D operations. With the exception of bump maps or gradient meshes, which benefit from 16-bit data, we've found it helps to process texture images in ACR as we normally would, and then crunch them down to an 8-bit file, with dimensions under 1000 × 1000 pixels. This improves performance quite a bit without a quality hit.

To get the most from 3D shape layers, you can create each one from an empty transparent document, using whatever resolution is appropriate, relative to the size of your final composite image. This allows you to modify all the material, lighting, and positional properties of the model without affecting other layers.

Mesh from Grayscale

Photoshop also offers the ability to create 3D depth maps with the Mesh from Grayscale command (in the 3D menu). The intent of this function is to re-create the topology of your 2D image or some other real-world surface with a 3D mesh (in other words, a grid that has been warped to have higher and lower points, based on how dark or light the tones in your source image are). Once done, you can then map a photograph onto the 3D mesh's diffuse layer to create simulations of terrain, close-up textures, and other structures.

In theory, this is a powerful tool that has a lot of potential, but in practice it can be frustrating to use. To wit, most photographs that depict terrain or other areas with obvious topological differences have both light and dark regions within the entire range of "topologies." For example, if you photographed the ocean from some cliff lookout point, the odds that the cliffs will proportionately and uniformly darken as they get close to the sea (which must then be the darkest area) are very low. This is what would be required for the Mesh from Grayscale function to accurately map that topology.

We'll talk more about this a little later in the chapter, but just keep this function's limitations and quirks in mind. We are anxious to see how this feature evolves down the road, but for now it may be more advantageous to focus your 3D learning on the other 3D features in Photoshop and, more important, on third-party modeling programs.

Understanding Textures

Working with textures in Photoshop is critical if you're going to take full advantage of the 3D tools. Though they're defined a little differently in other 3D programs, in Photoshop workflows, textures are the building blocks that define the appearance of your Materials. Materials in turn are applied to the various surfaces of your model or 3D Shape layer to define its appearance, when combined with different types of lighting and environments.

Several types of textures (sometimes called "texture maps") are available for working with 3D objects in Photoshop CS4 Extended. Each type serves a specific purpose, and some are a little more difficult to understand if you are new to the world of 3D modeling. Here are the nine supported texture types in Photoshop:

Diffuse. This is the actual pixel data that is mapped onto your 3D surface mesh. The texture can be an image or a solid color.

Self-Illumination. This is a color that does not rely on lights in your scene to display. It gives the object the effect of being lit from within, or glowing. Note that if the sides of your object are 100 percent opaque, this texture will have no effect.

Bump Strength. This is a bump map that affects the local topology or surface relief of your model. For models created as meshes from grayscale layers, you will also have access to a depth map.

Glossiness. This map defines how much light is reflected off the surface of an object. Black is the most reflective shade, while white is the least reflective.

Shininess. This is different from Glossiness in that it defines the specular properties of the object's surface, or the dispersion of reflected light. High values produce a smaller reflection with low dispersion, while low Shininess values create a more diffuse, dispersed reflection.

Opacity. This controls the local opacity of an object. White regions are 100 percent opaque, while black regions are 100 percent transparent.

Reflectivity. This changes the ability of the material surface to reflect other objects in the scene and the Environment map.

Environment. This map holds the image of the "world" around your object. It is what an object will reflect if there are no other objects in the scene. The Environment map is produced as a spherical panorama.

Normal. This is similar to a bump map, except a bump map uses only grayscale information. A Normal map uses color information to move the surface topology in the X, Y, and Z directions based on the RGB components of the map. These maps are often used to smooth models with low polygon counts.

You may not need to use every texture type in each model or each shape layer, but it's important to familiarize yourself with them, so that you understand the type of effect each one has on a given model or shape layer.

The Diffuse and Environment maps have an obvious effect on your object because they use pixel data directly. But Opacity, Bump Strength, Reflectivity, Shininess, and Self-Illumination rely on a kind of translation between grayscale value and visual effect, so their effects may not be as obvious without some experimentation. The textures used in 3D are essentially effects masks that control how a given effect is applied to a given surface area. With very few exceptions, texture will play a big part in all your images. Whether that texture is fine and soft like a silk fabric or coarse and rough like gravel, the way light falls across the varied surfaces of your model communicates its scale and appearance to the viewer.

Many kinds of textures exist, but for our purposes we will stick to textures that translate into surface topologies that are visible in a photograph, which means, in practical terms, features of scale with respect to the apparent size in your final image. Our gravel example might have lots of texture if you are standing on it, but that texture would not be visible if you were looking down on the gravel from 20,000 feet.

You can also talk about textures in terms of how often they are repeated across a surface (frequency) and whether they appear to have a different topology from surrounding areas (amplitude). If you look at a basketball, you can see that the texture has a pebbled surface. For this surface, the frequency is the number of "bumps," and the amplitude is their apparent height as measured from the surface of the ball. However, if you look at a large gym floor that is covered in basketballs, frequency now relates to the number of basketballs, while amplitude is the height of the basketballs relative to the floor.

Most important when considering texture in terms of 3D artwork is the level of detail in the final image. Looking at 25 basketballs in an image makes the exact surface texture of each ball a little less important. Now, let's say the 25 basketballs are placed in a 5 × 5 square pattern on a white floor filling our imaginary frame (**Figure 9.19**). For this arrangement, the balls exhibit "low" frequency but "high" amplitude. But if we zoom in so that one ball takes up the entire image, the texture becomes "high" frequency and "low" amplitude.

Figure 9.19 Keep in mind that scale is always relative, and this has a big impact on how we perceive—and create—textures in 3D images.

The same idea applies to all kinds of elements that you might use in a composite. Cloth, for example, can have a very high frequency if you look at the weave but can be low frequency if you are standing away from a sheet blowing in the wind. In the second case, the frequency is the pattern of folds and undulations, but if you move far enough away, even that becomes low frequency. Remember, scale is relative, not absolute! The earth itself is an enormous sphere from our perspective (so big in fact that we can't detect its curvature while standing on the surface), but from the surface of the moon, the earth seems much smaller.

Working with Materials

The Materials you use (and the textures that define them) help convey information about distance, scale, and light direction in both obvious and subtle ways. Careful visual hints about these elements through the use of placed textures give depth and realism to the scene. With the power of lighting tools available in Photoshop, you can fine-tune these visual hints, sometimes much more easily than you can with any photograph. For this example of a brick sign, we could not find a brick wall with exactly the right angle and quality of light, so we built our own brick wall Material; the resulting image element is believable and can be used to change the character of the scene (**Figure 9.20**).

Before Material Was Applied

After Material Was Applied

You can use Materials to build an environment, enhance or change the subject, or do both. Textures are most useful when they add realism in some way, which implies that they are truly interacting with the environment.

Figure 9.20 This brick sign was adjusted using depth mapping and a new light source to change the direction of the shadows on the final Material.

Adding Contour with Depth Maps

You can use the New Mesh from Grayscale command (3D > New Mesh from Grayscale) to build textures and materials with contour, using grayscale image data. However (because of reasons noted earlier in the chapter), we start with the default depth map, first taking a few minutes to modify it to fit our scene. The default provides a working template of the size of your map and an idea of the gray ranges involved. When working on the depth map, pay close attention to the base image for your texture. In the previous brick wall example, we used a small brush with a grungy, slightly random rotation and size to paint in the grout between the bricks. Then we created a cloud layer above that at reduced opacity and with the Darker Color blending mode to give the entire wall additional texture (**Figure 9.21**).

Figure 9.21 The depth map used for the brick wall texture. Note that it is hand painted to allow precise placement of the mortar and surface of the bricks.

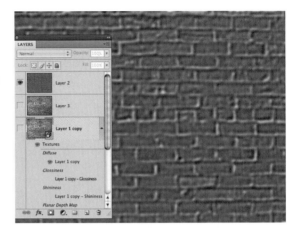

Here are some tips for working on depth maps:

- Work in 16- or 32-bit mode whenever possible.

- Keep the original texture image on a layer so you can use it as a reference by turning its visibility on and off when needed.

- Use "modifier layers" whenever possible so you don't lose resolution or depth data as you work. For example, you can use a layer at the top of your stack with a 50 percent gray fill with varying opacities to adjust the overall depth without losing relationships between gray values.

- Use gradients to add curves or large, low-frequency undulations to your textures.

Lighting 3D Content

Once you have a depth map that provides your Material with the contour it requires, you need to show it off with good lighting. It turns out that proper lighting can be difficult to achieve, even with the freedom of 3D lights and infinitely variable locations. Simulating real-world lighting may mean you have to trick the eye here and there. For textures, this is relatively easy, but keep in mind that the lighting you used to define your textures may need further adjustment when you bring it into your composite.

You can choose from numerous approaches, but we often start by leaving the texture perpendicular to the camera, which lets us control the lighting more precisely because we can readily see effects of small movements. The main difficulty with this process is picturing the final relationship of the texture to the larger composite scene. Then you must translate it into locations for lights and shadows. Keep in mind that the visual relationships created by objects and lights change as you move them around, while moving the camera leaves the relationship intact, though the view changes.

For subtle depth maps to be visible behind the texture image, you may have to place a close, hard light almost directly to one side of the model. You also may have to increase the total range of the depth map, beyond what reality would normally show, just to make the texture work in a meaningful way.

When to Adjust a Material vs. the Model

Sometimes a model cannot be rotated or positioned properly with the standard Photoshop 3D tools to achieve the correct perspective for your scene. Photoshop does not have any tools for adjusting the perspective of 3D models with virtual camera lenses, unlike many dedicated rendering applications.

For these situations we will attempt to modify the Material or individual textures. Converting a 3D layer to a smart object retains the 3D properties but allows transforms to modify the object's simulated perspective. The smart object layer can then be reopened for further editing of the 3D model if needed. Edits to the smart object layer affect all elements in the 3D scene on that layer, including lights and shadows.

RENDERING AND PERFORMANCE

Photoshop has a variety of settings you can use to view and render your 3D shapes and models to speed up your workflow. The various wireframe and illustration options are intended to help you position your model and lights, while ray tracing is meant for visualization and preparing for a final render. Starting with a few basic shapes and experimenting with the different kinds of render settings will help you figure out what works best. For most situations, we recommend using a wireframe view or basic shading options for the creation and/or rough positioning of your 3D content, lights, and camera. When you are ready to make a more "finalized" evaluation of your 3D content, you can use ray tracing to produce a more visually pleasing result. This method will give you the most accurate previewing only when you need it, to avoid long render times each time you wish to evaluate your progress.

Choosing Your 3D Environment

If you plan to use 3D content frequently and already feel comfortable working with models, lights, and textures, consider purchasing a dedicated 3D design environment, such as Cinema 4D, Strata 3D, or other reputable 3D package (there are quite a few to choose from and a huge range of prices). If you are less sure but want to give 3D a try, start with Google's SketchUp, which is free and easy to use. Another free product, Blender, is very powerful but unfortunately not very easy to use, so be aware that the learning curve is the price you pay for extra design flexibility over SketchUp.

The advantage to using third-party applications is that they are dedicated to the purpose of making and manipulating 3D models. They have a large array of shaping tools, light and render settings, material settings, animation options, and other impressive features. 3D applications, perhaps more than any other creative space, have made great strides over the past 10 years or so. It is now possible—with the right training and skills—to make movie-quality 3D effects directly from a high-end desktop workstation from Apple, Dell, or Alienware. Specialized hardware or software costing tens or hundreds of thousands of dollars is no longer required to get top-notch realism in a 3D design.

Both Cinema 4D and Strata 3D are industry leaders in ensuring that output from their products is easily "ingested" by Photoshop, and that is one of the primary reasons we choose to use them.

Cinema 4D

Among Adobe types, one of the more popular 3D modeling and rendering applications is Cinema 4D from Maxon (now on version R11). We could fill this entire book with techniques for using this program and still not have enough pages to cover all the important tools and techniques, so here we'll provide a glimpse of what the program can do so you can get a better idea of how popular 3D tools can fit into your compositing workflow.

continues on next page

Cinema 4D *(continued)*

Cinema 4D (C4D) provides extensive functionality for modeling, rendering, and animating, as well as for working with motion graphics. It is designed as a modular program, so its cost will depend on whether you include various add-ons that work within the C4D environment. For example, when building composite still images, you do not need some of the modules related to animation and rendering, while others that provide the building blocks for specific kinds of content—such as the special architectural or body painting modules—are essential in certain industries. Which modules you might need depends heavily upon your vision and on your appetite for learning new software.

As in Photoshop CS4, the user interface is designed to look and work in the same way on both the Windows and Mac platforms, though Mac users may need some time to get used to the menu system, which is built into the application window and also into the viewports. Using C4D, you have the option of viewing your models from four viewpoints by default, thus generating four viewports. Each viewport has its own menu and miniature toolbar with controls for manipulating which camera it uses, the camera's position, the distance to the subject, and the rotation (**Figure 9.22**). One of the great features of C4D is that it's easy to quickly jump from many views to focus on a single view and then move back again, without having to save new workspaces or drag window components around each time.

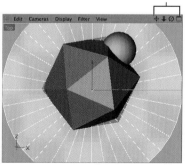

Figure 9.22 Cinema 4D viewport with menus and controls for defining your point of view

Viewing your model from a variety of angles can help you build and refine it more quickly, since you can see more of the scene or model at once. What we typically do is build and fine-tune our models using the various shape manipulation controls, add materials, and then render them out for inclusion in Photoshop projects.

continues on next page

Cinema 4D *(continued)*

Cinema 4D also uses toolbars, much like the ones in Photoshop. Many of the buttons contain more than one tool, which can be viewed by clicking and holding down your mouse button or stylus. Although most of the Photoshop tools are designed to directly manipulate the pixels on your canvas, C4D has several distinct types of tools. Fundamentally most of them either directly manipulate the shape or propagation of your model's shape, move your model, or allow you to select some small part of your model for further refinement (**Figure 9.23**). As noted earlier in the book, models are built from many smaller 2D shapes that are grouped together to form the illusion of a surface with depth, or 3D shape.

Figure 9.23 The tools in Cinema 4D are designed to modify your model's shape, select a small part of the model, or move the model around so you can edit it. The tool groups that share a button can be "torn" off into floating tool palettes as well.

The most important tools to familiarize yourself with—and that have similar counterparts in most other 3D applications—are the Move, Scale, Rotate, Objects, Splines, and Lights tools. Of course, there are many other important tools you will need to use, but these six are the fundamental building blocks of the C4D workflow, much the same as Move, Selection, Brush, and Clone Stamp likely formed the basis of your understanding for Photoshop when you first used it.

Objects is synonymous with the word *primitives* in C4D, and there are 16 types, ranging from the obvious Cube and Sphere to the more complex shapes such as Pyramid and Tube (**Figure 9.24**). Each of these, along with the other 12, can be moved, bent, stretched, and generally deformed into just about anything you want.

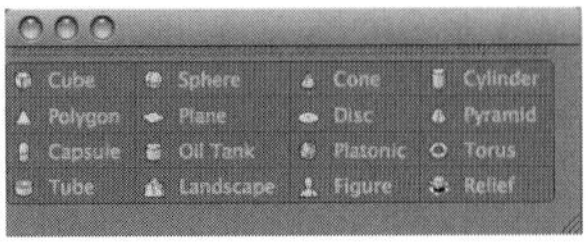

Figure 9.24 Sixteen primitive shapes will form the basis of most 3D projects in Cinema 4D, allowing you to build them together in an infinite number of ways to create new shapes.

continues on next page

Cinema 4D *(continued)*

Splines are another key part of the 3D workflow when you are generating subjects for your composites with complex shapes. They allow you to create the equivalent of predefined or freehand-drawn shapes (like a Photoshop Bézier curve) and then generate a 3D geometry from that. Using this process enables you to make organic shapes that are more useful in the world of still-image compositing. If you're trying to bring something into your scene that looks like a shape from a geometry text, the realism of your image will take a bit of a hit!

It's important to remember when using splines in a 3D program that it's generally not a brand new or foreign concept. You can employ many of your existing Bézier skills, in terms of manipulating shapes and transforming object scale and rotation, to create your 3D models for inclusion in a Photoshop composite. The images in **Figure 9.25** were created using spline objects and standard transformation functions (in this case, "Extrusion NURBS," which is just a fancy way of saying "the Extrusion tool." The Bézier and Extrusion tools that were used here operate on similar principles to the Bézier and Extrusion tools you would find in Adobe Illustrator, which can reduce the learning curve.

Original Spline and Bézier Shapes

Shapes with Base Extrusion Applied

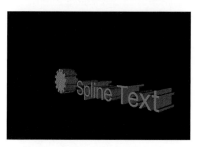

Rendered with Extended Extrusion
Materials Applied

Figure 9.25 Many of your existing Photoshop (and Illustrator) skills can be leveraged with programs such as Cinema 4D to create 3D content that will mimic real-world subjects.

continues on next page

Cinema 4D *(continued)*

The final topic we'd like to address is that the objects you build in Cinema 4D and similar programs are mathematically defined, and as such they have a great many properties that you can manipulate using the Objects and Attributes panels. These work much like a combination of the Layers panel and options bar, except that instead of selecting a specific layer and tool to access your options, you select a specific object (**Figure 9.26**). The Attributes panel works much like the analogous panels in a web editor like Adobe Dreamweaver CS4 or a motion graphics program such as Adobe After Effects CS4. In the Attributes panel you can find everything from an object's dimensions to its X, Y, and Z coordinates to the type of textures it uses to its name and the number of polygons it contains.

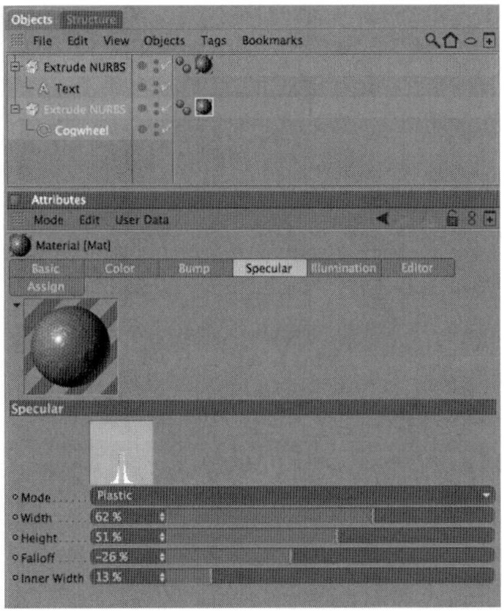

Figure 9.26 The Objects and Attributes panels in Cinema 4D and similar programs allow you to define and modify the many characteristics of your models.

CHAPTER TEN

Compositing Source Materials

This is where all the planning, brainstorming, photographing, and retouching finally come together and take shape as a composite image. Although no single sequence of steps or rigid list of tools will work best in all situations, you can use some time-tested—and new—techniques to produce high-quality results while maintaining an efficient and intuitive workflow.

QUICK SETUP

Strong foundations. It's important to consider how to set up your compositing workspace. Although some artists may start with their large background image as the "base," it can be useful to start with a new document as the basis for a composite. This enables you to precisely target an output type. More specifically, if your image is destined exclusively for the Web, there is little point in consuming extra processing resources, RAM, and time by using a huge image from your DSLR as the working file.

Web-targeted. The main considerations when targeting the Web are document dimensions, resolution, and color profile. Although many creative websites are growing larger as the average screen size increases, generally you won't find many situations where you need a final image that is more than 900 pixels wide. Furthermore, few LCD screens on the market display images at greater than about 96 pixels per inch (ppi). So to reiterate, working at your DSLR's native dimensions and resolution is not necessarily a good idea.

Give yourself enough leeway to make multiple edits (including tone, color, and scale/size) without needlessly consuming system resources (see **Table 10.1**). Finally, assign the sRGB color space to your working file. In fact, if you know from the start that your source images will be used only on the Web, consider processing raw files with an sRGB profile. This may limit the color quality of your images somewhat, but it will reduce the chances that you have an unpleasant surprise later, when you convert your pristine and optimized source image from a ProPhoto or Adobe RGB 1998 profile to an sRGB profile.

Table 10.1 Suggested File Setups: Web

Page Dimensions	Width	Height	Resolution	Profile
Large	1500 px	Variable	200 ppi	sRGB
All Others	1000 px	Variable	150 ppi	sRGB

These settings usually provide enough pixel data for any type of edits we need to make, while speeding up the process of editing and filtering layer data.

Print. For composite images that are destined for print, the options are more complex depending on your goals, but generally you can live by a few rules to avoid any headaches late in the process (see **Table 10.2**).

For starters, if you're not quite sure what resolution your ink-jet printer, paper type, art medium, or press requires, go with a 300 ppi file at a given print size. Although not quite a "universal" standard, it's pretty close. Every commercial press that we've worked with accepts 300 ppi files, and for professional ink-jet systems, we've yet to see one that produces suspect results from a crisp 300 ppi file, even though certain printers can produce slightly better results at 360 ppi.

The other print consideration is color space. Again, which one you choose will depend on—as with your source images—whether the composite file remains in your control or whether third parties will need to work with it. If the latter, we suggest choosing the Adobe RGB 1998 profile to minimize the potential for color matching problems and other color-related headaches that might otherwise rear their ugly heads during the digital production process.

Table 10.2 Common File Setups: Print

Print Type	Dimensions	Resolution	Profile
4/6 Color Press	Variable	300 ppi	Adobe RGB 1998
Pro Ink-Jet	Variable	240 to 360 ppi	ProPhoto RGB

Keep in mind that if you are using special print media such as canvas, vellum, or other art materials, you will likely need to experiment with your resolution to find the best results (make sure you have enough ink on hand!). Many labs have specific requirements for the different media they offer and provide tables that list the specific resolution and color space needs for different media and printers.

Television/cinema. Video-based media are another common application for composite images created in Photoshop (**Table 10.3**). Artists who use Adobe After Effects CS4, Adobe Premiere Pro CS4, and Adobe Encore DVD CS4 often create still art and other graphical content for their productions with Photoshop. Unfortunately, choosing output options for video media is an exercise in frustration for most designers and photographers. For this reason, if you are working on composites destined for the television, DVD, Blu-Ray, or cinema, talk to someone at the production studio before making important setup decisions. They may be able to provide specific advice that others cannot.

Table 10.3 Common File Setups: Video

Format	Dimensions	Color Profile	PAR
Standard-Definition TV	720 × 480 px	NTSC	1:0.91
Anamorphic-Wide DVD	720 × 480 px	NTSC	1.85:1
720p High-Definition	1280 × 720 px	NTSC	1:1
1080i High-Definition	1440 × 1080 px	NTSC	4:3
1080p High-Definition	1920 × 1080 px	NTSC	1:1

PAR for the course. The most important file setup considerations for the video world are the image dimensions, pixel aspect ratio (PAR), and color space. Like standard display aspect ratio (DAR), which refers to an image's width-to-height ratio, PAR describes the width-to-height ratio of a single displayed pixel in a video image. Entire books are dedicated to the process of creating and editing still images for video, so we won't go into too much detail here, except to say that the dimensions of your file will depend upon the medium's format.

For example, television shows broadcast in 1080i HD are 1440 × 1080 pixels. Shows broadcast in 1080p HD are 1920 × 1080. Standard-definition, wide-screen DVD (which looks a lot like HD on some sets) uses the same dimensions as standard-definition television—720 × 480—but the pixel aspect ratio is much larger, thereby having the effect of being "stretched" but without distortion. It's difficult to imagine a more confusing scenario!

NTSC or PAL? Color is another issue that can become complicated with files destined for video, unless the production is only for North American viewers. In that case, NTSC is most likely the color space you will need to use. Beyond those boundaries, things can get pretty complicated if your images will be used in other parts of the world, where PAL or SECAM is the standard. So, again, we stress the importance of talking to someone at the studio where the motion content is being produced before making any final decisions about your document setup.

Independence for all. File resolution (in most cases) is completely up to you. Choose the resolution that gives you the flexibility you need to make your edits, because broadcast formats are resolution-independent. Whether your TV is 22" diagonal or 52" diagonal, it receives the same signal and therefore the same number of pixels for every frame. Interpolation occurs inside the television. You configure these settings in the Advanced Options area of the New File dialog box.

TIP We recommend for most purposes that you work in 16-bit mode regardless of the resolution, dimensions, or color space of your compositing document. When the composite is finished, you can create a copy of the layered document and convert it down to 8 bits (and flatten and covert the profile if needed).

ADDING SOURCE FILES

Smart placement. At this stage of the game, your original photos, stock art, 3D models, and other source materials should be ready for inclusion in a newly created compositing file. To start, we frequently take advantage of smart objects and the Place command (File > Place) in Photoshop. This technique allows you to choose your source files (even layered versions) and place them as smart object layers into the composite document. When you place a file into another document, your initial view is with transform (Scale) handles so you can adjust the layer's longest dimension to fit within your composite. We zoom out before scaling the object, so the resize handles are fully visible (**Figure 10.1**).

Smart objects also respect transparency—including masking—in the original file, and in Photoshop CS4 each smart object layer's mask can (finally!) be linked to its parent. This means that while a smart object is repositioned on canvas, the mask follows the smart object, just like regular layers. These two capabilities alone should compel you to experiment with smart objects, even if you've been reluctant to do so with past versions of Photoshop.

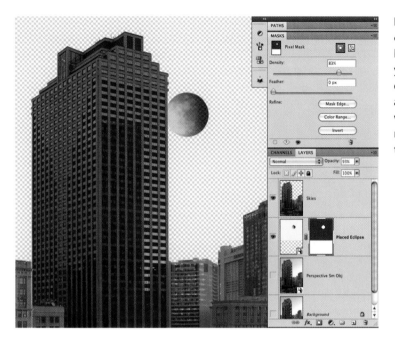

Figure 10.1 Placing source files into the composite document as smart object layers provides flexibility. They allow you to apply transforms and filters non-destructively, and to take advantage of adjustment layers or masks that are saved within the smart object source document. Smart objects can now be linked to their layer masks as well!

Nondestructive. Smart objects are extremely useful when compositing because they allow certain edits (such as filters and transforms) to be applied nondestructively to the smart object's content. This means the original pixel data for the smart object is preserved until you use tools that perform permanent edits, such as the Brush tool or Clone tool. As noted in Chapter 8, "Enhancing Source Images," nondestructive transforms such as Scale, Rotate, Perspective, Distort, and even Warp are techniques we use frequently when creating composite artwork. We'll provide more details on this later in the chapter.

To paint directly onto a smart object or apply other pixel-level edits, you have two choices. First, you can rasterize the layer by highlighting it and using the contextual menu or the Layers panel menu. If you want to preserve the smart object for future edits, you can double-click the icon and edit the PSB file—which contains the original image data and layers. When finished, save and close the PSB file, and your smart object layer will update.

Although smart objects do have a price for their flexibility (for example, file size will increase, and it can take a few seconds to open and close each smart object), they definitely make compositing a more forgiving process. For example, filters applied to a smart object (called *smart filters*) can be adjusted

Panoramic Smart Objects

One of the most inventive uses of smart object technology is related to the concept of *stacks*, which are collections of individual images stored in a single document. Prior to Photoshop CS3, when making panoramic images, you often had to manually place all your images into one document, positioning the overlapping image regions just right. From there you had to mask each layer, correcting tones and colors, and finally transform everything so that the images appeared as one photo. As you might guess, this was a tedious and painstaking process.

Using stacks as your starting point for a panoramic image, you can quickly group all your source images together and output them as a smart object file. Just open the Load Layers dialog box, as shown in **Figure 10.2** (File > Scripts > Load Files into Stacks), and choose the files you need to "stitch." From this point you can attempt to align your files in the Load Layers dialog box, or you can use the improved Edit > Auto Align Layers and Edit > Auto Blend Layers functions in Photoshop CS4 to create seamless panoramic images. We prefer the latter, because it tends to produce much more consistent results.

Later in this chapter, we'll discuss the full technique for creating panoramic shots from a smart object image stack, because panoramic images are one of the more popular ways to create a background, or *setting*, for your other composite source images.

Figure 10.2 Using the Load Files into Stack script in Photoshop CS4 allows you to quickly stack images together as unique layers in a single smart object document. This saves you a lot of time versus manually placing each image into a "base document" for your panoramic composites.

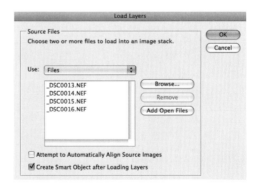

individually and changed at any time. You can also adjust the blending mode and opacity of each filter to dramatically alter the visual effects you create.

Outside help. One often-overlooked benefit of smart objects is that you can include vector artwork from Adobe Illustrator CS4 in your composite without rasterizing the original graphic or illustration. This can be quite useful to those creating advertisements or other business collateral that involves gradients, text effects, cartoons, or other artwork that may need to be updated as the composite's colors, tones, and overall theme evolve (**Figure 10.3**).

NOTE Editing a source file automatically updates all smart objects linked to that file. This is important if you use the same source file in different projects or multiple times within the same project.

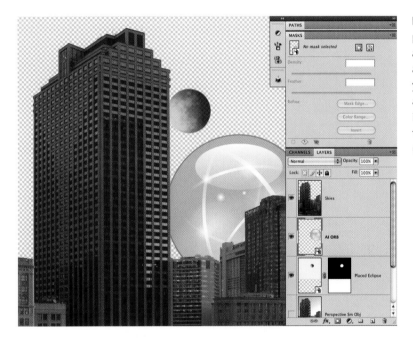

Figure 10.3 Illustrator files that you place within a Photoshop composite as smart objects allow you to include artwork without first rasterizing it. If you have both the original source file and composite image open, updating and saving the source will cause the smart object in your composite to update automatically.

Adding 3D content. You can also place your 3D models within 2D images so that you don't have to generate the entire scene in a 3D program. Although this doesn't usually give the impression of a "3D immersive environment," you can still create some compelling images using this technique, particularly for product-related images for advertising and similar commercial uses.

You can place and manipulate your 3D content—Photoshop CS4 Extended supports DXF, U3D, 3DS, OBJ, and DAE (Collada) file formats, among others—in two ways. First, if you are nearly finished editing your 3D content, you can add it as a smart object layer using the Place command. From there it behaves as any other smart object would. You'll need to first scale your placed object down to its rough size, and press Enter or click the green check mark on the options bar. To change the orientation of your 3D model once you've place it, double-click its smart object layer icon, and the model will open in a separate window, where you can then use the 3D object manipulation tools discussed in the previous chapter to rotate it or make other adjustments.

NOTE Be aware that a model created in other programs may use multiple materials. Often the textures are stored in separate files, so check with your 3D application Help files to determine what you need to do to get your textures into Photoshop.

Second, if you have more work to do on your 3D model once it's part of your composite document, make your changes by choosing New Layer from 3D File in the 3D menu (**Figure 10.4**). You will be able to manipulate your 3D object within the scene immediately, without having to open a separate window first. This also brings in any textures and lights that are recognized. We recommend positioning the lights within the 3D file before bringing the file into your composite. Once in your scene, you can use the Camera tool to position the model so you retain the relationship between the model and its associated lights.

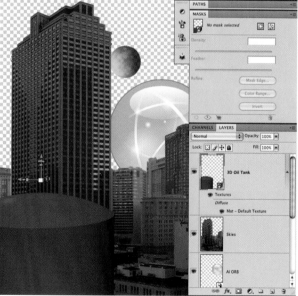

Figure 10.4 Adding 3D models to your 2D backgrounds, while maintaining the ability to manipulate them as 3D objects, is easy using the New Layer from 3D File option.

3D Layer Menu Option

Placed 3D Object

ADJUSTING SCALE AND PLACEMENT

Scale matters. Once you've added source images to a composite document, chances are good that you'll need to scale one or more layers (and possibly transform them in other ways as well) so the content appears to have the correct proportions relative to other parts of the image. Using smart object layers in combination with the Transform tools is the easiest way to achieve good scale, because they allow you to make more than one attempt (at different points in the compositing process if needed) to get everything just right.

The scale you should use depends on the subject's real-life size relative to other items in the scene, as well as its placement in the scene. For most situations, determining scale is a visually intuitive process that you arrive at with a bit of experimentation. For example, creating a surreal example of a pear (either a 2D image or 3D model) that is the size (and color) of a mountain is quite simple (**Figure 10.5**). Whether it ends up half as big as the mountain or 10 percent larger is immaterial because the viewer realizes right away that the intent is not to present a literal approximation of the objects in your scene.

NOTE If you scale a smart object beyond the pixel dimensions of the original photograph, you may encounter softness and possibly artifacts just as you would with a normal file-scaling operation. As long as you stay within the bounds of those original dimensions while scaling, no loss in quality should occur. For 3D and vector artwork, scaling beyond the original dimensions should not make a difference in most cases.

Figure 10.5 The scale you choose for the objects in your scenes will depend heavily on the intent of the scene and your understanding of people's innate perception of scale to sell the illusion.

However, making a pear fit onto a child's school table requires more attention to the details. For this example, you have a limited number of placement options that would look logical (in other words, you're not likely to place the pear on pencils or similar objects), and there are many items on the table with well-known scale. So, the pear has to be the right size relative to the scissors and other items if the viewers are to accept what they're seeing. It's best not to underestimate people's ability to intuitively know when something is not to scale. Usually viewers will pick up on this right away.

Some image elements will require more than simple scale transforms to look just right. For instance, you might decide to include a couple of man-made structures in your composite. Earlier in the process you probably straightened the perspective lines in those structures (individually), as we discussed in Chapter 8. However, you may find that even though they look straight on their own, when you place them side by side, things can still be slightly askew. A few extra tweaks with the Lens Correction filter or the Warp Transform command might be all that is required to give the subjects a more pleasing appearance (**Figure 10.6**).

Figure 10.6 Additional perspective corrections with the Transform tools can quickly remedy any minor variations between objects placed in the scene.

Completing the Illusion of Scale

Light and shading can also help sell the illusion that a scaled object fits into the surrounding scene. This is true of both 2D subjects and 3D subjects placed into a 2D world. Pay attention in your original photos to how the light falls across the subjects at a given location. Use this knowledge to make sure that any shadows or shadow-like effects you create look realistic.

For this example, it was quite easy to determine the direction of sunlight in the original image because of the shadows on the front of the pier. Based on this information, we created an approximate drop shadow for the fish. We used the Opacity, Blend Color, Angle, Distance, and Size controls to make the shadow's appearance consistent with other shadow regions on the pier (**Figure 10.7**).

We then broke the drop shadow out into its own layer so that we could mask the parts that don't apply to the image's light environment and move and shape it to be more realistic. The quickest way to create a layer from your layer effects is to right-click the layer effect in the Layers panel and choose Create Layer from the contextual menu. You can also choose Layer > Layer Style > Create Layer.

Once the shadow is in its own layer, you can manipulate it as you would any other grayscale layer. Usually a little scaling, masking, and placement are all that's needed. If you need to soften your shadow effect, you can do so by masking it with a soft brush and a middle gray, brushing around the edges and smoothing any odd angles.

Layer Style Dialog Box

Image with Drop Shadow Added

Global Light Dialog Box

Figure 10.7 If a simple scaling of your smart object layer doesn't sell the illusion that the subject belongs in a scene, a simple shadow can make all the difference.

Spatial relationships. As with photography, few things have greater impact on how the subjects in a composite are perceived than the spatial relationships created by changing their positions relative to one another. Ultimately, this is what sets the mood, or *attitude*, of your concept, along with the lighting, as discussed in Chapter 5, "Capturing the Scene and Subject."

The relationship between subjects and their environment can make or break your concept, so spend the time needed to experiment with different subject locations, and even different scales if necessary, to sell the illusion you want. For example, people who are placed behind or partially behind other people (or objects) can be perceived as lesser in stature or maybe even sneaky or suspect. People shown "front and center" with other props or people gathered around them are often perceived as having great stature and are central to the image.

Figure 10.8 The spatial relationships among people, animals, and even objects are very important in directing human perception of a scene, and often heavily influence the viewer's understanding of the scene.

There are many possible relationships between people and objects in a composition. For example, a woman with a calm expression on her face, standing in front of a park bench, might be perceived as sad or anxious, while a woman with the same expression, sitting on the same park bench, might be perceived as relaxed or content. Similarly, the image of a running dog, placed behind an image of a car, may be perceived as aggressive, while the same dog shown running alongside children is perceived as a faithful companion (**Figure 10.8**).

Distance factors. For compositions that are as much about the space your subjects occupy as the subjects themselves, recall that as an object moves away from the camera, its apparent saturation and contrast decrease (especially at great distances). Keep in mind that if you scale and place a subject such that it appears relatively far away from other subjects, you may need to make additional adjustments to saturation and sharpness and possibly even add a bit of "blue haze," as described in Chapters 7 and 8.

In **Figure 10.9**, the mountains are not far from the car; however, the effects of the afternoon sun call for a reduction in saturation of the red rocks and additional bluish tint. We accomplished this using a blue fill layer with the Soft Light blending mode at about 50 percent opacity and a layer mask to avoid making the car and sky overly blue. The original shot of the road and mountains, acquired from a stock agency, was a bit oversaturated (not uncommon for stock shots), so we opted not to process it in ACR before beginning our Photoshop work.

Before Adjustments   After Adjustments

Subject placement also has a pronounced effect on perspective in some compositions. As a subject—including a 3D model—moves very far away, it will appear much flatter, with the edges and surface details becoming less distinct.

Figure 10.9 Sometimes if you place an object into a scene that is to be perceived as being far from the background elements, you may need to tweak the saturation, color, and sharpness in spots. In this case, even though the car is close to these elements, the time of day dictated that we make things a bit bluer after inserting the car.

OBSCURING EXTRA PIXELS

Once you've placed, scaled, and positioned your images in a way that is consistent with your composite vision, there's a good chance that some of the layers will have content that is not relevant to your scene. As noted in Chapter 7, "Processing Raw Source Files," we try not to worry about how the non-critical parts of an image look while editing colors or tonality in ACR. This is because we intend to completely mask, or otherwise remove, these regions of extra pixel data when compositing them.

This process of creating "seamless edges" between subjects is what most people focus on when producing their first composites, and understandably so. This is the stage where a coherent visual picture of the final concept comes into focus. It's exciting! Relationships between the subjects in the composition are clarified, and as the extra bits are removed from view, the final composite starts to take shape. You can use many techniques to hide unwanted layer content; we prefer those that are nondestructive, but all have their merits, depending on the situation.

Clone, Patch, and Healing Tools

Cloning. As you likely are aware, this method allows you to cover unwanted regions of pixel information with different parts of the same image or even parts of another image. Cloning is a destructive editing technique because it permanently alters the pixels that are being cloned over. For this reason, if you expect to do a lot of cloning, you may want to use a layer specifically for cloning so—as mentioned in Chapter 8—you can start over at that stage if errors are introduced. A classic example of cloning involves removing power lines or other man-made "distractions" from your images.

Since the arrival of Photoshop CS3, cloning has become a more flexible process thanks to the Clone Source panel. This panel allows you to pull pixels from source regions in multiple documents and apply them to your target document. Source pixels can also be rotated and scaled so that if there is a slight mismatch (because of focal length or perspective differences between the shots), the pixels placed on the target layer will be correct in scale (**Figure 10.10**). Matching a clone source region to your target region is now more easily implemented with a new Photoshop CS4 feature, Clipped preview, that allows you to preview the cloned area inside the brush cursor.

Note that if you don't use the Clipped preview, the entire source *document* will be overlaid on your target document (which you can lower the opacity for so that you can see through to the target). We definitely prefer the Clipped preview for most purposes, although the original method can be useful when matching image content across frames of video.

Figure 10.10 The Clone Source panel makes it easier to see your source pixels in their modified state, before you replace the pixels in the targeted area.

Patching. Another important tool for permanently replacing the pixels in a targeted image area is the Patch tool, which works very well in concert with the Clone tool. There are many situations where the Clone tool alone—even with a perfected clone source—does not adequately do the job of replacing pixels, because it can leave behind faint patterns or other unusual visual cues that the image has been altered. The Patch tool will replace one area of texture with another, but it will also smooth out the texture replacement's tonal values to be more like the neighboring image regions, in effect, removing any obvious "contrast seams" (**Figure 10.11**).

Keep in mind that although you can use the pixels from one layer to clone over pixels from another layer, the Patch tool works only on and within the active layer. You cannot take a "patch source" from other documents or layers.

Target Area, No Patching   Target Area, Patched

Figure 10.11 The Patch tool—especially when used in combination with the Clone tool—can do a great job of seamlessly removing unwanted pixels on textured areas.

Healing Brush. The Healing Brush is, roughly speaking, a hybrid of the Clone Stamp tool and the Patch tool. Like the Clone Stamp tool, it allows you to define a source point for the replacement pixels you will use—press Option (Alt) and click the pixel location. But rather than cloning the texture alone, it also then "patches" the cloned area to smooth out its tonality. This is particularly useful when you want to clone something but don't want to leave any "seams" behind as evidence that changes were made. Like the Clone Stamp tool, the Healing Brush can also use multiple layers or images for its source point, which is a big deal when trying to match textures across images, for example.

From the options bar, you can choose from several brush parameters and special *blending modes* that can impact the edges of your healing zone. That said, we frequently use the (default) Normal mode, with a slightly soft brush edge and the Sample: Current Layer option active. Normal mode uses the aforementioned clone + heal behavior. The Replace mode, which is the equivalent of cloning without healing, is also an option if you want to make a few quick cloning fixes without switching tools.

The Spot Healing Brush works the same as the standard Healing Brush except it automatically chooses the source pixels from nearby regions. So, all you have to do is make a quick "blot" or brush stroke over the area, and Photoshop will take its best shot at making an accurate heal correction. In practice, we use the Spot Healing Brush mostly for removing water spots or dust spots (produced in-camera) and also for minor skin corrections such as removing freckles. However, being of the mind-set that it's always better to control the source area of the cloning, we usually opt for the Healing Brush to perform edits on skin tones, important texture regions, or other detail areas (**Figure 10.12**).

Figure 10.12 The Healing Brush allows you to clone and patch an area at the same time, which is useful for avoiding "texture seams" or unsightly artifacts on skin areas.

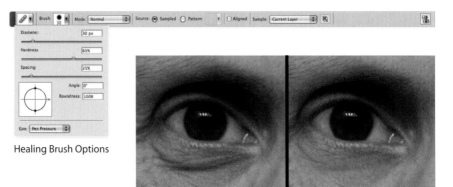

Healing Brush Options

Skin Area, Before and After Healing

Selections, Layer Masks, and Alpha Channels

Creating Selections. For situations where you need to cover something up but can't be 100 percent sure you won't need those same pixels later, layer masks are the best solution (yes, this is the selections section ... bare with us!). Layer masks allow the compositing artist to maintain precision and maximum editing flexibility, because no pixels are replaced or permanently removed. Instead, everything is covered with a virtual grayscale mask that you can shape and define with the tools described below.

To create precise layer masks, you often start with a precise selection. When we are selecting a complex subject that has contrasting edges relative to the surrounding pixels, it pays to try a simple method of selection before grabbing the Pen tool. The Quick Selection tool (press W or Shift-W if the Magic Wand is active) is a great way to make an accurate first pass at isolating your subject. For areas where the surrounding colors or tones are very different from the subject, we usually create brush settings with a Hardness value at or above 50 percent, and we leave the Spacing value very low.

With settings in place, drag the brush cursor around the periphery of your subject at a steady pace until most of it is selected. You can then zoom in and add or subtract away small bits of selection so that the contour of your subject is more accurately mimicked. The zoom level will often be between 50 and 200 percent, depending on how large your subject is relative to the image dimensions.

To remove bits, just hold down the Option (Alt) key, and the Quick Selection tool brush cursor will display a minus (-) sign, at which point you drag across the small areas you don't want selected. Using a small brush cursor at this stage is helpful and produces more accurate results in tight corners. This should leave a close approximation of your subject's outline (**Figure 10.13a**).

TIP In some cases, it may actually be easier to select your subject by subtracting it away from an entire document. To do this, choose Select > All; then choose the Quick Selection tool, hold down Option (Alt), and drag across your subject. When finished with the selection outline, choose Select > Inverse.

Figure 10.13a Although creating Bézier paths with the Pen tool as the basis for a selection is very precise, it's often not as efficient as using Quick Selection and other refinement techniques when you have "contrasty" subject matter.

Once you've made your selection, click the Refine Edge button on the Options bar to open the Refine Edge dialog box (**Figure 10.13b**). The Refine Edge controls allow you to slightly expand, contract, or smooth out the entire selection edge as needed. For subjects with "harder edges" in the real world, we find that usually a Radius value around 1 and a modest boost in Contrast—with final touches applied using the Expand/Contract slider—provide very crisp results. We generally use the Smooth and Feather sliders only for softer-edged objects or when we're trying to give something a slightly blurred edge or ethereal look. It also pays to experiment with the various Preview modes. We often find the three right-most options across the bottom (selection on black, selection on white, and "mask") to be the most useful. Figure 10-13b shows selection on black.

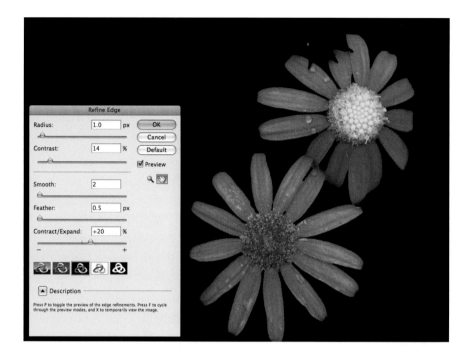

Figure 10.13b Regardless of how you create your selections, it is always a good idea to refine the smallest details of your selection (that is, refine its edge) by working with the Refine Edge dialog box.

When the "slam dunk" method doesn't work because you don't have great contrast across a complex subject contour, you can choose between either using the Pen tool to create a picture-perfect path around the subject's contour (read: accurate but more time-consuming), or creating an empty mask and brushing around your subject with black to create the mask directly. Which option you choose will depend on whether creating paths with the Pen tool gives you fits.

For many images, we prefer to mask directly when precise selections are required, because ultimately, we can turn that mask into a selection (and then an alpha channel from the selection if need be) just the same as we can create a selection from a Bézier path. Typically, the only time we go straight to the Pen tool is when we have a geometrically precise subject to outline, like the silhouette of an automobile or airplane, or the shape of an apple or pear that has similarly colored surroundings (thus making Quick Selections more difficult). To convert your selection to a layer mask, just click the Add Layer Mask button on the bottom of the Layers panel (third icon from left).

Creating Masks. If you are comfortable working with items such as the Quick Selection tool, the Lasso tools, the Pen tool, the Brush tool, and the Layers panel, you have all the basic skills necessary to effectively mask your source materials. Remember, all you are doing is covering up your subject with a malleable "transparency layer"; you aren't removing anything so don't sweat it. Experiment with and master these techniques! No 1-2-3 Photoshop guide can instantly transform you into a zen master of masking. Ultimately, you must practice with all kinds of images and all the tools available to make masking second nature. This section will cover a few basics, as well as some new tricks to make the process more precise and user-friendly.

To create an empty layer mask, click the Add a Pixel Mask button in the Masks panel (top right, left-hand button) or the Add Layer Mask button on the bottom of the Layers panel (third from left). To modify a layer mask's shape, select it in the Layers panel and then paint (in Normal mode for most cases) over the regions to hide with solid black. To reveal what's under a masked area, paint over it with solid white. To partially mask or reveal an item, you can paint with varying shades of gray—the darker the shade, the more the subject will be concealed in that area.

TIP Using a softer-edged brush when masking is akin to making the outer regions of the brush more gray than black, producing a partially opaque effect at the outer edge of each brush stroke. We recommend that you maintain slightly soft brush edges when creating precise mask boundaries, because very hard mask edges often produce an unnatural-looking effect in the final composite.

You can also modify the entire mask region's opacity by painting with black but reducing the brush opacity. This lowers the opacity of the black or makes it gray. In other words, masking with black at 50 percent brush opacity or masking with 50 percent gray at 100 percent brush opacity will produce the same effect. If you wish to increase or reduce the entire mask's opacity or grayness, you can do so using the Masks panel's Density slider, which we cover next.

Photoshop CS4 makes the direct masking process (or the process of creating selections from masks) a much easier one with the new Rotate tool. This tool allows you to instantly (and temporarily) rotate your entire image preview as you are painting your masks, making it much easier to work tight corners and awkward shapes, such as those seen on urban rooflines, for example. Just zoom into your document so you can see the subject boundaries clearly, press the R key, and drag your stylus on the document to spin it around into whatever orientation makes it easiest for you to paint a mask along the edges of your subject (**Figure 10.14a**). One of the most time-consuming aspects of masking with older versions of Photoshop—trying to angle the brush into tight spots with standard orientations—is a headache no more!

Figure 10.14a The process of creating masks is now a much more intuitive and efficient process, thanks to the Rotate tool.

For the example shown in **Figure 10.14b**, we needed to remove the windshield area so that we could add a different background later. We used the Quick Selection tool to make a first pass at the basic window shape. We then converted the resulting selection into a layer mask, zoomed in to 100 percent, and used the Brush tool with a soft-edged cursor to smooth the contour of the mask around the edge of the windshield and steering wheel. As we worked our way around each edge, we rotated the canvas so that we could paint in the mask lines using relatively straight, horizontal strokes. Trust us: This is much easier than tilting your head as you try to make an accurate brush stroke in corners, or along odd vertical angles! We also made a more precise masking shape around the wiper blades, fuzzy dice, and other objects that "overlap" the windshield area.

Figure 10.14b You can use the Quick Selection tool to select a basic shape, such as the window in this image.

TIP To create an active selection from a mask, right-click on the mask in the Layers panel and choose Add Mask to Selection. If there is no selection active on the canvas, the result will be the shape of the layer mask; otherwise, the mask's shape will be combined with the existing active selection on the canvas.

You can further refine and perfect the large majority of complex layer masks—regardless of how they were created—by clicking the Mask Edge button on the new Masks panel, which we will discuss next. (By the way, we're not sure why Adobe calls the button "Mask Edge" when the dialog box that opens is called "Refine Mask," but we all have our quirks!)

The Masks panel. Adobe has also improved the options for creating masks and enhancing mask characteristics with the new Masks panel (**Figure 10.14c**). This panel is a mix of existing and new features. The Density control (which might seem like a new concept) actually takes the entire mask and modifies the darkness of the masking pixels. It has the same effect as painting with shades of gray, but it affects all mask pixels. So if a region of your mask is 50 percent gray and another region is 100 percent gray (that is, black), reducing the Density slider to 90 percent results in a region that is 45 percent gray and one that is 90 percent gray (the opacity of all masked regions is reduced by 10 percent).

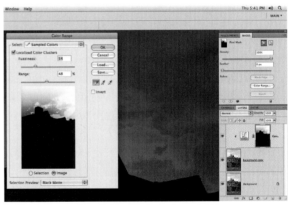

Figure 10.14c The Masks panel in Photoshop CS4 offers several options for creating and enhancing layer masks (either pixel- or vector-based).

You can also create new masks from the Masks panel, and one of the best ways—especially for masking adjustment layers where you may want to isolate changes to specific regions of color—is to use the Color Range button. Clicking this opens the Color Range Selection dialog box and allows you to set up a localized color selection using the new Localized Color Clusters option. When you click OK, Photoshop generates a precise layer mask for the layer you selected.

The Feather slider works as you'd expect, and the Mask Edge button opens a dialog box with controls identical to those used by Refine Edge (which we used with our selection in Figure 10.13b). It allows you to make precise adjustments to the boundary region of your mask. The same guidelines discussed for using the Refine Edge command apply to the Refine Mask dialog box when tweaking your mask boundaries.

Using Alpha Channels. Alpha channels are a scary concept for some people, mostly because of the technical-sounding name, but they really are simple to understand. For many images like the ones shown in our masking examples, you will want to save the initial selection (we'll get to why in just a second). That's what an alpha channel is: a selection saved as a grayscale image, instead of marching ants. The underlying information is exactly the same; it just looks different sitting in the Channels panel. Alpha channels are vital because they allow you to reuse complex selections very quickly without having to remake them from scratch. To create an alpha channel from an active selection, open the Channels panel and click the Save Selection as Channel button (**Figure 10.15a**). That's it!

Figure 10.15a
Creating alpha channels from an active selection is a simple and useful technique that ensures that you don't waste time recreating complicated selections or masks.

To create a new selection from your alpha channel (for use with a different layer in your image), highlight the target layer and the channel, and then click the Load Channel as Selection button. As an alternative, choose Select > Load Selection; then choose your channel from the Load Selection dialog box (**Figure 10.15b**). Of course once your selection is recreated on your canvas, it's easy to make a new layer mask from the same source. Another useful trick is to create masks that are the opposite of the original selection. Once your selection is loaded, choose Select > Inverse and create the new layer mask as needed.

Photoshop does not have unlimited space for alpha channels, but you can store over 50 of them as noted earlier in the book, so there's no reason not to save your complex selections as alpha channels, even if you're not sure you will use one or more. You can always remove them later if needed, but you can't get your selections back once you've run out of history steps or when you're reopening a document from a previous edit session.

Figure 10.15b
Recreating selections from alpha channels is a very simple process.

Alpha channels are also extremely useful for defining and protecting regions of your image that are affected by specific filters, like Lens Correction or Lens Blur, or by new transform capabilities like Content Aware Scaling (all of which are covered in this chapter).

Alternate Removal Methods

Content-aware scaling. One method of removing unwanted pixels involves a new feature in Photoshop CS4 called Content Aware Scale (CAS). Also referred to as *seam carving*, CAS allows you to push together two regions of an image without creating the appearance of overlaying the regions manually. You do this with the use of alpha channels to protect important regions of the image and to tell Photoshop which regions can safely be "devoured."

This tool has many potential uses. Any photograph with subjects that you want to use but that are spaced too far apart, or with a subject that needs to be closer to an edge of the frame but you don't want to crop out details, is a good candidate for CAS. To use this feature, make a selection around the areas of the image you want to *protect* from being "carved," and convert the selection into an alpha channel. Then choose Edit > Content Aware Scale.

You will be greeted with transform handles that you can use to scale the image inward from whichever sides you need. Don't forget to use the Protect menu (in the options bar) to choose your alpha channel so Photoshop knows where to tread. You'll also see an Amount slider (which frankly is a bit of a mystery to us, because it doesn't always seem to have the intended effect). You may need to experiment, but in general this technique is quite simple and, if performed carefully, can produce great results (**Figure 10.16**).

Figure 10.16 The Content Aware Scale command in Photoshop CS4 offers the ability to seamlessly "compress" your image without harming important details.

Original Image

CAS Scale Handles in Place and Alpha Selected

Final Result

As you might expect, this is a processor-intensive operation, so like the Lens Correction and Lens Blur filters, CAS can take a minute or two to process before you see the final results onscreen. For this example, we determined that there was too much water between the landmasses, so we protected them with an alpha channel and then scaled downward. Notice that the top and bottom sections have not been scaled at all, but the image is much shorter. The best part is that with many nature scenes there is enough chaos in the image texture (the water, in this case) that when CAS is done, it has a very believable look to it as long as you don't go overboard (no pun intended).

Eraser tools. Erasing your image pixels is rarely a good idea, since this is a destructive approach. The only exceptions are if you have very small regions along the periphery or other instances where you know there is no chance the pixels can be utilized in your composite. For these unusual situations, erasing some of the pixel data does have one minor benefit—it can decrease file size for images with many layers. If you must erase potentially useful material, it is best to work on a copy of your compositing document.

Typically the only erasing we do is with the Erase tool along the periphery of an image (if distracting material appears there) or with Background Eraser tool, which does a surprisingly good job of removing continuous regions of high-contrast color from images. However, even in this situation it is usually better to use the color channels to build a mask for these color regions.

Perfecting Focus

Once you have your layer content in place, scaled, and masked as needed, it is sometimes necessary to create the illusion of continuous and smooth changes to focus levels, from the foreground to the background. This can be less an issue with commercial images such as advertisements, because they tend to blur the backgrounds and focus on the products or people in the foreground (in some cases there's no discernable background detail at all).

Focus work is commonly required for composites that involve landscapes and other images with relatively long distances between the farthest discernable object in the frame and the viewer. Airport terminals and train platforms are also good examples of images that might require some real focus work on the individual layers placed within the scene (**Figure 10.17**).

The trick is to set up each layer so that there is no break in the focus progression. For example, if your image is designed to quickly blur from the middle ground to the background, setting a sharpened subject in the background won't help your cause. Even for images with a long depth of field, you still need to pay attention to where the details begin to blur slightly.

Properly Sharpened Layer, Relative to Placement

Figure 10.17 For images with longer focus distances, pay attention to the details, and note where the sharpness starts to trail off. The amount of perceived blur visible in the immediately neighboring regions of the image dictates the sharpness of a given layer.

Improperly Sharpened Layer

Lens Blur. The Lens Blur filter works on a simple principle (**Figure 10.18**). It uses masks (when enabled as a smart filter) or both masks and alpha channels (when applied to a standard layer) as a "sharpness map." This map tells the filter which parts of a layer should receive the maximum blur (based on your settings), which parts to leave untouched, and any variations in between. As you might expect, anything that is masked with pure black will not be processed by the filter, while lighter and lighter shades of gray have more and more of the filter's settings applied, until everything that is pure white uses the full effect.

The blur effect is defined by the Radius, Blade Curvature, and Rotation settings, though it's never been entirely clear to us what the latter two settings do in terms of blur style. Experimentation is the only answer we've found that works every time. For this example we used the Gradient tool to draw a "protection mask" from the bottom-left half of the image toward the center of the shot, where it tapers off so that the full blur effect takes over at that point.

Figure 10.18 The Lens Blur filter can apply precise amounts of simulated lens blur to your individual layers. Based on each layer's placement in the scene and the relative sharpness of nearby objects, you can build a layer mask or alpha channel to tell Lens Blur where to make its changes.

Lens Blur Users Beware

Although the Lens Blur filter does a high-quality job, you should be aware of a couple of drawbacks. The first drawback is speed. For all its elegance and power, the Lens Blur filter is heavily processor-intensive. For even moderate-sized images, it can take a few minutes for the filter to be applied when using older hardware. Even on top-end desktop workstations (with multiple, multi-core processors) like the Mac Pro, it can take a couple of minutes for the Lens Blur effects to be applied to larger images. The good news is that the results are usually worth it, and if necessary, you can click the Faster option at the top of the dialog box when working on large image layers; then when the result is almost right, you can switch back to the Accurate setting and click OK to apply the filter.

The second Lens Blur quirk is that by default it isn't "activated" as a smart filter. However, there is a simple remedy for this condition that is often overlooked. To add smart object support for the Lens Blur filter, choose File > Scripts > Browse. Navigate to your Adobe Photoshop CS4 folder. The script you'll need is located at Scripting > Sample Scripts > JavaScript and is named EnableAllPluginsForSmartFilters.jsx. Select this script, and click OK. You will be asked whether you want to run the script; click Yes. You now have all the filters—including Lens Blur—available to you for smart object workflows!

Keep in mind that if you choose to work with Lens Blur as a smart filter, you will want to set up your blurred regions using a layer mask rather than an alpha channel, because of possible technical issues with the latter in smart filter "mode."

Keep in mind that the kind of blur you apply to your composite layers may change depending on the layer's content. If your source image was shot with more detail than your scenic or base image, you may need to use the Surface Blur filter or Gaussian Blur filter, instead of Lens Blur.

Surface Blur. This filter allows you to remove some surface detail (and also camera noise in some cases!) without destroying high-contrast edge details. The Surface Blur filter can also help eliminate luminance noise in some cases. Very small amounts of surface blur can help soften the details of textures while preserving the larger view of your subject, as shown in **Figure 10.19**. Here we removed the raindrops from the surface of the vehicle, without blurring the edges of the rear door.

Figure 10.19 The Surface Blur filter can be useful when trying to soften the subject matter in a given layer so that it blends better with its surroundings, while not losing the higher-contrast edge and contour details.

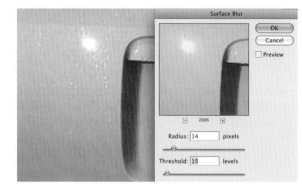

Gaussian Blur. An old standby for many Photoshop artists, this filter applies a uniform blur across your image. This is the quicker solution when the entire subject is far enough away that edge detail would be lost or when depth of field would not have any noticeable effect. This is a good solution for background or foreground elements that are included for visual texture more than story telling (**Figure 10.20**).

Before Gaussian Blur   After Gaussian Blur

Figure 10.20 The Gaussian Blur filter helps soften the entire content of a layer, and when needed, you can use the layer mask and the Gradient tool to show a gradual blurring or sharpening effect from "front to back" on a given object.

Here the basketball in the background takes on a completely different feel once blurred. The focus of the image now looks more realistic, as if the basketballs were photographed in the room (rather than having been placed there electronically). Obviously this is not a completed composite; however, it clearly demonstrates what a little bit of selective blurring can do in leading the perception of the viewer.

Motion Blur. One significant (and very common) challenge in compositing is producing the illusion of motion for objects that were not photographed while in motion. This is not a slam-dunk process by any means and usually requires some experimentation with the layer's orientation and placement, as well as the amount and direction of blur being applied. **Figure 10.21** illustrates how the Motion Blur filter gives the appearance of an object in motion. Here again we've given the basketball a completely different context, just by applying the blur.

Before Motion Blur   After Motion Blur

Whether the Motion Blur filter by itself resolves your particular situation will depend a lot on whether the intended effect is meant to be taken literally (in other words, you're trying to fool the viewer into believing that the photographed object really was in motion at this location) or figuratively (such as an advertisement showing a bicycle "zooming" across a nondescript backdrop). Usually, a mix of overlapping layers works best (each layer having the same content but a different blur amount, and stacked on top of one another to give the impression of a single blurred object).

Figure 10.21 The Motion Blur filter can do a serviceable—if not perfect—job of creating the illusion that the subject in your smart object layer is moving.

For some situations, a powerful 3D application like those mentioned in Chapter 9, "Creating 3D Content," can actually produce a much more realistic motion blur, though it will take more time to find the right settings and values to create the perfect motion blur.

LIGHTING ENHANCEMENTS

The techniques discussed in this section are used to control visual focus and balance and, in some cases, to add drama. Most are surprisingly easy to create, while providing great visual impact. Lighting layers, as we call them, are typically little more than brush strokes on a layer that rests above your target subject in the layer stack. The layer is then blurred and blended in different ways to give the effect of additional lighting in the scene.

"Lighting Layers"

Shaped light. For creative, vignette-like effects, use the Brush tool to create a simple white shape with soft edges on an empty layer. Setting the brushed layer to Overlay causes the painted areas to brighten whatever is beneath them. In **Figure 10.22**, the pine tree in the snow was already reasonably well lit, but the shaped light layer adds a completely new dimension and feel to the image. Lighting the tree in this way might make it easier for the tree to fit into a dark composite, because the black and near-black areas can blend together without much interference or extra work.

Figure 10.22 Creating shaped white brush strokes on an empty layer above your intended "brightening target" and changing the blending mode to Overlay is a simple way to create visually pleasing results.

Original Tree Image

Shaped Light Layer

Finished Image

Rays of light. This is a refinement of the shaped lighting layer technique, where the painted shape looks like a ray from a light source. This variation gives a solid visual direction to a composition and is effective at helping tell a story or set a mood (**Figure 10.23**). Here we've enhanced the drama and emotional effect of a beautiful canyon by adding the beams of light coming down from the side of the image.

We created them by first using the Polygon Lasso tool to draw out the "light fingers," which we then filled with an off-white color based on the surroundings. From there we softened the edges and lowered the opacity by a large amount to give the appearance of light beams. These types of beams can be used to draw the viewer's eye to an important subject.

Canyon with Light Ray Selection and Fill

Softened Beam Rays

Finished Canyon with Subtle Rays

Figure 10.23 Creating rays of light (sometimes called *God beams*) is surprisingly not as difficult as it might seem using simple brush techniques to shape the beams while keeping perspective lines in mind. In the real world, these beams are wider at the bottom than at their origin in the clouds, for example.

Render Clouds. If we want to add some variation to the landscape, we sometimes use the Render Clouds filter to fill an entire layer with black and white splotches. Once you have found the Blend mode that works best and have reduced the opacity, you can immediately see the effects. Blurring this gives a nice mottled look, and you can use a Perspective transform to make it fit the scene, as shown in **Figure 10.24**.

Once you've masked out the parts of your sky that shouldn't be mottled, you can take a sample from a variegated light source and use that as the basis for your rays. For this example, we took a 1-pixel-wide selection of light coming through the leaves near the top of the scene and stretched it with the Transform tool to simulate the shape of rays we wanted. This approach provides lots of variation and texture for the light, and appears more natural to the scene, since it has a visual anchor.

Figure 10.24 The Render Clouds filter can create a mottled light effect for landscapes or other shots with large ground planes visible in the scene.

NOTE For 3D content, we strongly recommend using the lighting tools built into your application of choice to create photorealistic lighting for your 3D layer content.

And since we are directing focus with light, you can use the same technique with shadows. The only changes you make are to paint with black and then lower the opacity of the shadow layer. This is usually done to simulate a vignette effect around the edges of photos but can easily be applied to any regions that need individual shadows or darkening. We prefer this method for more detailed work, including creating shadows on objects that exist on different layers.

Creating Shadows

To create cast shadows on other objects, you will have to rely on your artistic skill to properly assess light fall. This is no easy task for complex surfaces and subjects. We suggest using the Pen tool to draw shadow outlines first, which allows you to adjust the shadow at any time by modifying the path you create. Predicting how shadows will look takes experience, though you can "cheat" a bit with images that have less complex lighting and subject contour. Obviously, the more light sources there are and the more complex the subject, the more difficult it is to create a realistic-looking shadow.

Shadow from layer. Looking at a simple case of a subject isolated from its background, we often create shadows by duplicating the subject layer, locking the transparent pixels, and filling the duplicate with black. From here, we move the shadow layer away from the original and then use the Transform tools to rotate, stretch, and warp the shadow so it can be "placed on the ground" (or whatever surface you're using) (**Figure 10.25**). You can even use Transform > Warp on the shadow to give the impression of a curved surface!

Figure 10.25 For simpler shaped images, creating realistic-looking shadows is a fairly easy process once you commit a few basic steps to memory.

Original Image Composite without Shadow

Partially Rotated Shadow Layer,
Prior to Final Transforms and Placement

For this example we made sure that the dog's front foot was placed in a darker, dug-out area of the sand, from which we could give the appearance of a "shadow origin." Once objects are placed, it is often necessary to experiment with the shadow shape, width, and opacity until they match the surrounding shadows, if there are any. Here our original shadow wasn't quite blue enough, so we added a bit to the shadow layer using a clipped Photo

Filters (cooling) adjustment. The finished image was shown in Figure 10.8.

TIP If you need to draw your own shadows by hand, it helps to first make a temporary sketching layer so you can keep track of light direction and intensity with notes or markings.

Shadows the hard (but more accurate) way. Sometimes it's necessary to create shadows from scratch. Usually this is done with the help of Ruler Guides and the Pen tool.

The gladiator in **Figure 10.26** was originally standing on a street with somewhat diffuse lighting. The base shot of the ruins has strong light at a severe angle, just in front and to the right of the photographer. That meant the shadows would be prominent so they had to be very precise. After placement of the gladiator smart object was complete, the major challenge was building the shadows.

The first task was to figure out the angle of light fall, using one of the columns as a reference. Using the Pen tool, we constructed a triangle that went from the top of a column to the peak of the shadow, then back to the base of the column and up to the top again. That gave approximate angles for a shadow on a flat surface. However, the stairs can be approximated as a sloping plane to determine the length of the shadow. As the plane slopes downward, the shadow gets longer. Next we moved the path node down along the shadow line until it reached the stairs. That also rotated the bottom line.

Figure 10.26 Creating shadows along undulating or geometrically contoured surfaces takes more effort but is possible using the Pen tool as the basis for your shadow shape.

When a shadow is cast down stairs, the length of the shadow is the same whether it is cast on the stairs or a flat plane. What changes is that the tops of the steps are flat, and there are right angles to deal with. We filled the outline of the gladiator with black on a new layer, then transformed the shadow, stretching and applying a little perspective until the top met the right point on our guide, and the bottom was anchored at his feet.

Using the Pen tool again, we outlined the shadow, making sure to put transform nodes where the shadow crossed a right angle. Because the shadow crossed several steps, we had to treat each flat plane of the stairs individually, dragging one node at a time down the face of the steps. At the leading corner for each step, the shadow stayed with the bottom line guide. But at the inside corner, the node moved that part of the shadow to the right.

Once the outline was completed, we took a look at the other shadows and adjusted the density and color of our new shadow to match. After that, we applied a layer mask to our shadow layer and filled it with a gradient to use as a guide for a very slight Lens Blur treatment. The masking proved to be difficult at the transition from shadow to dark, so after we finished the blur and added a little noise, we created a flat, merged layer above everything and used the Patch and Healing tools on the seams.

3D Shadows. For the time being, creating shadows that are cast from your 3D Photoshop models or layers onto a 2D layer or image plane is a very complex and time-consuming task—so much so that we recommend that you not attempt to create 3D-generated shadows from Photoshop. Instead, duplicate your finished 3D layer, rasterize it, and then create the shadow in the same ways noted earlier.

FINAL TOUCHES

By this point, you have taken the time to make sure all your subjects have been placed into the scene with a scale, a relationship to one another, a level of focus, perspective, and believable lighting and shadows. The scene now looks real (or surreal if that's your goal) in the basic sense. But what it lacks might be a bit of moodiness, humor, or just some intangible quality that you can't quite put your finger on, but you know it when you see it.

It's time to make the (frankly random) small changes that every image requires to become that much more believable. These changes can include everything from tweaking the color and shininess of a wood-grained dashboard using techniques such as painting with Vivid Light to making the clouds in your scene look a bit more ominous, to warping a tiny corner of your faux shadow into the crack in the sidewalk so it looks a little more "there."

Many compositing artists will benefit from taking a few hours or even a few days off and not looking at their "almost-finished" work. Invariably, when you come back and look at it again, you will see variations in the color and lighting of your subjects (or the scene as a whole) that just don't quite look right. While it is somewhat subjective, this phenomenon is true whether you're retouching photos, drafting an illustration, or compositing 2D and 3D elements together.

Color and tone tweaks. Probably the most common "extra tweaks" that any image needs (particularly images with outdoor or otherwise complex lighting) are a few added brush strokes here and there to make the subject "pop" a little bit more. For this example (**Figure 10.27**), everything looks great for the most part, but we noticed that some of the houses were somewhat dull in appearance. They're not underexposed or unsaturated ... just a bit lifeless. (And, yes, we know that houses are not alive!) To remedy this problem, we used the Brush tool and Option-clicked (Alt-clicked) the regions we wanted to liven up, which gave us a color to work with. From there we reduced the brush opacity to less than 15 percent, softened the edge a bit, and went to work on sprucing things up!

Figure 10.27 Using the Brush tool in combination with sampled colors and various blending modes painted at lower opacities can help lend that extra something to your subjects.

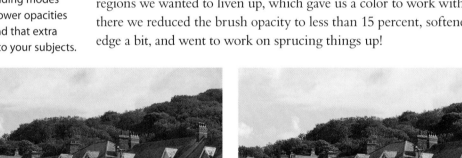

Before Brushed Enhancements · After Brushed Enhancements

Mixed bag. Another useful technique comes into play when you want to mix regions of grayscale detail with color detail. For example, perhaps some part of your layer or concept is so striking that you want to maintain the detail around it but focus solely on the subject in question without throwing all sorts of beams of light on it or warping it. For these situations, the Black & White adjustment layer, combined with a layer mask to isolate the color regions, can have an impressive effect (**Figure 10.28**). And, by using a mask to selectively apply your settings, you can also modify the amount of those settings via the opacity.

Without Black & White Adjustment   With Black & White Adjustment

Auto-Align, Auto-Blend layers. For the simplest of all composite images—panoramic photographs—the first compositing steps are often the last. Earlier in the chapter we mentioned the usefulness of smart object stacks as a means of finishing your panoramic images quickly. But the real power of Photoshop CS4 comes to light when you use the Auto-Align Layers and Auto-Blend Layers commands (both in the Edit menu) first to place and transform the images in your stack and then to seamlessly blend their tonality and color (blending dissimilar regions of sky being the most common example).

Figure 10.28 The Black & White adjustment layer has many potential uses in compositing as well as in traditional photographic retouching.

The Auto-Align Layers dialog box (**Figure 10.29**) offers some new options in Photoshop CS4, but we're ashamed to admit that the Auto option works so well that we often try that first without experimenting with the other methods of layer alignment. Fundamentally, what these alignment options do is examine each image layer for common visual details; then Photoshop overlaps the layers using these details as "registration points" and, finally, uses various transform algorithms to remove the distortions that would otherwise prevent a smooth-looking panoramic scene. After building our smart object stack of source files, we typically perform this step second.

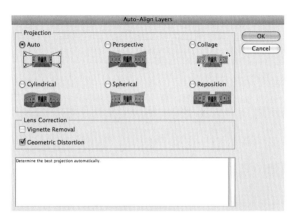

Figure 10.29 The Auto-Align Layers dialog box makes it simple to create the initial alignment for your panoramic composite image.

Auto-Align Layers Dialog Box

Aligned Files without Blended Tones or Colors

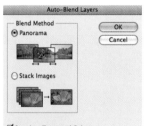

Figure 10.30 The Auto-Blend Layers dialog box provides the final blending of tone and color across multiple source images, giving the illusion of a single photographic image.

Third, we use the Auto-Blend Layers dialog box to smooth out the uneven tonality in the bordering image regions and handle any color differences (**Figure 10.30**). Since we always align the images prior to this step, we select the Stack Images and Seamless Tones and Color options.

When using these two features, it really is quite amazing how "automatic" the results can be, even with very complex panoramic composites, such as the ones shown in **Figure 10.31**, which contain details along the ground plain that could easily confuse lesser panoramic software.

Figure 10.31 The final panoramic image shows that even with fine details such as tree branches and complex patterns such as corn stalks, Photoshop CS4 is more than capable of handling the task. Making perfect panoramic images is a much simpler process now.

Selective sharpening. We've spent some time in this chapter talking about focus and blur relative to depth in a composition, but sometimes something minute or odd, such as a random shoe or part of a structure, will need to be sharpened up just a bit—have its edges honed, as it were. In such cases, it's possible to sharpen only small bits of an image while leaving the rest untouched. We use the trusted High Pass sharpening trick to apply a modest amount of sharpness to slightly blurred details, and we use a layer mask when necessary to avoid unwanted sharpening in other areas (**Figure 10.32**).

Figure 10.32 High Pass sharpening can be a quick and effective way of bringing out small details in a specific layer or part of a layer, if using a mask.

Before High Pass

After High Pass

To apply a High Pass sharpen to your smart object layer, duplicate your target layer (and mask out the regions you don't want to show up as sharpened). Then choose Filter > Other > High Pass, and set a value (usually at the low end of the scale) until you can barely see some haloing in the filter preview; then click OK. From there, change the sharpening layer's blending mode to Overlay (some compositors also use Screen). Turning the sharpening layer on and off will make the changes you made more obvious.

Of course, you can use many combinations of tools and techniques to shore up the details in your image, but these are among our favorites and should really help make your finished pieces exactly what you envisioned them to be (back when you were brainstorming!).

The Appendix demonstrates many of these techniques as part of two detailed image examples, so you can see a typical "start to finish" process. We also provide other finished composite images to show you some of the types of images that are possible.

FILE VERSIONING OPTIONS

The final point we want to reiterate is image flexibility. As noted in Chapter 8, working with layers, masks, alpha channels, and smart objects is key to any compositing workflow. As such, when you've finished the job, the worst thing you can do is flatten your image. Rather than one version, you should have several versions of your file when finished to account for multiple output types.

For example, we recommend you not only keep your master edit file (which should have plenty of the goodies noted earlier and be a 16-bit file if at all possible), but you should also back it up on a separate drive. The following are the file types we usually keep on hand for any important compositing project:

- 16-bit, layered master file (plus backup)

- 16-bit, flattened master file (for resizing the image later with third-party tools such as Genuine Fractals or, for example, making minor Curves corrections)

- 8-bit, flattened file tagged with Adobe or ProPhoto RGB (for ink-jet or commercial printing purposes)

- 8-bit, reduced and flattened file converted to sRGB (for web purposes)

Although every workflow is a bit different and not everyone needs as many versions, for those who intend their work to be used commercially, a file workflow similar to this one at the end of the process is a good idea. Don't get stuck with an 8-bit flattened file when you may have to make multiple additional corrections to tone, color, or size!

Output Options

Once you've created your composite image and are ready to output it to your medium of choice, you have a few options to consider that may help you produce better-looking prints and web images. This stage of the process is less of an issue for those working in the video space, because the Adobe Media Encoder that comes with Adobe Premiere Pro CS4 and Adobe After Effects CS4 usually handles the output options. For video-related composites, about all you can do output-wise in Adobe Photoshop CS4 is to make sure you've created a file with the correct dimensions, pixel aspect ratio, and color space.

COMMERCIAL PRESS OUTPUT

One of the more difficult and frustrating aspects of any Photoshop workflow is making sure the images you create maintain their visual integrity when printed on a four-color (or six-color) printing press. So many variables are at play even within supposedly similar press setups that there is plenty of opportunity for your colors to become muddled and your contrast to lose all of its punch. We wish it were as simple as providing you with a formula for getting great CMYK prints, but unfortunately no such formula exists.

The only way to make sure you get quality press output is to keep the lines of communication with your printing house's account agent open so they understand your goals and concerns, and to perform your due diligence with respect to soft-proofing and converting your document from an RGB working space to the correct CMYK space.

Choosing the Right ICC Profile

TIP Once your document has been soft-proofed/corrected for CMYK (more on this later in the chapter), use the Edit > Convert to Profile function to convert your document's color data into a "color language" the printing press can understand.

Before you send your composite file to the print house, you should understand the variables that will help you maintain the contrast and colors in your RGB document as much as possible for final press output.

First you need to know something about basic color management and the color profiles and printing presses that you will utilize. As noted earlier in the book, color management is a complex topic—but it's key to working successfully in Photoshop. For example, we're assuming that you're familiar with ICC profiles and how they relate to the documents you are creating and the devices you are using.

Handling profiles. For those printing their images in North America, some Photoshop users (and even press operators) suggest that it's OK to just convert your RGB document to the Photoshop default U.S. Web Coated (SWOP) v2 CMYK profile and hope for the best. However, this is not the best approach. The problem is that some print houses do a fantastic job of optimizing CMYK files tagged with a particular profile, while others do a less than stellar job. Don't leave it to chance.

The best defense against unwanted results in commercially printed output is to educate yourself on how CMYK processes work. Although a full-blown discussion of handling CMYK workflow is more than enough to fill its own book, it is ultimately beyond the scope of this book. Our goal is simply to give you some pointers that will help you get started. If you want to learn more about working in CMYK, take a look at *CMYK 2.0: A Cooperative Workflow for Photographers, Designers, and Printers*, by Rick McCleary (Peachpit).

The first thing to understand about CMYK workflow is that most of the CMYK profiles in the Color Settings dialog box in Photoshop are based on the most common types of commercial printing presses currently in use (**Figure 11.1**). Most print houses will likely use one of two kinds of presses to print your composite CMYK image: a sheet-fed press or a web press.

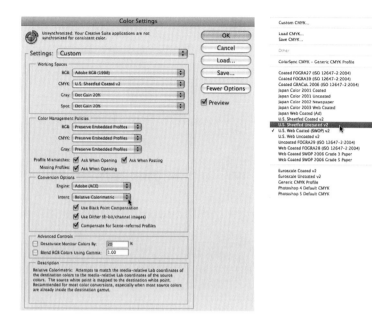

Figure 11.1 Familiarize yourself with the ICC profile options and CMYK settings available in the Color Settings dialog box; it's crucial to ensuring good commercial press output.

Sheet-fed presses. This type of printing press works just as the name suggests; individual sheets of paper are fed into the press to create your print (**Figure 11.2**). Usually this type of press is used for projects that aren't mass distributed, such as posters, brochures, limited-edition prints, or company reports. Typically, sheet-fed presses are a better option for photographic output because more paper types are available. However, many print houses use only one or two *sizes* of sheet-fed paper to keep costs down. We discuss this in more detail later in the chapter.

Web presses. Web presses rely on a very different "feed process" that uses huge rolls of paper (often weighing 2,000 pounds or more) that are continuously fed through the press and later cut to size per the final output specs (**Figure 11.3**). This is how newspapers and most large-circulation magazines are printed. Web presses are extremely high-volume machines; they can often print several thousand impressions of whatever content they're reproducing per hour! As a natural consequence of this volume, the paper types that are available for these presses are usually not as adept at photographic reproduction (otherwise the cost of the print run would be enormous). Some exceptions do exist, such as high-end glossy photo magazines (in other words, the ones that usually cost $10 a copy!).

Figure 11.2 Example of a sheet-fed printing press

Figure 11.3 Example of a web press machine

TIP For a cool look at how a CMYK press works, visit http://computer.howstuffworks.com/offset-printing.htm.

As you might suspect, the first step in choosing the right ICC profile for your document is deciding whether it will be reproduced on a sheet-fed press or a web press. If your composite image was designed for an ad agency that is placing the work in a major magazine, chances are good it will be output on a web press. If this is a lower-volume project where you are choosing the print parameters, then a sheet-fed press is almost certainly your best option.

Coated vs. uncoated. The second variable in determining which CMYK profile to choose when converting your document is the paper type. Though the range of paper types is vast, they all fall within two simple categories: coated and uncoated. The former is much better for any type of photographic reproduction and typically is more expensive as well. Whatever printed medium you are using for your composite, a coated paper type is likely the best candidate.

Profile choice. At this point, you can probably deduce from Figure 11.1 which CMYK profile best suits your situation. For most prints done commercially, the U.S. Sheetfed Coated v2 profile is the one we end up using. Before making the final conversion, though, check with your print representative. Whatever CMYK setting you're going to use, verify it, even if you're confident that it's the right way to go!

Returning for a moment to the discussion of sheet-fed presses, the paper size your press uses (your rep can also provide this information) may dictate whether additional changes to your final document size or canvas size will be needed. Ideally, your document should be sized in such a way that one, two, four, or eight (and so on) full copies can fit onto a sheet, depending on how large the sheet is. Documents with odd dimensions that require the press sheets to be cut down after printing will cost you more money, since the printer will have to use more sheets to create the same number of prints.

NOTE Some print providers have websites that guide you through the process of ensuring that your document's dimensions can be divided evenly into their sheet size and that your document uses the appropriate guides to define any "full-bleed" print regions (areas beyond which content will be cut off the page). Many sites also provide templates for commonly printed items such as company letterhead, business cards, placards, and several other types of printed material.

Soft-Proofing Your Work

Once you know which CMYK profile you should use, it's easier to accurately (and we use that term loosely) "soft-proof" your RGB document's colors so that you can estimate what they will look like when converted to a chosen CMYK space and printed on a press. Although it is not a bulletproof process, soft-proofing your images is really not that difficult and can spare you some monster headaches if done carefully.

What is it? Although you may not need tips on how to operate the basic control points of a Curves adjustment or how to set the opacity and blend mode for your brush-based tools, a large number of Photoshop users are (intentionally) inexperienced in the black art of soft-proofing. Fear not! Soft-proofing simply involves leveraging your high-quality, calibrated

LCD (you didn't forget to calibrate your monitor, did you?) to mimic the limitations of the CMYK printing process. This allows you to temporarily see where the colors (may) become faded or where the contrast (possibly) decreases. In other words, soft-proofing is a monitor-based simulation of printed CMYK output.

Soft-Proofing: An Imperfect Solution

The limitation here should be obvious: It's difficult for any collection of software engineers (no matter how talented they might be) to accurately mimic the appearance of a printed (or reflected) medium on a device that projects colors. So, keep your expectations realistic: The bottom line is that some of your perfect color and tonal fidelity may be lost when printing your composite images on a CMYK press. Soft-proofing is just there to minimize that condition, not alleviate it entirely.

In fairness to print houses everywhere, we should note that often there are small regions of color that your monitor can reproduce from a given working space (such as Adobe RGB 1998), which your fancy Epson 4800 series printer cannot reproduce (and vice versa). However, most CMYK press machines are unable to duplicate even the range of colors that can be printed by today's professional ink-jets. So, the limitations of reproducing all the colors you see on your monitor are somewhat lessened when using a professional ink-jet versus a commercial press.

Proof setup. To get started with your soft-proofing duties, choose View > Proof Setup > Custom. This opens the Customize Proof Condition dialog box, which allows you to define a few basic parameters to help you simulate your chosen CMYK colors as accurately as possible (**Figure 11.4**). The various Proofing Conditions controls are fairly simple to set up once you understand what each item does and whether you need to use it (here again, your press representative will be *the* source for such information).

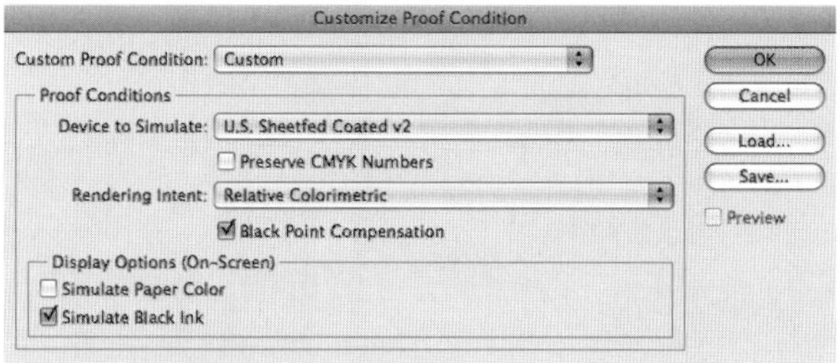

Figure 11.4 The Customize Proof Condition dialog box is where you set up all your important proofing options in Photoshop (Select View > Proof Setup > Custom).

Device to Simulate. This menu allows you to select the CMYK "device" profile that you intend to convert the document to so its color characteristics can be simulated on your screen. The word *device* is used because, as noted earlier, the ICC color profile you choose has more to do with the type of printing press and paper you use than anything else. For many of our images, we select U.S. Sheetfed Coated v2, just as we do when converting our document profile in the Convert to Profile dialog box.

Preserve CMYK Numbers. Most of the time you can leave this option deselected (assuming it is available to be selected). Its purpose is to simulate how your image colors will look without being converted first.

Rendering Intent. This menu/option essentially allows you to define how the colors and tones in your image will shift when the document is printed or converted. For most projects that contain a photographic material, Perceptual or Relative Colorimetric is the option you should use. For those occasions when we try both methods, it's not uncommon for the resulting prints to be indistinguishable.

Black Point Compensation. This option ensures that the full dynamic range of your device (in other words, the range of gray tones, including the blackest black) is temporarily "mapped" to the tones in your image so that you don't lose shadow detail. Leave this selected when setting up your conditions.

Simulate Paper Color. This option attempts to map the white point in your image to the white point of the simulated paper. We rarely use this option. Although it can be useful in a few circumstances, there are so many variations of white paper that it is impossible for one function to accurately mimic them all. Photoshop assumes that the least white paper among the common paper types is the one being simulated (it is in effect the "lowest common denominator"), and as a result, this option will put an obvious (and frankly, inaccurate, in most cases) haze over your image.

Simulate Black Ink. We typically leave this option selected because it will give you an idea of where your near-black RGB tones might turn a bit gray. This is easier for Photoshop to simulate on-screen than it is to simulate a paper color (white).

Once you have created a proofing condition setup that generally is representative of the press and paper type you're using, save the settings as a preset so you can return to those settings quickly later if needed. It's usually a good idea to name each setup after the company whose press you are using. Every print house operates differently and may provide different setup advice as a result.

For the actual proofing, we generally recommend you stick to onscreen evaluation and corrections, because most ink-jets (even the professional variety) have a hard time creating really accurate press proofs unless you've set them up specifically to mimic the conditions at the print house and are using the same paper type. For most users, this will not be a practical option.

To proof your CMYK colors onscreen, make sure the aforementioned preset is selected, close the Customize Proof Condition dialog box, and use the keyboard shortcut Command-Y (Control-Y). This creates the simulated view of your image (**Figure 11.5**) and gives you an idea of how much the colors or contrast will shift (remember, it's not exact!).

Figure 11.5 Using the Command-Y (Control-Y) shortcut in tandem with your chosen proof condition setup allows you to get a general idea of how the colors and contrast in your image will change when it's printed to a CMYK press.

Standard RGB View   Onscreen Soft-Proof View

You can also use the Gamut Warning feature by pressing Shift-Command-Y (Shift-Control-Y) to show a color overlay on the areas of your image that fall outside the CMYK device space being used. This works in much the same way as the Shadow and Highlight Clipping warnings in ACR. You can select the color (and opacity of color) used for the Gamut Warning feature from Preferences > Transparency & Gamut. The default is a middle gray.

Making Corrections

The final step is to make some (let's hope minor) corrections to your image. Remember, you don't want to make CMYK corrections to any of your master RGB files. Instead, make sure you create a layered or flattened CMYK version that you can use to experiment with different settings so the quality of the original remains intact!

To make CMYK corrections, we usually leave the onscreen soft-proof active and first use a Curves adjustment layer to bring back any lost contrast (**Figure 11.6**). Typically, the darker regions of the image will tend to move "toward" the midtones a bit, thus decreasing contrast. Fixing this can be a little tricky and may require more than one attempt, but usually you can start with a simple S-curve to see whether that removes any of the grayness and restores the image's punch without creating unwanted effects such as banding. Take advantage of the new on-document Curves control in Photoshop; targeting one small range of tones might be all the correction you need!

Figure 11.6 Use the Curves adjustment layer with your onscreen proof active to add the contrast and tonal changes needed to make sure the CMYK converted document is a close approximation of your RGB master file.

Occasionally it may also be necessary to correct one of the color channels with your Curves adjustment, as well as to make a Vibrance adjustment. This can restore your image's color "punch."

Once you've achieved the desired look, save your CMYK master document and create a duplicate. Take the duplicated copy, merge any new adjustments down to the background layer, convert to 8 bits, and save your file as a TIF, keeping in mind any suggestions your print provider offered for compression settings and the like. Every provider is a little different and often uses different versions of Creative Suite components, so don't assume the TIF options available to you will be available to the print house.

Ink-Jet Printer Output

Somewhat simpler than CMYK soft-proofing and correction is the process for producing a pleasing ink-jet print from Photoshop. Although several variables are in play, the Print dialog box for Photoshop CS4 has been redesigned, providing a more intuitive layout of controls and also some useful new features.

Prints, Not Proofs

This section is specifically geared toward those who are creating fine-art prints or prints for sale, not those who are printing CMYK proofs. Although there are some nice improvements to the way that Photoshop CS4 sets up printed proofs, you still cannot assume your ink-jet printer will accurately reproduce the color characteristics of a commercial press, unless it has been specifically set up to do so, starting with the same paper type, which may be difficult to acquire.

Some no doubt will find ways to successfully create always-accurate proofs in-house, but for the majority of users, creating printed proofs locally might produce a false sense of security in what they're seeing. Therefore, we usually soft-proof and make corrections and then send the file—along with any special concerns or instructions—to our printer's graphic design department, and they take care of the rest.

NOTE Many third-party paper manufacturers provide ICC profiles for several popular printer models, usually freely available for download (along with installation tips) from their websites.

We provide these ink-jet tips with the assumption that you have generated a custom ICC profile for your printer and paper type or, at the very least, have installed manufacturer ICC profiles for your printer model and paper type.

Print-happy. The new Print dialog box in Photoshop CS4 is easy to set up and use once you know your way around the different menus and modes (**Figure 11.7**). We have a few simple recommendations to help make your life easier when printing.

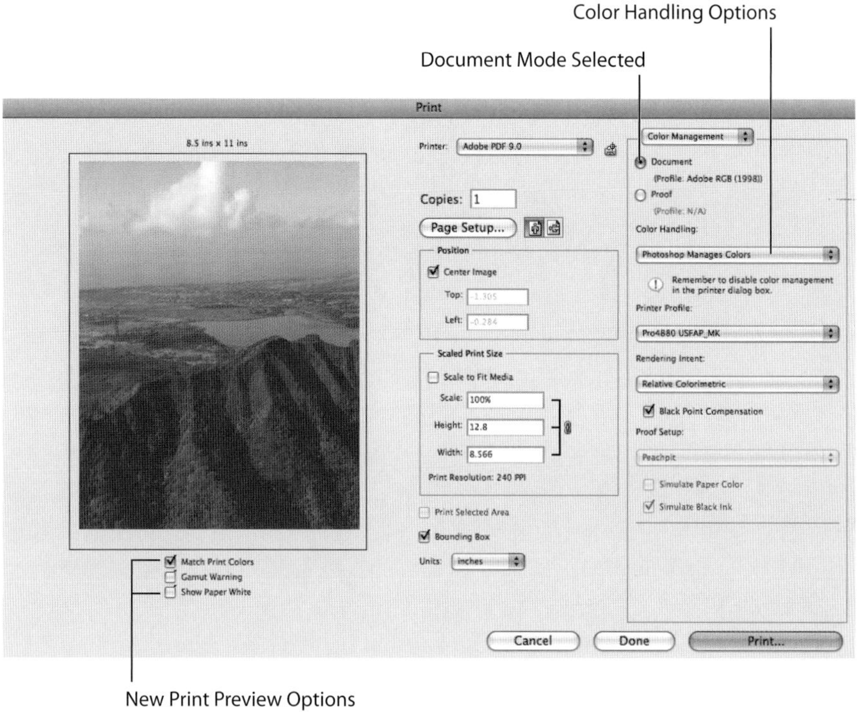

Color Handling Options

Document Mode Selected

Figure 11.7 Photoshop CS4 has a new Print dialog box with a more intuitive layout and some extras that make it a bit easier to preview your print in the dialog box. For our purposes, we focus mostly on the Color Management settings (top right) using Document mode.

New Print Preview Options

Photoshop Manages Colors. This is a big one. In the Color Handling section of the dialog box, the default setting for this dialog box is still Printer Manages Colors. For the vast majority of your composite printing situations, we recommend choosing Photoshop Manages Colors. The way this function works gets into the nitty-gritty of color management theory, but really the reason for using it is simple. Much more often than not, Photoshop CS4 does a better job of interpreting the colors in your file—so that the printer has a better chance of getting them right—than your printer's driver software. When trying to remember the last time we intentionally let the printer manage our document colors, we drew a blank, because we never intentionally let our printers (even the fancy ones!) manage our colors.

Printer Profile. Another important step is making sure you have assigned the correct printer/paper profile in the Printer Profile menu. To do this, choose your custom or manufacturer-supplied profile for your printer *and your paper type.* That last bit is important. The accuracy of your prints will largely depend on your printer's knowledge of which paper type is being used so that it can adjust—on the fly—the amount of ink it puts on the paper. If you don't have a custom profile but you have, for example, an Epson 4880 printer and you are using Epson Premium Semi-gloss paper, then that is the profile you should choose. Ignore this setting at your own peril!

Rendering Intent. We mentioned this setting earlier in the chapter. Again, for output that is mostly photographic in nature (that is, not an illustration), either Perceptual or Relative Colorimetric should work well for you. Typically we use Relative Colorimetric. This is just a fancy way of saying, "Photoshop understands what kind of content you are printing and will make sure the color data handed off to the printer is optimized for this purpose."

Black Point Compensation. This option—as with our proofing setup—maps the black point of your image to the black point of your printer. Whether you should select this option is something we can't definitively answer, because we don't know anything about your specific image or printer. If you have a high-end, professional ink-jet and are using the Adobe RGB 1998 profile with your document, chances are good that leaving this selected will produce a pleasing result. If you use ProPhoto RGB as your working space for compositing, it's probably best to deselect this option because the ProPhoto color gamut far exceeds that of any printer or press.

16-bit printing. Photoshop CS4 now offers the ability to send 16-bit color and tonal data directly to your printer. You can activate this option by jumping from Color Management to Output in the menu (top left) and then, at the bottom of the output options, checking the Send 16-bit Data box (**Figure 11.8**). This option is worth using if you are printing a document that uses ProPhoto RGB as its working space, but in practice we haven't often seen marked differences in 8- and 16-bit prints—especially at normal viewing distances. However, as printer technology continues to improve, this will become a more important capability, so keep it in mind as you upgrade your hardware.

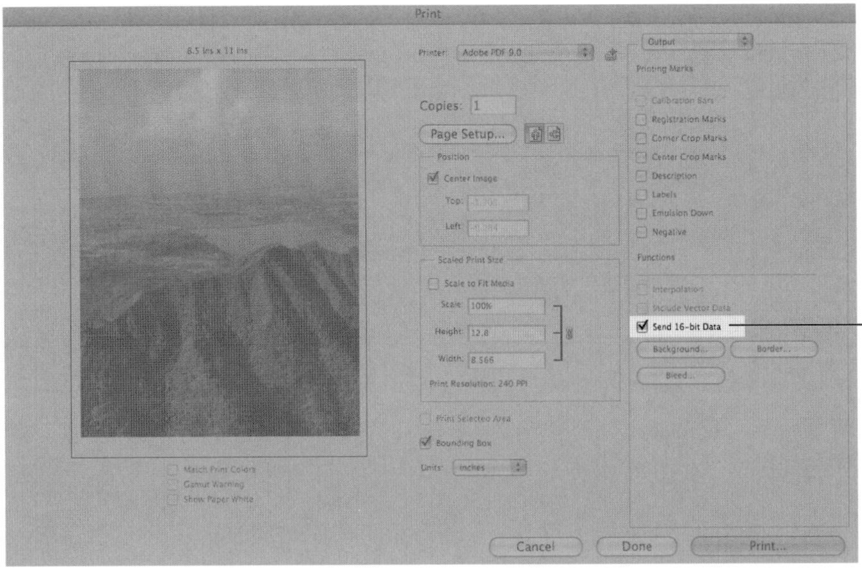

Figure 11.8 Sixteen-bit printing is now possible in Photoshop CS4.

Select this to send 16-bit color data to the printer.

The last thing we want to emphasize deals not with the Print dialog box in Photoshop but with your printer driver's dialog box. Most high-end ink-jet printers offer the ability in their driver menus to turn off color management. We implore you to do this every time you print! This relates to whether the printer (or, more specifically, your operating system via your printer) handles the colors in your print or whether Photoshop does. Photoshop is almost always the better option. So, turn off your printer's color management before you click Print!

WEB OUTPUT

Fortunately, outputting your composite images to the Web is a much simpler process than working in the world of CMYK presses or even in the world of ink-jet printing! Photoshop CS4 has introduced some major changes to the always-appreciated Save for Web & Devices dialog box (sometimes referred to by the acronym SFW) that allow you to make all the necessary adjustments for your web-bound image in one place!

SFW improvements. One of the biggest changes to the new SFW dialog box—aside from a more streamlined layout—is that it allows you not only to optimize the color and web compression settings for the various image formats (JPEG, PNG, GIF) but also to perform image size changes inside the dialog box, using all the familiar interpolation methods, such as Bicubic Sharper (for reductions) and Bicubic Smooth (for enlargements) (**Figure 11.9**).

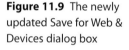

Figure 11.9 The newly updated Save for Web & Devices dialog box

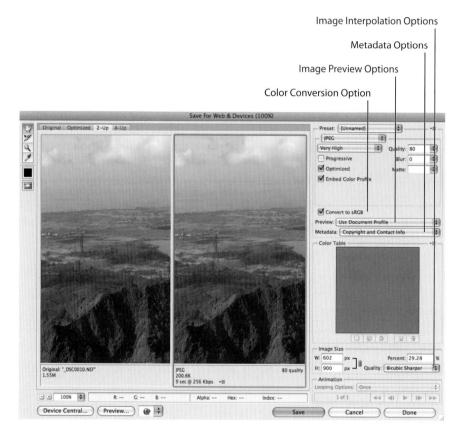

Other useful improvements to SFW include the ability to convert your document's colors to the web-safe sRGB profile and the ability to append metadata to the web file you are creating.

Typically our process for creating a web version of our composite involves the following steps:

1. We open our 8-bit flattened master file into the SFW environment.

2. We use the 2-up view to compare (at the appropriate magnification for the subject matter) our JPEG or PNG optimization settings with the original file quality.

3. Once we find a look that's acceptable and fits the document size requirements, we select the Convert to sRGB option and apply copyright metadata.

4. Finally, under Image Size, we choose our document dimensions (which are usually much smaller than the master file), set Quality to Bicubic Sharper (unless we're enlarging the image for some reason), and then click Save to name and place the file in the appropriate directory.

The new Save for Web & Devices dialog box in Photoshop CS4 really does make web output a simple and pain-free process most of the time, though opening large files into it can be a little slow.

Project Examples

This appendix provides an A-to-Z look at many of the techniques discussed in Chapters 7–10 and shows you how a typical composite image progresses through the entire workflow. The idea is to reinforce the many concepts described in this book by showing them in action and in the sequence in which we might apply them to a real project.

Ultimately what will make you a successful composite artist is finding new ways to adapt Adobe Photoshop CS4 to your habits and workflows, not the other way around. So, even with the examples you're about to see, there's no set-in-stone process in terms of the sequence of steps. Find the techniques here that work for you and adapt them to your imaging goals.

Later in this appendix, we'll show several completed composites, ranging from the very simple to the complex and covering a variety of subjects. This is just a way for you to see a few examples of how you can bring together some seemingly dissimilar images.

PROJECT 1: BLUE MOON

For this example, I wanted to use an early morning shot of the New Orleans skyline that I had captured as the basis for a fun and futuristic-looking composite that included photographs, vector art, and 3D content. The source images for this project are the skyline shot, a shot of a full lunar eclipse, an Adobe Illustrator CS4 "orb," a 3D "orb" generated only with Photoshop, and a background image (the starry sky) from NASA. The idea was just to let the imagination go; sometimes compositing is just about having fun, so don't be afraid to experiment!—Dan

Step 1: Process the Raw Source Image

Figure A.1 shows some of the settings that were applied to the lunar eclipse shot to make it stand out more, including tonal corrections and HSL adjustments, as well as sharpening of the "crater details." This shot was taken on a winter night where it was so cold that even the camera and tripod were shaking! The point here is that it's important to work the tones and colors in your raw images with the final composite in mind, rather than process the shot as if you were going to just make a nice print.

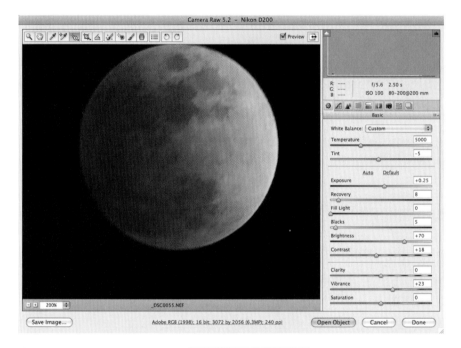

Figure A.1 Most corrections for this shot were taken care of in the Basic and Detail panels. I used the HSL panel (you can use the Targeted Adjustment tool for the same task) to give the moon more of an orange tone, rather than the original, faint red hue.

Step 2: Correct the Perspective on Buildings

The skyline shot was originally a medium compression JPEG, so I opted not to perform any ACR processing, since it might exaggerate any JPEG artifacts present. The shot was taken near dawn, so the color and quality of light was very good anyway. The warm glow added to the futuristic look that I was going for; all I needed to do was to make a perspective correction (**Figure A.2**), crop out the transparent edges, and remove the sky. I removed, rather than masked, the sky because those pixels wouldn't be needed later for the composite.

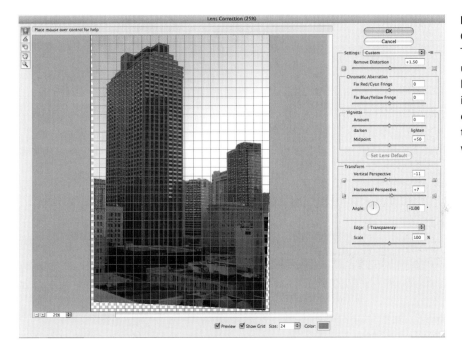

Figure A.2 The Lens Correction filter and the Free Transform command were used to straighten out the buildings a bit. The buildings on the right were not a concern because the parts that remained distorted would be cropped out.

Step 3: Create an Illustrator "Orb"

Since I wanted to add some graphic pizzazz to this composite, I decided to use Illustrator to create a glasslike orb (though ultimately I would remove the glassy properties to make it look a little more realistic). I accomplished this by using the Symbols panel and choosing Web Buttons and Bars from its menu. I dragged the icon onto my document, removed several of the strokes and other items that were not consistent with the lighting in my composite scene, and saved the orb (**Figure A.3**) as an Adobe Illustrator file (.ai).

Figure A.3 Creating graphics for use in composites is much easier with the advent of the Illustrator symbols technology. Drag an item onto your canvas, modify it, and save it. You can then place the graphic as a smart object, and each time you update it in Illustrator, your (open) Photoshop file will automatically update.

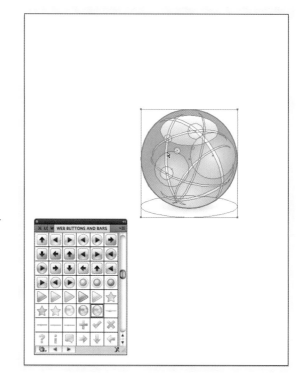

Step 4: Create a 3D Photoshop "Orb"

The next step was to use Photoshop's built-in 3D tools to create an orb that had a watery, slightly translucent appearance. I also wanted to create the illusion that it might be reflecting some of the surrounding buildings. To do this, I opened a new empty document about 800 × 600 and used the New Shape from Layer feature in the 3D menu to generate a sphere. Next I used the 3D panel to remove two of the default Infinite lights and position the third Infinite light so that the sphere appeared to be lit from an unseen source near the horizon and to the right of the viewer. A smaller version of the New Orleans skyline shot was used as the Environment texture (to provide some faint, reflective properties). I made changes to the Opacity, Reflectivity, and other settings in the Filter by: Materials view until things looked right (**Figure A.4**). One finished, I chose the High Quality Anti-Alias setting and Raytracing as my render option.

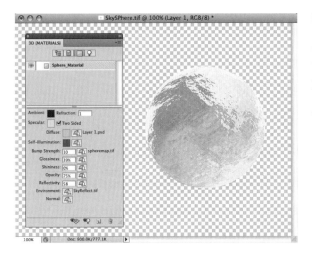

Figure A.4 Using the 3D panel to define the lighting and surface characteristics of the third sphere yielded an otherworldly-looking orb to place into the scene.

Step 5: Place Files as Smart Objects

Once I finished tweaking the moon image and the two orbs, the next step was to use the File > Place command to add them (as well as the stars) to the skyline file as smart objects. This ensured that for the moon and the two orb files, any edits I needed to make were just a double-click away. **Figure A.5** shows the document with all the placed files I needed to finish the composite image.

Figure A.5 Whenever possible, try to use File > Place to add the source images to your composite project as smart objects. This makes editing and transforming them a nondestructive process that you can experiment with freely.

Step 6: Position, Scale, and Rotate

Having already placed the night sky into the scene and reduced its brightness so that the stars looked far away, I experimented with different sizes, orientations, and locations for the moon and the two orbs, settling on the moon and Illustrator orb being mostly obscured and the 3D orb floating in plain view. I find that placing parts of a given subject behind another subject lends credibility to the illusion (**Figure A.6**). Real urban environments rarely have unobstructed views of anything, so don't be afraid to obscure parts of your source images if setting them in a complex environment. Although it's clear that this is an illustrative piece, placing everything out in the open would not make for an interesting composition. To scale the 3D object, I double-clicked its layer to open the original file. From there I used the 3D Scale tool, saved the document, and then switched back to the composite window, which updated automatically.

Figure A.6 We scaled the moon and Illustrator smart object using the Free Transform command and changed their stacking order in the Layers panel so that they could be set partially behind the buildings.

Step 7: Mimic the Evening Light

As the composition started to come together, something was obviously not right with this "picture." Several of the buildings, including the largest one, were too bright. They didn't look as if they could plausibly be under a night sky with moons and city lights providing partial illumination. To fix this I made a series of adjustment layers and clipped them to the building layer to create a more realistic ambient environment that wouldn't affect the other content (**Figure A.7**). I also toned the stars way down by placing a black fill layer behind them and pulling the opacity down until I had an effect I liked.

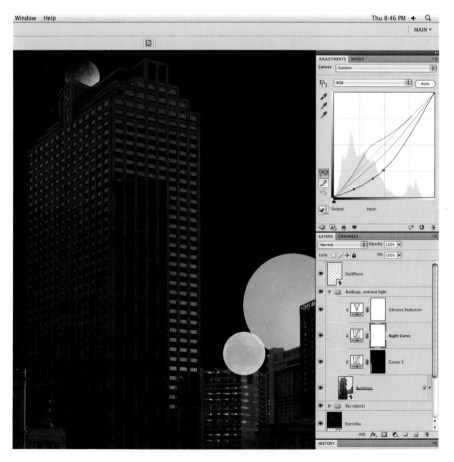

Figure A.7 Once everything was in place and roughly proportioned the way I needed, it was time to use adjustment layers and layer masks to work some lighting magic.

Step 8: Adjust the Focus

At this point, the buildings were almost finished, but they were still too sharp (in focus) for even a well-lit night, and the moon and Illustrator orb both needed to be blurred some as well, based on their positions in the frame. I left the 3D orb sharp because I wanted to give the impression that it was close and floating among the buildings like a giant bubble. For these blurring tasks, I used the Gaussian Blur filter (moon and orb) and Lens Blur filter (buildings) to make things look more realistic. For the latter, I also used a gradient layer mask on the building's smart object layer, so that the effect would taper off near the bottom of the building (**Figure A.8**).

Figure A.8 Before the image was finished, it was necessary to blur parts of it so that their focus level was consistent with their apparent distance from the viewer.

Step 9: Add the Final Touches

To make the final edits, I added several adjustment layers and clipped them to the moon layer and Illustrator orb layers, making some final creative touches. No scene is complete without a blue moon! **Figure A.9** shows the final result.

Figure A.9 Once the primary tasks in your composite are done, it's a good time to look at the individual lighting and colors of each element and see whether small tweaks using adjustment layers and layer masks can help you get things just right.

PROJECT 2: ALLEY MAN

This project was conceived with the idea of mixing creative lighting techniques and Lens Blur techniques to create an image that had the feel both of a real street scene and of a scene in miniature—almost as if you were looking at a movie set. This project had only two source images, and most of the work revolved around creating accurate masks for the various light sources and drop-off points for the blurring effects. I also spent some time working on the man's shadow so that it fit the time of night and light sources. Don't worry, though; if you meet this cat in the alley, he's harmless!—Scott

Step 1: Match the Tonality and Color

Figure A.10 When blending images that were shot (as JPEGs) in very different lighting conditions, my first task is often to match the tonal character of the two shots.

Once I brought these images together (both started as JPEGs, so no ACR processing was needed in this case), I set immediately to fixing the lighting on the man's clothes. This had the side benefit of making the placement an easier task, so it's not always necessary to place and scale first. I needed to create the appearance that the man was walking under streetlights at night, and the colors needed to reflect the same. As a start, the image of the man was treated with a gradient on a clipping layer to control the light fall, and the highlights were dulled down with gray paint on a separate layer, with lowered opacity, as shown in **Figure A.10**.

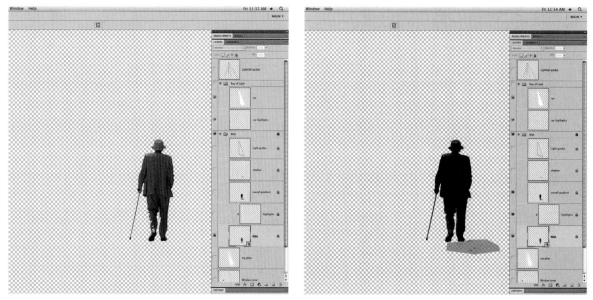

Before Highlight Adjustments   After Highlight Adjustments

Step 2: Place the Man in the Alley

For the project discussed earlier, the positions of the moon and orbs were arbitrary, but here the placement has to match the reality of the alley. The man in the scene was originally flipped the other way so that the lighting came from the opposite direction. He also had a shadow, which made for an easier start. Because the subject was photographed from 180 degrees (in other words, directly behind) and the alley is straight, there was little choice but to match up the highlights.

I painted some guides to determine the correct angles. Starting at the center of the closest streetlight, I made several straight paint strokes with a small brush on an empty layer (clicking with the brush on the starting point, then holding down Shift and clicking again at your destination produces a straight line). With a few of these rays in place, it was easy to choose the right one by moving the man's layer around until they lined up. **Figure A.11** shows the final placement of the alley man.

Figure A.11 The placement of the alley man was based on the lighting environment and the look of his clothes so that they would match in a believable way.

Step 3: Achieve Accurate Scale

Here again, the scaling could not be arbitrary. This was one of the most important parts of the image to make the illusion look authentic. The size implies distance, since our brain "knows" how tall someone should be. The highlights on his clothing meant he had to be close to or directly across from the streetlight. Looking at the windows, doorways, and curb, I estimated the size and scaled until it "felt" right. A few nudges to avoid the appearance of a "floating man," and the placement was set (**Figure A.12**).

Figure A.12 The scale of the alley man was based on the proximity of nearby objects. I used the height of the door relative to the height of an average-sized man, and his distance from the door, to approximate his height.

Step 4: Set the Focus Points

The next trick is to set the focus for the background and then make sure the man—based on his placement—blends in correctly. I built the Lens Blur mask used in this image in pieces to control the individual areas more carefully. One limitation of using masks to control the filter is that you don't have real-time feedback on adjustments. To overcome this limitation, I converted the base image to a smart object to allow editing of the filter. The mask itself was created first on the smart object to isolate the background buildings, and then I saved that mask as a new layer via copying and pasting. Starting over, I masked the foreground and then saved it to a new layer. Finally, I merged the two grayscale layers and reapplied them to the smart object layer mask (**Figure A.13**).

Figure A.13 The focus was a two-pronged task: first getting the overall scene to have the creative look I wanted and then matching the man to that scene.

Step 5: Work the Shadows

One of the last steps was to put the finishing touches on the image by creating a believable shadow. The shadow had to fall across the curb, so I used the Pen tool to outline the original shadow, leaving extra corner nodes where the shadow met an angle of the curb. I then used the Node tool to select all the points to the right of the lower 90-degree bend and moved them so that the path went straight up the curb, just as a shadow would in real life.

This allowed the outline of the shadow to look right as it went over the curb. I filled the path with black, added a little monochrome uniform noise, and blurred slightly. I added a gradient layer mask and applied the Lens Blur tool to simulate the shadow getting softer as it got farther away from the light. Finally, the shadow's blending mode was changed to Multiply and the opacity lowered until it matched the density of other nearby shadows (**Figure A.14**).

Figure A.14 For any image of this kind to be believable, the shadow must be made so that it "interacts" with the contours on the ground plane and also (in some cases) so that it matches the color and density of other shadows in the environment.

MORE COMPOSITE EXAMPLES

This section provides additional examples of composite images we created for different purposes. We initially conjured up many of these composites just by looking through photographs and finding common visual threads or themes. Others are more academic in nature, but the point is that there are endless possibilities if you have a large collection of images to work with.

Figure A.15 The purpose of this image is to demonstrate how the human eye can be momentarily tricked into accepting what it sees. This concept includes a couple of (intentional) visual cues to tip the viewer off that it is, in fact, not a real place. From there you're left to wonder what was added or subtracted as you scan the image, almost like solving a puzzle. This image was created by layering multiple source images and carefully masking away different parts of each. Finally, we applied similar levels of Lens blur along their boundaries and gradient masks to control the amount of blur relative to distance.

One reason this image works is that the original photographs were taken under similar weather conditions, and the brickwork (as well as other details) images were very similar. All were processed together in ACR so that the White Balance and other settings matched precisely. Little photographic details like these—which were discussed in Chapters 5 and 7—can make all the difference and save you time in Photoshop.

Figure A.16 This is the final composite that was used in prior examples from Chapter 10, "Compositing Source Materials." The first trick here was to make the mountains look a bit more realistic. Sometimes when you purchase stock images, the original author or the agency will have made too large a hue or saturation correction, so be aware! Here the saturation was toned down, and the Difference Clouds filter was used on a separate layer to add a "singe effect" to the face of the mountain. Other modifications included matching up the lighting conditions implied by the bright blue skies with the car, as well as selective blurring. We also gave the clouds a slightly warm treatment to stylize the image a bit and applied a gradient to the rear window of the car to match the bright skies.

Figure A.17 This composite is designed as a proof of concept for a scene in a first-person, 3D video game. The idea was to use ordinary-scale images and give the appearance of a completely different scale, as well as an other-worldly effect. The main focus here was to set up the base image (columns) so that the right parts were masked out and the overall color character was that of a moonlit night. This way, most of the Curves adjustments would be to the composite RGB channel rather than to individual channels. After-ward, other images were placed into the composite, scaled, and given vari-ous treatments with Lens Blur, Curves, and Gradient masks. An artistic filter was also used on the foreground material, though not on the columns themselves. The columns look as they do purely with treatment from ACR, Curves, and Lens Blur.

Figure A.18 This image was designed to mix naturally occurring elements from the forest with a surreal element (a young woman given wings, a new skin color, and a tattoo to match). Obviously, much of the challenge here was to provide a stylistic impression using focus levels and color, and to affix the fairy's wings in a believable way. This composite is a great example of how everything doesn't have to be literal; we encourage you to experiment and try new things. Scott even gave it a cinema-like letterbox effect!

PARTING WORDS

In closing, we would like to thank you for purchasing this book! We wanted to share what we know with you, without turning the book into a series of simplistic 1-2-3 examples or covering materials that are already well done in other Photoshop books such as toolbar basics, selection basics, and the like.

We hope you have enjoyed this book and gathered some useful ideas and techniques for your own workflows. If you have feedback, we would love to hear from you. Tell us what kinds of techniques and concepts you'd like to see in future editions, and we'll do our best to accommodate the most popular requests. You can send comments to rwcompositing@colortrails.com.

IMAGE CREDITS

Figure 1.8, Motorcycle in Cinema 4D, courtesy MAXON Computer GmbH.

Figure 2.1, "New Skies" © 2008 Dan Moughamian.

Figure 3.1, "Rainy Road 2" © 2007 Marco Coda.

Figure 3.2 (left), "Warm Glow of Sandstone at Sunset" © 2008 Charles Guise.

Figure 3.2 (right), "Red Rocks Sunset" © 2008 Alexey Stiop.

Figure 3.3, "The Law" © 2008 "DNY59" (iStock).

Figure 3.4, "Moraine Lake" © 2007 Matt Naylor.

Figure 3.5 (left), "Iguacu Falls" © 2007 Greg Brzezinski.

Figure 3.5 (right), "St. Basil Cathedral" © 2007 "cloki" (iStock).

Figure 3.6, "Modern Professional Business Woman" © 2008 Nicole Waring.

Figure 3.6, "Punk" © 2008 Valentin Casarsa.

Figure 3.6, "Schoolboy Playing" © 2008 Michael DeLeon.

Figure 3.6, "Photographer" © 2008 Jess Wiberg.

Figure 3.7, "Subject Montage" © 2005, 2006 Dan Moughamian.

Figure 3.8, "Earth Melon" © 2008 Dan Moughamian. (Earth Image courtesy NASA).

Figure 3.9, Angel image © 2006 Dan Moughamian.

Figure 3.10, "Shanghai at Night" © 2007 David Pedre.

Figure 3.11, Hallway image © 2005 Dan Moughamian.

Figure 4.5, Hubble telescope, image courtesy NASA.

Figure 5.1, Woman © 2008 Scott Valentine.

Figure 5.6, Child looking out window © 2008 Scott Valentine.

Figure 5.7, Lantern, Cathedral Wall © 2005, 2006 Dan Moughamian.

Figure 5.9, "Sunset Columns" © 2006 Dan Moughamian.

Figure 5.12, "Atom power station" ©2007 Petr Nad.

Figure 5.13, "Mountain Retreat" © 2005 Dan Moughamian.

Figure 5.15, "Clock Tower" © 2004 Dan Moughamian.

Figure 5.16, "Park Overlook" © 2006 Dan Moughamian.

Figure 5.17, "Hanging Mask" © 2005 Dan Moughamian.

Figure 5.18, Nikkor PC-E 24mm lens, courtesy Nikon USA.

Figure 5.19, Cathedral Ruins © 2006 Dan Moughamian.

Figure 5.20, LensBaby, courtesy LensBaby, Inc.

Figure 5.21, Nikon D3 DSLR, courtesy Nikon USA.

Figure 5.22, "Lake Michigan Sunset" © 2008 Dan Moughamian.

Figure 5.24, Nikon Speedlight, courtesy Nikon USA.

Figures 6.7, 6.9, 6.10, Fall foliage © 2005 Dan Moughamian.

Figure 6.14, Helicopter shots © Scott Valentine.

Figure 7.2, Peninsula © 2006 Dan Moughamian.

Figure 7.3, "Sunset Prairie" © 2008 Dan Moughamian.

Figure 7.10, Cathedral Columns © 2006 Dan Moughamian.

Figure 7.17, Various Flower Close-ups © 2006 Dan Moughamian.

Figure 8.1, "Tumble Flowers" © 2006 Dan Moughamian.

Figure 8.2, Forest Preserve © 2004 Dan Moughamian.

Figure 8.4, Maple Leaf © 2005 Dan Moughamian.

Figure 8.5, Flowers © 2007 Dan Moughamian.

Figure 8.12, Lakeshore © 2006 Dan Moughamian.

Figure 8.13, Fish © 2005 Dan Moughamian.

Figures 8.21 and 8.22, Building © 2006 Dan Moughamian.

Figure 9.20, Highway scene © Scott Valentine.

Cinema 4D Figures © Dan Moughamian.

Figures 10.1, Skyline with moon © 2008 Dan Moughamian.

Figure 10.6, Buildings © 2006 Dan Moughamian.

Figure 10.7, Fish on pier © 2008 Dan Moughamian.

Figure 10.8, Chasing Dog © 2008 Dan Moughamian.

Figure 10.9, Car on highway © 2008 Scott Valentine.

Figure 10.13, Flowers © 2006 Dan Moughamian.

Figure 10.14, Classic Auto © 2006 Dan Moughamian.

Figure 10.16, Welsh Harbor © 2006 Dan Moughamian.

Figure 10.17, Buddha in terminal © 2008 Dan Moughamian.

Figure 10.22, "Winter Light" © 2008 Scott Valentine.

Figure 10.23, "Canyon Lights" © 2008 Scott Valentine.

Figure 10.24, Mottled Landscape © 2008 Scott Valentine.

Figure 10.26, Centurion on steps © 2008 Scott Valentine.

Figure 10.27, "Colorful Row" © 2006 Dan Moughamian.

Figure 10.28, "Rustic Beach" © 2006 Dan Moughamian.

Figure 10.31, "Empty Field" © 2008 Dan Moughamian.

Figure 10.32, "In a Park" © 2008 Mitja Mladkovic.

Figures A.1 through A.9, "Big Easy Night" © 2005, 2008 Dan Moughamian.

Figures A.10 through A.14, "Alley Man" © 2008 Scott Valentine.

Figure A.16, "Pleasure Cruise" © 2008 Scott Valentine.

Figure A.17, "Giant Columns" © 2006, 2008 Dan Moughamian.

Figure A.18, "Forest Faery" © 2008 Scott Valentine.

The following talented artists' photography appeared as part of a composite image example featured in this book. To learn more about them, visit www.istockphoto.com:

Daniele Barioglio, Tamara Bauer, Ronald Bloom, Julien Grondin, Hazlan Abdul Hakim, Ben Klaus, Maciej Laska, Maria Latnik, Skip O'Donnell, John Prescott, Witold Ryka, Nick Schlax, Denis Tangney Jr., Georg Winkens, and Edwin Verin.

INDEX